# HERE I GO AGAIN

## BRITT AMSLER

### A MEMOIR

Copyright © 2021 by Britt Amsler

# HERE I GO AGAIN

Quantity sales special discounts are available on quantity purchases by corporations, associations, and others. For details, contact the publisher at the address above.

Orders by U.S. trade bookstores and wholesalers. Email info@BeyondPublishing.net

The Beyond Publishing Speakers Bureau can bring authors to your live event. For more information or to book an event contact the Beyond Publishing Speakers Bureau speak@BeyondPublishing.net

The Author can be reached directly at BeyondPublishing.net

Manufactured and printed in the United States of America distributed globally by BeyondPublishing.net

BEYOND
PUBLISHING

New York | Los Angeles | London | Sydney

ISBN Hardcover: 978-1-637920-91-6

ISBN Softcover: 978-1-637920-79-4

# SPECIAL THANKS & ACKNOWLEDGEMENTS

Telling my journey has been the most humbling experience of my life as reliving many broken-hearted memories has been the greatest therapy a human can get. Yet there have been many rewarding times in my life, there also have been many challenges, trials and tribulations along the way that I had to overcome. I learned a very valuable lesson in life the hard way by wishing to live in someone else's tree versus my own, a wish God granted me but a wish that was very costly, but in the end, made me a better man and humbled my soul. I have also learned how to forgive and to the many who have hurt me, I have forgiven you.

Though I have many more goals to accomplish in my journey ahead, having my story available for the world to read is a milestone goal accomplished for me. My goal is for my story to touch people in ways they couldn't ever imagine and to show them that people can overcome being knocked down, but only to get up and bounce back time after time after time!

I would like to thank God for walking with me through my journey in life. He caught me when I fell and lifted me back on my feet during the many hard times throughout my life. Loving thanks to my family, brother Aaron and wife Katie Amsler, stepdad Bobby Manning, nieces Abbie & Allie Amsler, nephew Bryant Amsler and especially my mom, Joy Manning for being my rock! I would not be the man I am today without her. Love you mom! My uncle Jim & aunt Cathy Sanders, cousins Amy & Chad Pikens, Burl, Sabrina, Tyler, Chelsea & Davis Richards! To my deceased grandparents Lero & Weyma Sanders. You both were so very special to me and are greatly missed RIP!

To my dear & special friends that have stood along the side of me over the years and who have touched me in so many ways JMAC, Neil Duran, John Eric Henry, Robert Olivares, Rodney Allison, Anthony & Melissa Baker, Bryan & Lauren Boeck, Forbes & Gretchen McMullin, Bob & Michelle Day, Pat & Frank Allums & family, Charles & Sherrie Britton, Phil Boeck, Ginger Malone, Scott Deffebach, George Rauch, Chris Courtney (RIP), Matt Lampo, Chuck Stavorowski, Tim & Nicole Dlugos, Curt & Mindy Liles, Bob & Doreen Camillone, Paul & Carmen Shortino, Chelsie Davis, Stewart Davis (RIP), Kelly Davis, Paul Leto, Rick Call, Danny Jester, Dan Zeigler, Don & Cathy Emig, Paul & Kelle Blalock, Gerry Machia, Mackenzie & Janelle Castillo, Becky Petty, Seth Stokes, Jon Holz, Rick Westbrook (RIP), David Slocum, Chris Barecky, Gavin Copeland, Barry Lefroy, Lindsey Lockhart, Sean Gilligan, Cathy Bogaerts, Frank Aguilar, Ivonne Zambrano, Steve Sanders, Doug & Daniela Aldrich, Christine Scott (Ghost Writer), Joe & Ronnie Politi, Dave Hein, Kelly Stang, Vinnie Paul Abbott, Jeff Molitz, Scott Thompson (Carrot Top), J.J. Raterink, Tanner Varner, Bob Hendrickson, Rudy Castello, Jeff McKinney, John O'Donnell, Christian Brady, Carlos & Vicki Cavazo, Jerry Natividad, Kristine Williams – Anderson, Jim Ross (JR), my many friends in Cabo San Lucas, MX – Oscar Paye Sanchez, Miguel Zuniga, The Office Rambo, Julian, Cabo Johnson, Ricardo Hernandez & Hugo Castillo, the boys from Oklahoma – Mikey Owens, Brent McMullan, Todd Kahoe, Mitch Griffith, Jordan Poliski, Eddie Spencer & Steve Hixon, thank you all for being a part of my life. I wouldn't be where I am today without all of you!

Lastly, thank you to Michael Butler for believing in my story, publishing my book and making a dream come true!

## SPECIAL THANKS

Special thanks to Christine Scott for writing my story and making a dream come true! - Big Love

# TABLE OF CONTENTS

# PROLOGUE

How do I define me? How do I define my life? Well, that for sure is not a one-word answer. There's a lot that comes with being me and experiencing things in life that can only happen to me. I've been struck by a car, poked in the eye with a drumstick, hit in the face with a cue ball, and kicked in the eye with a high heeled shoe that lacerated my right eyeball. I've been arrested five times, one of which got me my "Hollywood Moment of Fame" on WFAA Channel 8 News in Dallas. I've fled from police during my high school days and enjoyed many a good car chase with my friends back then. I've literally roasted my hand in a fire when I was a little boy, and then played with fire on a greater scale which led to me filing for bankruptcy at the age of 27.

I've been a Co-Owner with a rock star partner of a professional Arena Football Team that went bankrupt, and I've dated women of all kinds. I've engaged with Playboy playmates, pro lingerie football players, strippers, and I've even been on a date with a porn star! Fourteen of those women all had names starting with the combination of either Chris or Krys.

I've partied at the Playboy Mansion, partied on tours with rock stars, and have bumped noses with the elite. I've even been in situations where people asked me for my autograph and wanted pictures with me!

I have a grown daughter that wants nothing to do with me, a non-existent father, and I have suffered the tragic loss of two pregnancies.

I feel like I have lived the life of three men, take the good or the bad. There are things that I would do over again, and there are things that I don't even want to remember let alone do over. Aside from it all, aside from the wild ride that has been my life, a lot of people tell me that they think my life is awesome, but they don't know the true story and the facts. Sure, they see the positive end results, but they don't see what went into achieving that end result. They don't see what a hard road it has been for me at times.

I don't recommend for anyone to take my path unless they are looking for a rollercoaster ride of disappointment, pain, and at times, fatal consequences. Learn from me, don't mimic me. Travel with me through my life's journey and the many lessons learned. Witness with me my trials and tribulations, my bad decisions, and the heartache and disappointment that has shaped and formed me into the man I am today.

I will tell you this. Live your own life. Live it for you and for no one else. Take chances, take risks. It's much worse to wonder "if" than it is to know something as a certainty, even if it's an ending.

# IN THE BEGINNING

## PART 1

# GROWING UP

I was born on April 20, 1971, at Good Shepherd Hospital in Longview, Texas, which is the very same hospital that brought Miranda Lambert into the world and located in the very same town where Matthew McConaughey graduated from High School. I still think that's cool … fuck any haters, haha!

The basics are that I was the first born to my parents, John and Joy Amsler, and was named after one of my mom's former bosses who was officially named Britton. As a young child, I moved around a lot and lived in several different states because my father was in the military. We lived in Alabama, Georgia, Washington State, and Texas while my dad served in the Army.

I started kindergarten in 1976 in Longview at a school named Pine Tree and right after that, we moved across town where I started the first grade. We stayed there for a while, and I graduated from Spring Hill High School. As a kid, I really didn't apply myself in sports or my studies and to make matters even worse for myself, I was also extremely shy. And I mean *extremely* shy. It wasn't until after college that things started to change for me in that department. But all that comes later.

During those wonderfully naïve and simpler times, my grandparents lived in Arkansas and my brother Aaron and I would go stay with them every single summer for anywhere from four to six weeks, depending on when Little League Baseball ended.

I really loved my grandparents and I loved spending my summers with them even more. I was beyond blessed to be able to spend every summer with them right up until I turned 12 years old, which was when my mom and dad divorced.

I'll never forget the exact moment when it all ended, too. That exact earth-shattering moment when all that happiness, all that comfort, just dissipated into thin air like a vapor. *Poof!* All gone. Buh-bye. Show over.

I remember that night like it was last night. It was Halloween of all nights, and my mom took my brother and me to the Friday night high school football game. Right before we left to go to the game, my parents got into this huge ugly fight, but my mom didn't let it ruin our night and she took us anyway. She knew how much we loved to go to those games, and she was more than used to my father being a dick. And did I mention that it was fucking Halloween? Come on!

When we got home after the game and were pulling into the driveway, my mom calmly looked at both of us and told us to go inside and grab a few personal things, that we were going to go stay with our grandparents for a little while. We were totally confused by this, but we did as our Mom told us to do.

Unbeknownst to us, our grandparents had just moved back to Texas from Arkansas, so they weren't as far away as they used to be. Mom added that we were leaving immediately so we needed to be quick about getting our things. We scurried inside, collected our things as fast as we could, and as we began to walk out of the house another fight ensued between our parents. Only this time, the fight turned a side of ugly that we had never seen before, and one that I won't ever forget.

While my dad had the fucking audacity to strike my mom right in front of us, my 8-year-old brother had the balls to start punching him while screaming, "Leave my mom alone!"

My dad immediately turned to me and grabbed me by my left arm while my mom grabbed my right arm, and the Britt-o-War tug game began. Back and forth they both went. Back and forth. Back and forth. My head swirled while trying to get a grip of what was actually going on. It was more than just a physical tug of war that would end in either the strongest winner or one of my arms being pulled out.

Go with my dad. Stay with my mom. What do you want to do, son? This was truly a tragically defining moment in my young life because how the hell do you decide between your two parents? How do you choose just one in a moment of pure insanity and emotional distress? I mean, what the hell?

Shit. A minute earlier, I was sitting on the bleachers, checking out the cheerleaders in their Halloween costumes and watching them kick their legs in the air, watching football, and then, the next thing you know, I'm living my own version of Sophie's Choice. Move over, Meryl Streep, we've got a new contender on the block!

The drama didn't matter, though. It really didn't have any impact on what I already knew would be my decision. I knew damn well I wasn't going anywhere with my dad, and neither was my little brother for that matter. I was going with my mom, my brother was staying with me, and that was it. No debating it. I knew in my young, developing soul, that we both needed to be with our mom.

In a split second, vaporizing into thin air was the Amsler family as we knew it. In a split second, my mom and dad shared their final moment as a cohabitating husband and wife, as a couple. In a split second, a mother of two walked away from her husband and married life and she would never look back. Not even once.

Unfortunately for me, the early memories of my father all embody the dysfunctional elements of alcohol and disappointment, and then some. My biological father never once took the time to be the "dad" that I always wanted him to be, to be the "dad" that I thought he could be if only he wanted the same thing. He just never did. He never wanted the same thing as me when it came to our relationship, and over time it became obvious that's how he truly felt about it.

He always drank a lot. Always. And he always had a Merit cigarette in his hand. Always. He mostly just laid on the couch watching TV rather than spending any time whatsoever with his family, no matter the reason or occasion. I recall my dad having multiple jobs over the years when I was growing up. Nothing was ever long term with him. He would exert just enough effort to get us by and that was it. Once he hit his minimum goal, he shut down and never cared to go beyond that, no matter the reason or occasion.

My mom always somewhat defended him by saying that he was a very smart man and that he, at one time, had achieved these tremendous grades while attending the University of Houston. I wasn't impressed. Not then, not now. To this day I still don't understand how he could have been so smart yet still be able to abuse and neglect his family. Can someone explain that to me? I mean, stupid people do stupid, self-absorbed shit, right? Careless, reckless, ignorant, narcissistic men do that kind of shit to their families, not the men who possess intellect and awareness about themselves, right? Right.

Men who go to church don't act like that, either, right? Tell me another one. Our family attended Church on a regular basis at Elmira Chapel Cumberland Presbyterian Church *and* my father sang in the choir. He sang in the fucking choir! It was impossible to grasp how this hypocrite could devote so much time to God yet still treat his family like he did, leaving them in pure anguish and wreckage. God-fearing, God-loving men don't do that to others. Evil, sociopathic, monster-like people do that, and it doesn't have to be Halloween for them to come out of hiding. They're out and about in broad fucking daylight. Every damned day, too.

This fractured shell of a fraudulent man, this "big" man who sang in the choir at church, was a certified monster behind closed doors at home. Though he gave up drinking and joined AA in 1980, the damage had already been done to his mind and to his body. And to every relationship he ever had. It was way too late for any long term effects to be reversed, even just a little.

He roughed up my mom on so many occasions, there are no words left to describe those moments. It was agonizing to witness that shit as a kid and not be able to do anything about it. You just sit there and watch it unfold right in front of you, helpless, hopeless, and scared. There really are no words that can properly define it.

My mom put up with a tremendous amount of abuse while married to my father, and I honestly have no idea how she survived it. What I *do* know, however, is that my mom has always been a strong, devoted woman, and she remains one of the toughest human beings I know. When I tell you that she did whatever it took to survive and take care of my brother and me, I mean, she did whatever it took.

Before the divorce, some of the best times in my life were spent when it was just the three of us, my mom, brother, and me, operating like a close-knit, three-tiered family unit. That was, until my dad came home. Once he was home, everything went to shit. Every time. He really was just a miserable bastard.

I remember one night my mom and I were sitting on the couch, hanging out, watching TV. The couch was against the living room wall, on the other side of which was the garage. On that night, we were lucky that the wall acted like a bumper-car barrier. My dad came home from one of his nightly drinking binges and drove into the wall so hard the impact literally knocked my Mom and me off the couch and onto the floor.

Chalk it up to just one more hole in that wall from the car. I guarantee you the possibility of him crashing through that wall and killing his family never once entered his alcohol-soaked mind. Not once. Such an asshole he was drinking and driving like that all the time. Such an asshole he was for not caring how it affected the rest of us once he got home.

When the three of us moved away from that, it was such a sense of relief. It was nice to be able to sit on the couch and not have to worry about getting hit by the family car. Imagine!

***

My dad was a physically big man back then, especially to a kid, and he always looked intense. Standing at 6'2" and weighing about 220 pounds, I feared him just as he feared his dad when he was younger. You see, my grandfather, John Carl, was utterly horrible to my dad when he was a kid. Thus, my dad chose to pass on that shitty quality instead of killing the vicious cycle and starting anew, doing it better, being better. Nope. Guess that was too much to aim for in his life, too much to want better for his own sons, too much effort needed to be a better person. It wasn't worth it to him.

I remember meeting John Carl, which was the one and only time I ever stood before him. He never, *ever* came around the family, and my dad never talked about him. Ever.

My dad only mentioned his mom/my grandmother when he spoke of his immediate family, which didn't mean a rat's ass to me because I never met the woman. She died of colon cancer before I was born, and the only stuff I knew about her was what my dad wanted people to know about her. From what I can remember, there weren't any glowing reviews or anything like that other than my mom said she was a "good woman" and left it at that.

Looking back on it now, I see it as a blessing in disguise not knowing these individuals. I mean, if those two people are the ones responsible for creating the sheer mess that was my dad, I'm not sure having them in our lives would have been much of a pleasant experience, to say the least. Some omissions in life are actual blessings, and I can honestly say that this was one of them. For sure.

Luckily for me, I did have wonderful grandparents on my mom's side of the family. When I was five years old, my grandpa, Lero Sanders, took me fishing at Duran's pond, just outside Henderson, TX, where they lived. To this day I remember what happened on that fishing trip like it happened yesterday.

I was sitting on the bank watching my grandpa and my cousin Bryant Robinson wade in the water, bass fishing. While I was watching them, my fishing pole suddenly took off at rapid speed and headed towards the water. I jumped up to grab it and felt the resistance of what was on the other end of that line. That resistance was such an awesome, weird feeling. I mean, to think that an invisible battle had begun with something that was still in the water was an incredible, unexplainable rush.

I really didn't know what the hell to do, so I just looked over my shoulder and copied what my grandpa and cousin were doing and reeled in my very first catch – a catfish. Man, I was so proud of that catfish I could have died embracing it right then and there on the bank. I couldn't wipe the ear-to-ear grin off my face. It was stuck there, permanently frozen in time. See, this was more than just catching a fish. I loved my grandpa so much that having him there *while* I caught that fish was the real glory, the real conquering moment. He saw it! He saw me do it!

That feeling of pride is something that I have never forgotten, and I never will. That memory also brings back that instant moment when I fell in love with fishing, and I still love it to this day.

The Channel Catfish I caught weighed almost three pounds and my papa told me to turn it into that night's dinner for the family. I couldn't wait to get back home and proudly show my catch, to show my Mom and Dad what I had accomplished, to show them what I had achieved for the very first time, what I had conquered that day at the pond. I wanted to show them my prize, my pride, my joy.

As what should have been no surprise to me, the first thing that I noticed when I got home was that my dad was already at his standard level of shitfaced drunk. So, instead of getting the reception and gratification that I so desperately wanted from my father, I got shot down by him instead. Dismissed. Invalidated. Derailed. Debunked.

Instead of being proud of me, he looks at me through his alcohol-soaked eyes and with slurred speech tells me that this catfish was a mudcat and unfit to eat. Catfish. Big fucking deal I caught a catfish. He immediately let me know that this fish wasn't anything I should be proud of catching and didn't stop there. He stood up, took a knife, stabbed the fish in the fucking head with it, and walked out the back door, off into the woods, and tossed it out like garbage.

I was shattered. Just fucking shattered. That was my trophy, laying out in the woods with a knife puncture in its fucking head. Man, you just can't imagine what that feels like to a kid. Shit, even to an adult if it happened that way.

I always hated Sunday nights, too, because *60 Minutes* was one of his favorite shows and it was on during the catfish debacle. The family only had one TV with about three channels on it, so it was always about what he wanted to watch. If my brother and I made ANY noise during one of his shows, he would sit there and turn the volume up louder and louder until we got quieter. Never looked at us, never asked us to be quiet. Just turned up the volume on the TV to drown us out so he didn't have to communicate with us or acknowledge we existed.

To this day, I still hate that fucking soundtrack to *60 Minutes*. Every time I hear it, I shudder, and my skin starts to crawl. Screw Chinese water torture if you want to torment me, just play that. It will be way more effective, trust me.

My father was the kind of man that never should have had children and that's the cold hard truth of the matter. He never should have been given responsibility over another living being. He was the type of guy who coached Little League Baseball, yet never took the time to teach me how to throw, catch or hit the ball. He never felt it necessary to give me that individual daddy-to-son time, that one on-one interaction that is the foundation for any father-son relationship.

For the six years that I played in Little League, our teams were grouped by age. We had the standard 7- and 8-year-old group, the 9 and 10-year old group, and the oldest kids comprised their group of 11 and 12-year old kids.

During each of the odd-numbered years I played, I struggled through each season, yet during the even numbered years I made the All-Star Team – every single time. Was there a reason for that? Damn straight there was a reason for it, and it wasn't a coincidence. Those losing years were the years when my dad was coaching my team. I was a winner when he wasn't coaching, and a loser when he was, finishing in last place under his guidance for three out of the six years. It was a consistent losing streak piloted by a consistent loser. My dad used to call me the "Strike Out King," yet he was the one who struck out on everything he did. Game. Set. Match. Asshole.

It's true that I didn't have any confidence in myself at that point of my life, and it's also true that I couldn't get out of my own way to save my life. But to be fair to myself and call a spade a spade, I also didn't possess some of the things that I needed the most to develop into a better person at that time. I was never given the leadership or guidance that I needed to succeed like every other kid would need. I wasn't given the proper materials to learn from because I didn't have the positive male example to give them to me. I didn't have any male lead. I didn't have any positive male exposure. All I could do was sit back on the sidelines and enviously watch as the other dads in the neighborhood supported their sons.

All I ever got from the male figure in my life was to be constantly degraded and told how bad I was, how worthless I was, how much of a disappointment I was to him. He never gave me anything, he never did anything of substance for me, and he never cared about any of it. Hell, my mom is the one who taught me how to ride a bike and throw a baseball.

I can think of only one thing that he gave me that was worth anything to me. One. One thing. Yes, there is *one* thing. He gave me the ability to defend myself. He did. My dad loved boxing and it was through this love that he taught me those skills. I was one of the younger kids in the neighborhood and when I got picked on by the other kids, my dad would watch, almost like he was the referee or something. He would make me stand my ground and fight the other kids. He made me face those fears. Most of the time I won and when I did, it made that smug bastard happy.

Funny. The *one* thing he taught me was the *one* thing that made him outwardly happy. He used to put up his dukes to me and say, referring to his fists, "This is ole buck and this is ole ball, when one of them hits you, you are bound to fall…Mohamad Ali…" And then he would just laugh. It was amazing that such a cold bastard even knew how to laugh, but apparently, he knew how to do it, he was just very selective about showing it.

Odd as he was, everything he did and everything he touched was also done at the same level of odd. Yep. That crazy bastard would have made Lewis Carroll proud in proving his statement: "We're all mad here." Ain't that the truth, though?

With the turn of the fall leaves, I went into 6th grade and Little League Football came into my life. It was the first year for the league and I made one of the teams. Unfortunately for me, my football career was extremely short lived thanks to a few C's on my first report card that year. After playing only one game, I was grounded and forced to quit the team. My friends got to play football on Saturdays, and I got to stay home and feel ashamed and embarrassed. #Winning.

The shining light, though? That was also the year my mom left my dad. That's when life really started to change for the better, and I mean *really* started to change. The future was about to take a sharper, more sober, happier turn. Finally.

***

It came time for me to go into the 7th grade and start Jr High School. I couldn't wait to start junior high for one major reason – they had snack machines in that building. Sweet, right? Hey, you laugh. That was a big deal back then and was one of the perks of getting older. I made the football team that year and earned the position of running back.

I was beyond pumped that I was going to be carrying the ball and standing behind the QB. Yeah, baby. What a stud position that was for me. I always loved Terry Bradshaw and Franco Harris of the Pittsburgh Steelers and here I was, at the age of 12, playing the same position as my hero Franco. Wow. Snack machines *and* playing Franco's position? Fuck ya, life was *goooood*!

Unfortunately for me, yet again, that level of cool didn't last for very long, either. Shortly thereafter, my mom remarried and after only getting to play one game like one of the cool kids, we moved 30 miles away to the teeny tiny town of Beckville, Texas. And I mean tiny. Beckville had one flashing traffic light, one Affiliated Food Store for groceries, and one convenience store, Bearcat Grocery, that sold gasoline. (I would later work there when I turned 13.) It was also a town that didn't offer much in terms of social activity and worldly experience, but it was home. For now.

I was terrified when we moved to Beckville. All my friends and everything I ever knew were back home in Spring Hill, and when you're 13, it's not like you can just hop in your car and go see your buddies whenever you want. Shit, back in those days, there were still "toll calls" on your home phone bill if you called outside your county. You were basically in another solar system being 30 miles away, at that.

Living in this small town brought something out in me, though. Feeling isolated caused my soul, my essence of being, to take an unexpected sharp left turn. It started on my last day of school at Spring Hill. At the time, I was so in love with a girl named Teri Hardy, it was ridiculous. When I had to say goodbye to her, I was so devastated I cried over it. Yep. I cried. It didn't matter that she wasn't my girlfriend, either. I was in LOVE, man. LOVE! This girl owned my heart, and everyone knew it.

My mom, being the cool person that she was, took me to buy a gold necklace that had a "T" charm on it. Since I was too chicken-shit to give it to Teri myself, I had one of my friends give it to her on my last day of school, after I had already left school property.

I thought about that day for years afterwards, and at our 25th high school reunion, Teri and I got the chance to laugh about it together. It was pretty frickin' awesome when she told me that she still had that necklace. Gave me such an odd sense of validation for some reason. Geez. It even made it worth crying in public.

After the reunion, she drove me back to my mom's house and as we came to a stop in my mom's driveway, I leaned over and kissed her, making the comment that it only took 30 years to get that kiss, but I finally got it!

We both laughed out loud with each other again, kissed each other goodbye one more time, and away she went. It's amazing how situations like that can give a person a sense of peace and worth when finding out that it mattered to someone else, too, back then and now. Maybe it's the innocence of it all. Maybe that's what true love is really supposed to give you. A sense of peace and worth.

I don't know what to call it, but I do know that the memory will always be one of the most gratifying memories of my life. Thank you for that, Teri. Thank you *very* much.

***

During the Junior High days, my mom married for a second time to a real dick of a guy named Fred. Fred promised my mom the world and promised to be the father that my brother and I never had, but he never did any of it. He, too, was nothing more than a cheap fraud of a man, just like my father.

Fred had two daughters and was a shitty parent to them, so there really was no incentive for him to change his ways for us. His biggest problem was that he thought he was something special, something unattainable to most, when he was nothing more than a huge dipshit of a human being.

He liked to have nice things and constantly tried to compete with the Joneses off a lower middle-class salary, which, needless to say, didn't work out all too well for him. He desperately wanted everyone to think he was something that he was far from being, and because of that, he always came across as being a totally fake, pompous ass. We didn't get along much as I couldn't fucking stand him, but I did genuinely like my two stepsisters, Monica and Kim. They were cool people, and it was hard to believe they were created by such a jackass of a man.

***

In 7th grade, when I played defensive end, I had no clue what I was doing. (I KNOW…Lil' ole me playing defensive end!?) No clue. During the first week I was there, I played my first game ever as a Beckville Bearcat and played with kids that were total strangers to me. I barely knew anyone's name at that time and of course my father never came to one game to watch me play. Not one.

The only saving grace of my 7th grade year was the introduction to rock-n-roll. By the time I entered 8th grade in 1984, my life was set on a rockin' path and set to change forever.

Back in the 80's, kids brought their "jam boxes" to school to rock out with during recess and lunch. Man, all those cool songs that were coming out then – songs that have stuck around to modern day. Those were the songs that paved the way to what has become my lifelong passion: The World of Rock-n-Roll.

It was a world where "Hot Girls in Love" by Loverboy, "Looks that Kill" by Motley Crue, "The Warrior" by Scandal, "Bang Your Head" by Quiet Riot, and "Bark at the Moon" by Ozzy Osbourne had fists pumping in the air and crispy hair sprayed hair tossing in the wind. The first rock-n-roll album I ever bought was Loverboy's *Keep it up!*, followed by *1984* by Van Halen, *Midnight Madness* from Night Ranger, and last but certainly not least, Ratt's *Out of The Cellar*.

I remember standing in my bedroom, rocking out, constantly rewinding the cassette tapes over and over again. I swear, it was my salvation. My Zen place. I can't tell you how many times I played the intro to Van Halen's "Jump." It started with just a keyboard playing a strong staccato rhythm, then built with drums and a signature scream by lead singer David Lee Roth. The lyrics spoke to me: "I get up…..and nothing gets me down… You got it tough, I've seen the toughest around."

That was it. I was hooked and never looked back. I found my niche. I found my compatibility and coping methods. Finally.

\*\*\*

MTV was the shit back then, back when they played music videos and not these stupid reality shows that are long around now. Back then, MTV changed the path of my entire generation because every dude on the planet wanted to be David Lee Roth, and every chick had David Lee Roth posters on their walls. Before turning the rocker leaf, I was a country boy who loved bands like Alabama, Johnny Cash, Kenny Rogers, Conway Twitty, Oak Ridge Boys, and Ronnie Milsap. That's damned good music and all, but once I was introduced to Rock-n-Roll, I was like a snake that had to shed its skin.

In an instant, the cowboy hats and Wrangler jeans were out and the long hair, acid washed jeans, and devil horns were in, baby. Rock and Roll! YEAH! Oh, and the boots. The cowboy boots. Ya, I kept those.

Despite my newly fashioned devil horn toting ways, I faithfully attended church at the Calvary Baptist Church. I always felt safe there, and I always looked forward to seeing certain folks. Brother Cox was a great preacher and a good man, and I often think about him to this day.

While living in Beckville, I sat and waited on many occasions for my father (who rarely showed up) to come and get me. When he did show up, it wasn't anything great to me because the weekends spent with him always sucked and were nothing more than a total waste of time.

One weekend, I made him watch the Motley Crue VHS video titled "Uncensored" in an attempt to share a part of my life with him. All he had to say was "Look at these washed up, no good, dope smoking, hippy fags, AIDS-ridden, Losers," and laugh in disgust. No matter how I tried to defend my band and my passion, he would just repeat himself all over again. What sucked most of all is that it seemed to me his spending any time with my brother and me was a total waste of time to him, a huge inconvenience.

It was Hell. Pure Hell. I had two wannabe father dicks in my life, and neither one of them cared that I was alive. I was suppressed by all that dark, hazy, negative male energy with only one small ray of light and hope that came from my neighbor, Frank Allums. He was the one that became the male mentor in my life besides my grandpa. I am still in touch with Frank to this day and love him and his family as if they were my own. I owe him a lot for being there for me back then. I don't know what I would have done without him.

***

I hated going to school at Beckville. I hated it. It was an exceedingly small school with grades K 12 all on the same campus and the buildings very close together. I was always being bullied by the older kids. I felt out of sync there because I just didn't fit in and didn't know how to go about fitting in. I still wasn't handling the stress of my parents' divorce very well, my dad was an absentee dad, my new stepdad was a total fucking dick, and on top of all that, I'm now the new kid at school.

All my good friends were back home in Longview, and I missed them so much I couldn't stand it. How do you possibly top that? Not to worry. I managed to do it. Now add an embarrassing medical condition to my roster of issues. Just what an outcast kid needs to be able to fit in with the crowd, right?

The level of stress that I was under caused massive stomach issues, giving me cramps so bad that at times I would have to bend over or lay down until they lessened or went away. Was really an awesome time for me when it struck at school, let me tell you. I could barely walk when they were in full swing, and they lasted for what seemed like an eternity. There were times they got so bad, I sincerely thought I was going to die, right then and there in the nurse's office or right there in the hallways.

As time wore on, the cramps became the norm, so my mom decided to take me to the doctor and see what the hell was going on with me. The doctor ordered an upper and lower GI, which, back in those days, was not common for someone my age. So, I went for a procedure where they stick one camera-tube thing down your throat and one up your ass. The prep alone for this was awful. Shit. For days after it was done, I still felt violated, not to mention I was raw on both ends for a few more days after that.

The tests came back indicating I had a spastic colon, caused by, oddly enough, stress. Hmm. Go figure. Stress caused it. No way. I was prescribed some over-the-counter products and a laxative, but none of it worked.

Eventually my mom made the decision to move back to Spring Hill, going right back to the house I grew up in, and I couldn't have been happier. Turns out, my smart cookie of a mom rented out the house versus selling it and we could now go back home. I couldn't wait to be back with my friends, and, of course, back to Teri.

Turns out Teri had moved to Carthage, TX, so, you know, I was a bit bummed to find that part out, but nevertheless, I was back home. Home! As soon as I was back in my happy place, the cramps went away overnight, and I was no longer being picked on or bullied at school. I was back where I belonged, and I felt like a 10,000-pound boulder had been lifted off my shoulders. My soul felt lighter. I felt freer. I felt more confident.

Once I got back to Spring Hill, I slipped right back in sync with my friends and my attitude did an immediate 180-degree turnaround. I was alive again. I was lighter, wiser, happier. I had positive thoughts again. I immediately went back to being involved at the New Beginning's Baptist Church and faithfully attended throughout the rest of my high school days. It was like waking up from a bad dream and being grateful for it.

During high school, I was extremely athletic and played both varsity football and baseball for all four years. Three of those baseball years were played at Spring Hill and I split football with two years at Beckville and two years at Spring Hill. I lettered all 4 years in both sports and earned a letter jacket from both schools.

All my accomplishments weren't magical enough to change things with my stepdad, and I still struggled with my confidence at times because of that. Not having a father figure in the house gravely affected me, even though I always had my grandpa to lean on.

I remember back in the 10th grade when I was the starting 3rd baseman at Spring Hill in a game against Beckville, I couldn't wait to play them. I didn't like most of the boys on the team from days past and there was nothing I wanted more than to beat the shit out of them and prove that I was better. In the first inning, a hard line drive was hit directly to me and "wham," I snatched it for an out. Then later, a hard ground ball came my way and "bam," I scooped it right up and gunned the guy out at first. I had a couple of hits in that game, too, and we ended up with an easy win.

I was filled with so much excitement that it was almost overwhelming. It was like sticking a fork in someone's eye, but on a more pleasurable level, if there is such a thing. I had a gun for an arm that many players would kill for, and I could throw someone out at first like nobody's business.

It felt so good to be back playing sports, feeling good about myself. I was wild, though, and had a hard time with control, therefore throwing errors became the norm. Back in the 11th grade, I recall a hard line drive was hit to me at 3rd base and like always, I scooped that ball right up but had a difficult time making the throw because I always over-thought it. There was a runner on third and I had to decide whether to throw it home or go to first base. I panicked and when I threw the ball, I sent it between home plate and first base. What a fucking idiot. I stood in disbelief and devastated as I watched the ball hit the fence by our dugout.

The runner on third scored and the boy who hit the ball ended up on second base. I remember the reactions of our fans when I made that horrible throw.

I could hear the rumblings.

"What the hell are you doing?"

"What is this kid thinking?"

"Get him out of there coach!"

See, the fans had witnessed me making so many amazing stops at third base but had also seen me overthrow our first baseman so many times, as well. Now they're watching me throw the ball into no man's land and giving up runs. No medium ground there.

During practices I would over concentrate during warmups, and I couldn't hit my partner with a throw from 10 feet away. He would spend more time running after the ball than we would spend on the warmup. When it came to hitting the ball, I was known as a "crusher," at least when I was at practice.

Our coach used a pitching machine, and when he would load that ball, it would spit out the best-looking fastball you had ever seen. "BOOM!" I would hit the fucking ball out of the ballpark, pitch after pitch after pitch. If only I could hit the ball like that during a game, that would be great, but it just didn't happen that way.

Remember, when I was in Little League, my dad called me the "Strike-Out King," so that demon was still alive and kicking inside me. It was so frustrating that I couldn't get a hit to save my life now. Dammit! My batting average was below 200, and I eventually asked my coach to bench me for a couple of games to let me gather my confidence. He granted my wish too quickly and I immediately lost my starting position, and never started again.

By the time senior year rolled around, my baseball career was a total bust. There was a new baseball coach, and he was a 100% pure asshole. Ah, Coach Tidwell. How I will never forget you, you fucking prick. He was a total meathead, and we butted heads from day one, stemming back to football season.

I will say this, though. I can look back now and recognize how some repercussions were direct results of my own actions. Yes. I know. I said it. I have learned that being disrespectful doesn't get you anywhere, it just causes you pain and regret. It causes you to make further bad decisions and it forces you to carry around the negativity associated with it all. No, thanks, I'm good. I've found that forgiveness is key. Well, forgiveness combined with the ability to put the past behind you and not take it so personally that it destroys you. *That* is the key. Right there. Learn from it. Don't be destroyed by it, and then move on from it.

***

During my senior year I was the starting wing back on the football team. I would line up in the back field as a tailback or line up behind the tight end and go in motion to start the snap. I had the luxury of running the ball from the backfield or catching passes in the flat or down the sideline. I had great hands and could catch anything that was thrown to me, but unfortunately, I was too slow. I was 6'2 and 172 lbs and ran a 5.0 in the 40 yard dash.

I wasn't the biggest nor the fastest, but my whole heart went into playing on game night. I admit that I could have been a better performer if I would have taken practices more seriously and studied the game more, but I guess I was content with being just an average player. When you don't have a father figure teaching you greatness, you don't know any better than to settle for mediocrity.

True, I could have applied myself more, but I just didn't. We went 3-7 my senior year and finished last in our district. When I finally realized I was talented, it was after high school and too late to do anything with it at that point.

I did manage, however, to receive a partial scholarship to Kansas Wesleyan University in Salina, Kansas, to play both football and baseball, but blew that chance. I had gone on a recruiting trip there with a few of my friends and signed a letter of intent to play, but after my friends bailed out, so did I.

What a huge fucking mistake. Huge. It felt so good to be back in my "accepted" group that I failed to pay attention to my future, a future that wasn't going to include that same posse of high school friends. Huge mistake. Live and learn, right?

Throughout my days at Spring Hill, I was part of the "In Crowd" so to say. Senior year, I was one of just four guys nominated for the three Big Titles. I was King Shit! Now, I never won the crown for any of those Big Titles, but I *was* on the ballots for Homecoming King, Valentine King, *and* Mr. Spring Hill, thank you very much, so that totally counts.

Man, it felt so good to be popular finally. I enjoyed going to high school at Spring Hill and loved my friends dearly. Times were so good then. All I wore to school was 80's band concert T-shirts, representing bands like Poison, Def Lep, RATT, Cinderella, Bon Jovi, Motley, & Whitesnake.

I had one really cool Monsters of Rock T-shirt with Van Halen on it that I wore on my last day of high school. Loved that shirt, and I still have it. Okay, so I don't wear it anymore, but I do have it. I'll always have that shirt. It will never get thrown away. Ever. I also wore acid washed jeans and black Reebok high top shoes – you know, the ones with two Velcro straps across the top? Stylin'! Oh, and of course my jeans were rolled up. That was a fashion staple.

My hair was shoulder length in the back with wings in the front. Yes. Wings. Man, I used so much Aqua Net hairspray that it was like wearing a brick on each side of my head.

Back then, we all carried binders with clear outer sleeves to slide pictures or drawings in. I would cut out pictures of rock bands from Metal Edge & Circus Magazine and insert them into the sleeves to show support for all my favorite bands.

At home, my bedroom was plastered from ceiling to floor with cut outs from the pages of cool rock magazines like Circus, Hit Parader, and

Metal Edge, matched with the latest posters from local record stores. Each band had their designated spot on my wall, and by the time I entered my senior year, there was literally no visible paint. The walls were literally covered with my rock idols. It's what I saw every day. It's what I lived every day.

Since I was now King Shit, I had to have a cool King Shit ride to support all that ego and go along with the whole package, and I did. I had one of the coolest cars on campus, a 1969 Camaro SS, a real "hot rod" if you will. I bought that car for $2,800 back when I was only 13 years old and could only dream of the blessed day where I would be able to legally cruise around in it. Man, my car was the bomb.

I went through more sets of tires on that car than any other car I've ever owned. All it took was revving up the gas, popping the clutch, and the front tires would come off the ground and smoke would be coming from the rear. That car always left two perfect black tire trails on the pavement, too.

Looking back, I can honestly say I was a mischievous kid, but I was still a good kid. I was a fair student, falling somewhere in the B- to C+ range. To tell the truth, I just didn't like the academic side of school. I hated to fucking study and it didn't come easy to me, anyways, so there wasn't any real motivation there. Studying required a lot more work than I was willing to do, so I did just enough to get by in those days.

I liked school for my friends, sports, girls, and all the social settings that came with it. I graduated from that comfort zone the first week of June 1989. I couldn't wait to get out of school, but I had no clue what I was going to do. I had no real understanding of what being a young adult meant. I was just getting the hang of being a teenager, let alone deciding on what needed to be done for my future. Shit. One step at a time, right? What is that about Rome not being built in a day?

# THE COLLEGE EXPERIENCE

## CHAPTER 2

After graduation, I ended up going to Kilgore Jr. College for a year and transferred to Stephen F. Austin State University the following year. It was now 1991, my first week at SFA, and I was laying in my bed one night in my dorm room when someone pounded on the door and yelled, "Panty raid! Let's go!"

Instead of being excited, my first reaction was the dork in me coming out to wonder what the hell a panty raid was because I truthfully had no idea. Thankfully, another student filled me in, telling me it was a yearly tradition where the guys go over to the girls' dorm, the girls open their windows and throw down their panties to them.

I was totally down for that, so along I went with my heathen brotherhood, marching across campus to one of the dorms, with the hopes of acquiring some girl's underwear. I'll never forget the sight when we got there. There were like 100 dudes stretched across the front of the building, all of them standing under the windows, looking up and yelling for the girls to throw down their panties to them.

I remember seeing two girls looking directly down at me, so I did what everyone else was doing and yelled to them to throw me their panties. I mean, that's why I was there, right? Right. But what I didn't expect was for one of the girls to yell back to me, telling me that I had to show her my goods first.

Ya, it took me by surprise, but I didn't hesitate. Not for a second. I flipped around, mooned her, and "BAM" she threw down a yellow thong.

I remember holding that thong (I still have that, too) and within 3 seconds, I was tackled from behind, taken to the ground, and taken down hard. Before I knew what was happening, my hands were behind my back, and I was in handcuffs. Two officers picked me up, and through the haze, I asked them what I was being charged with. I found out I was getting nailed for indecent exposure. Ha. They walked me over to the police car, opened the door, and stuffed me in the back.

Yep. Cuffed and stuffed. Now, if you have ever been arrested, you know how difficult it is trying to stay balanced while getting in a police car with your hands cuffed behind your back while someone is pushing down on your head. I was scared, too, don't let me fool you. I had never been to jail before, and I had no idea of what to expect once I got there.

When we got to the police station, the police officers pulled me out of the car and took me inside to the booking area. I looked like such a tool, too. I was wearing green shorts, Rebooks, and no shirt. Everyone's reaction when they saw me was quite comical, I have to admit. If I saw some guy walking in looking like me, I would have laughed, too. Fuck ya, I would have!

I was told I could make one phone call and that I would be detained for at least four hours. After that, I could make bail. I called my roommate Kevin to see if he could bail me out and he began the mission of rounding up some cash to get me out. After the four hours were up, bail was posted, and I was free to go. When I walked outside into the lobby, a group of my friends was there, clapping and just howling at me. They couldn't believe it was me that went to jail out of all of us. I felt like the young Henry Hill in Goodfellas the first time he got popped selling those cigarettes out of his trunk. The bail was like 80 bucks and all my buddies chipped in. Remember, back in 1990, $80 was a lot of money for college kids to come up with, especially on short notice.

I remember calling my mom the next day to fill her in on my jail experience. I think the worst part was telling her that it all stemmed from a panty raid. Man, how embarrassed I was having to tell her that part. Meh. It's all in a day's outing when you're young, in college, and live by the creed of just living life and having a good time, no matter how stupid or juvenile the reasoning behind it.

*** 

I went to Southwest Texas St University after putting in one year at SFA. Did I have a blast there, you ask? Hellyeah! Maybe a little too much. I had so much fun that after an entire year, I only completed seven course hours, earned my first college "F," and got kicked out at the end of my second semester.

It was now Spring of 1992 and I had two choices to make: One, go to summer school to get my grades back up; or, two, take a year off. I knew that the second option wasn't going to jibe with my mom, so instead of staying in San Marcos, I ran home, back to Kilgore Jr College.

Okay. So, I wasn't running from school. I was running away from this girl named Leigh. Leigh was from Columbus, TX, and was a beautiful blonde with beautiful skin. I fell in love with her at first sight when I met her at a country bar in San Marcos. She was wearing tight faded blue jeans with tall black boots and a leather multicolored jacket with lots of red in it.

Man, that girl played me like a fiddle for well over a year. I never really had her to myself either, because she was still seeing her boyfriend from back home. The more she played me, the more I chased her. The more I chased her, the more it led me to devastating disappointment. Basically, I got the beginner's 101 lesson in getting played. I became obsessed with the thought of having Leigh as my girlfriend to the point where it drove me crazy. I had no choice but to run back home and get away from her.

Believe it or not, she still reaches out to me every now and then, but at least I no longer feel the need to run away from her.

I had some great times at Southwest Texas with its beautiful campus and beautiful coeds walking all around it. I remember one girl from my biology class. I don't recall her name but man she was smoking hot – *That* I remember. She had long blonde hair, the most beautiful, tanned skin you have ever seen, and she was an absolute 10 in my book.

One day, out of nowhere, I got the balls to talk to her. Lo and behold, we hit it off. We went out one night, and she ended up staying at my place. I was pumped that she was sleeping next to me in my bed. It was like a dream coming true.

The next morning, we were laying on my couch watching MTV when Kurt Louder came on the MTV news. He announced that Vince Neil had been fired and was out of Motley Crue. I was like WTF? I jumped up, totally feeling distraught for some reason, and told my blonde 10 that she had to go home. Immediately. I told her to go *home*. I mean, I realize I couldn't wrap my brain around the thought of Vince no longer being in Motley, but kicking out a hot blonde that you connect with, what was wrong with me?

I'll tell you what was wrong with me. My idolization and soulful connection that I felt to a band completely took over my senses and sensibility. Holy shit, Motley is done! They're done! Fucking over! Now what? Seriously. *Now* what?

My roommate at the time was a cool, little bit older guy named Jody. He transferred with me from SFA, and we lived in, well, a dump. Hey, that's all we could afford back then, and we were content with being on our own and having a roof over our heads. Ah, yes, Shalamar Apartments is what they were called. I called them "Shitamar Apartments," because they were so nasty. We had roaches out the ass, the carpet was grey from years of built-up stains, and all of the appliances were outdated, but we made the best of it.

It was the perfect party house, and we partied our asses off there. We didn't have to worry about ruining the place. Jody owned a bass and an electric guitar with a decent amp, and had a microphone rounding off the set for the homemade band that would merge at our parties.

That's when I jumped in. I couldn't sing for shit, but always wanted to be a "rock star." So I had fun with it. The bars closed in San Marcos at midnight during the week and closed at 1 am on Saturdays, so it was only natural to bring the party back to our place after the bars closed.

The cops became a permanent fixture to the point that Jody and I would take turns getting the ticket for disturbing the peace. And let me tell you something. When you're flat broke, a $35 ticket dips into your eating and drinking money big time.

One night, these same cops knocked at our door, and I will never forget this one officer. He was a huge black man, stood like 6'6," and always looked mean as hell. That night, Jody and I thought it would be funny to crank up the amp and taunt the cops a little bit. Jody whammed his guitar loud as hell and we shouted out through the microphone "keep a-knocking, but you can't come in!"

Yep. That went over like salt in one's eye and earned us a court date. When it was our turn to stand in front of the judge, he told us that if he ever saw us in his courtroom again, we would be taken straight to jail. No further questions asked. No further opportunities given. No get out of jail free card. No collecting $200.00.

As fast as the parties started to happen and gain momentum, they abruptly stopped. May have been an end to our party place, but it sure as hell wasn't the end of the partying.

There was one night where Jody, me, and one of Jody's friends went to a frat party at the TKE House. It was a Friday night, so bars and beer sales in stores closed at midnight. While there was still time, Jody and his buddy decided to take my badass Oldsmobile Cutlass 442 to the store to grab more beer for an after party. My car was awesome, too. It was white with gold trim and gold wheels, and it hauled ass. I loved that car.

Anyway, my buddy and I waited and waited and waited back at the frat house, and well, they never came back. I was wrecked with worry until I got the knock at the door, and it was Jody. His buddy apparently was the one driving my car. He had lost control of it on an S curve and plowed into someone's yard, clipping a telephone pole. Jody told me that if it weren't for a huge tree stump in the front yard, my car would have plowed right into the house.

Fucking car was totaled, and when I called home in the middle of the night to tell my mom, guess who got on the phone and was a total asshole about it all? Yep. That would be Fred. Fred, the dick.

 Shit really hit the fan when he drove down to San Marcos the next day. I couldn't believe he was being such a dick, more than usual, but I also wasn't surprised by it. What he didn't grasp is that originally, I was going to ride with them to the store, but my buddy and I decided to stay behind and chat with some girls we met.

Luckily for me my hormones won over that night because the back seat of my car was destroyed. There's no way I would have survived that hit. Didn't matter to Fred. Not one bit. The thought of losing me didn't affect him in any way, shape, or form. It was more important to him to always make me out to be some unworthy dumbass.

***

I left San Marcos in 1992 and moved back home to be with my mom. I attended summer classes at Kilgore Jr College to improve my grades, and then transferred back to SFA where I began my third year of college as a freshman. You know, the six-year plan. Yikes. Three years of college and still a fucking freshman. Wow. That's like some really bad After School Special right there. Still, I couldn't find the proper motivation to apply myself to getting an education. All I wanted to do was chase girls.

I stayed away from alcohol until I was 21 because I feared becoming my father, but by the time I made it back to SFA, the partying and drinking kicked into warp speed. Once back at SFA, I lived in another wonderous dump of a 4-plex apartment building. My unit was a two-bedroom shithole that must have been built somewhere back in the 60's. Maybe even the 50's. Everything was a dingy brown color. Everything. From the walls to the carpet. Brown. It worked well, though, with the black light and Miller Genuine Draft neon sign I had in my room. I thought that was the "cool" thing to do, you know, by creating some mood lighting when girls were spending the night.

Seriously, I was maniacal about the girls, though. That's all I wanted to do. Meet girls, party, meet girls, party, have sex with girls, keep partying, which was easy to do because my four-plex was party central.

My roommate was Robert, and later Kurt, but there were others that filtered in and out like temporary boarders. There was Curt, Scott, Chris, Steve, and, of course, there was James. We had a softball team on campus, and we named it "9 Dudes and a Beaner" in honor of James being Mexican. We had a great team and shared great times, but the best thing we did together was drink cheap beer (Busch Light, Miller Genuine Draft, Natural Light & Bud Ice). I shudder at the thought of that now.

It was an easy life, though. We played wiffleball, ate ramen noodles, grilled $1.99 round steaks in the front of our building, and kept studying away in the distance.

Thursday through Saturday, everyone that was anyone would come to our place for the kegs of beer and the chicks.

One drunken night, Steve and I decided that we were going to stay up all night and drink until the sun came up. Next thing you know, as we're rocking out to Pantera we hear a BOOM!

We opened the door, and there stood Chris, with a shotgun in his hand. Jackass just blew a hole in the wall for the hell of it. Didn't faze us, though. Steve and I kept drinking, air guitaring and singing until the sun rose in the morning sky until we were the only two crazy idiots still up. There were passed out bodies all over the floor, on the couch, and in my bed. That's when Steve and I shook hands and called the drinking truce.

The next afternoon was gross, I have to tell you. The keg was floating in bathtub water that had puke floating in it. That's when I realized that Steve and I were drinking from the spout all night and dropping it back in that water. Fuck. That almost made me vomit, but that's what went on at the animal house. Sad to say you got used to it. You became immune to certain things.

During these crazy party days, I became acquainted with a girl, Jenny, who was the most incredible woman I had ever laid my eyes on up to this point in my life. Like the many before her, I had a huge crush on her from the moment I first arrived at SFA in 1990.

It was a Friday night when I saw Jenny walk up to one of our parties and I was like *Holy shit, Jenny is at my house*! It was like the Universe sent her to me, telling me that I was given back my chance.

I was still relatively shy and had a hard time walking up to girls and starting a conversation. If I was introduced to a girl, no problem, but walking up and introducing myself, I still had a tough time.

But there was something about this girl. I knew that I had to meet her, so I asked my buddy to crack the ice and introduce me to her. We ended up exchanging numbers and she quickly became an obsession of mine.

I remember one rainy Thursday night shortly after we had met, after the bars closed and the streets were flooded, a few of the guys decided to strip down and play in the nasty muddy rainwater. I'm not exactly sure whose brilliant idea it was to do that, but, nevertheless, boys will be boys and we did it. I saw Jenny pull into the parking lot, so I walked over to her car wearing nothing more than a tight pair of boxers. Wet boxers. I was flattered when she came by and when I leaned over to talk to her, I noticed my dick was sticking out through the slit in the boxers. Ah, well. Shit happens. It didn't seem to bother her any, and it was just another day at our animal house.

At the end of that spring semester on a Friday, we all went to Crossroads, which at the time was the coolest bar in town. The only bad memory I really had from there is when I threw up outside in the bushes, walked back inside, and then gave Jenny a big kiss. Oh, man. How gross. That night was the one and only night Jenny spent the night with me, too, and the one and only time we had sex. She dumped me right after that. Not sure why, but it left me broken hearted again.

***

I'll never forget one special day, June 17, 1994, when summer school was in session and the Rockets were in the NBA Playoffs. The game was interrupted by the OJ Simpson white bronco chase on live TV. We all tuned in for what seemed like forever, and we all sat around and got smashed watching O.J. roll down the 405 Freeway in LA. That was some crazy shit to watch that as it was happening.

Shortly after the chase, June 25th, Motley Crue was playing at the Starplex in Dallas. The tour was with John Corabi as the front man – the first Motley tour without Vince Neil. Spontaneously, four of us loaded up in James' SUV and made the 3-hour drive to Dallas. Chris was from Dallas, and we were going to stay at his parent's house. Once there, we made the introductions, dropped our stuff off, and then we headed to the Starplex for the show. We were poor college kids and could only afford lawn seats back then.

Once we got to the venue, the drinking began and by the time the opening act, Type-O Negative, was done performing, we were in rare form. Kevin and I got separated from Chris and James as soon as the lights went out. Kevin and I bulldozed ourselves to the front by climbing over seats and pushing people out of the way until we made it to the front row. Now in today's world, I would probably have been body slammed or clotheslined for doing what I did to get to the front, but that night, I was on a mission. No fear, baby. No fear.

I stood right in front of Nikki Sixx, screaming word for word to each song and being belligerent as hell. At the end of the show, Nikki broke his bass guitar in two pieces, looked at me and said, "Come get it."

You're damn right I'll fucking come get that. #Hellyeah! I climbed up onto the rail and when I grabbed the guitar, I fell between the stage and the front row barrier right to the floor.

When I tried to get up, two security guards grabbed me and a third one snatched Nikki's bass guitar right out of my hands. They picked me up, hauled me off to the side, and told me to get the fuck out of there. That was sobering, let me tell you. I mean, I just had Nikki's bass guitar in my fucking hands and had it ripped away. WTF! I couldn't believe it. What the hell kind of luck or karma is that? I knew I would never get that opportunity ever again, too. Or would I?

\*\*\*

On August 20, Motley was playing in Tyler, TX, at the Oil Palace with the same lineup as they had in Dallas back in June. I went to the show and made my way down to the front row, yet again. This time I knew the drill, though, so I was going to be ready when Nikki broke his guitar. I'll be damned if I didn't have déjà vu. Right after the song "Kick Start My Heart" and before the encore, Nikki reached out, grabbed my hand, pulled me on stage and as he gave me his guitar, telling me, "Break this motherfucker, you big bastard!"

I was blown away and the holy shit factor was in full force and effect. I had a ton of friends there and it's too bad we didn't have cell phones back then to capture that moment. Do you know how cool that would have been to have a video of me on stage bashing Nikki's guitar over one of the front speakers on the stage? Come on, that would have been fucking stellar.

I broke that guitar in half in one swing, leaving the strings holding it together. It made one hell of a sound as I crashed it into that front speaker, too.

Nikki looked at me and said, "Holy shit, you crazy mother fucker. You broke my guitar in one swing. You are coming backstage after the show."

And just like that, one of the stage roadies came over, grabbed me, slapped a backstage sticker on my shirt and told me to "stand over there." Looks like I got a second chance after all.

I had no idea what was about to happen for the encore. Once the stage was set, I was given a chair right behind Tommy's drum kit, and I sat there while the band finished the show. I remember "Home Sweet Home" was playing and Tommy had a cigarette in his nose.

Now, if you followed Tommy back then, you knew that was one of his tricks. He inhaled the cigarette up his nose, blew the smoke out of his mouth, and would then stick the cigarette under his bottom lip, roll it down over the cigarette and grin with that cigarette sticking straight out. I looked at Tommy, he looked at me, and I motioned for the cigarette.

I'll be damned if he didn't give it to me. I put that cigarette right up my nose and did everything that I watched him do. Holy shit did that drag give me an instant buzz. Hell, I thought for a split second that I was going to fall over. Once I put that cigarette under my lip, he cracked up and I thought that was so cool.

After the show, I was sitting backstage with the broken guitar in my hand, when John, Nikki and Tommy walked into the room. There was a cheap, $9.00 blue swimming pool on a table stocked with iced down Coronas, and when Tommy walked in, he grabbed one, slammed it down, and then threw it against the wall where it shattered into a million pieces. He said, "Let the party begin!"

When the backstage party was over, Tommy invited me on his bus where I drank more Coronas and downed a fifth of Seagram's VO with him. Holy shit, I was hammered.

When it was time for the buses to pull out, Tommy asked, "Do you want to ride with us to the next show in Salina, Kansas? You can come with us, but you will need to find your own transportation home."

I thought that was the most awesome offer I'd ever gotten in my entire life, but even as drunk as I was, I knew I had to pass on it. I shook John's hand, high-fived and hugged Tommy, said thank you and then said goodbye.

When I got to my car and sat down behind the steering wheel, the world began to spin, and spin fast. I opened my door and threw up so hard I think I felt my brains move. As shitty as I was starting to feel, I was psyched it didn't happen in front of the guys.

Yes, I was still cool to Motley Crue. Safe!

***

Flash forward to 2017 where I was sitting with John Corabi after his show in Dallas with the Dead Daisies at the W Hotel bar in Dallas. We were having drinks and my good friend Doug Aldrich, who has played in several great bands like Whitesnake, Dio, and now the Dead Daisies, was telling John how he and I met in Vegas. Turns out, I was lucky that I didn't make the trip with them to Kansas because there was some major bus issue on the loop in Tyler and the night turned into a disaster. Hard to believe that I made such a good decision while inebriated, but I did.

***

It was now the fall of 1994 and to me, college was still all about partying, chasing girls, and skipping class. This was when my Mom put her foot down on my irresponsible lifestyle and told me that I wasn't going to get any more financial support from her after this year.

Can you say, "Cut off?"

Man, that was a rude wakeup call. At the same time, I realized that all my friends in college had graduated and moved on and yet here I remained at the age of 23, still in college, and still getting help from Mommy. I felt like such a moron and needed to change things. Pronto.

I got off my ass and registered for 21 hours that upcoming fall semester and registered for another 23 hours the following Spring semester. I worked hard and made the Dean's List both semesters for the first time ever and finally graduated in May of 1995.

My mom had made the decision to go back to school, and on my graduation day, my mom crossed the stage before me. How cool is that? I mean, how many people can say that? I was so proud of her. And I was proud of myself.

It was amazing to walk across the same graduation stage as my Mom to collect our degrees. It was so awesome it almost made the Jagermeister hangover bearable. It didn't matter that I woke up that morning with my face stuck to the carpet. My mom and I both graduated college. Together. Wow. By the Grace of God, we did it.

That morning before I walked into the arena, I spoke to my dad, and he told me he couldn't make it to my graduation because of some back pain he was experiencing. I was pretty sad and disappointed that he didn't come, but it was nothing new. I knew he was never going to come and support me, or my Mom for that matter. I knew it was a pipe dream of mine to think that he would be sitting in the audience while I walked across that graduation stage.

It's amazing you never get used to that type of disappointment. I never did, unfortunately for me. The only difference this time is that I was a disappointed college graduate.

# MIA

## PART 2

# DALLAS

## CHAPTER 3

This chapter is extremely difficult for me to relive because it forces me to re-feel some of the most painful memories of my entire life. Aside from how it makes me feel to do this, I want to be fair to the woman involved in this chapter and not force her to have to go through these painful memories again at my doing. So, out of respect to the entire situation, I'm using a fictitious name. If she ever reads this, she will absolutely know who she is, and that's good enough for me. But I do hope that one day, she sees the respect that I still have for her and realizes that my intention in writing it all down is to simply tell my story. Nothing more.

She was a big part of my journey – *my* journey. I can't speak for her or where she is in her life now, or even to where she was in her life back then, even when I was a part of it. This has nothing to do with her current life's journeys, for which I only wish her the best of everything that life has to offer her. Cheers to you, Mia!

Immediately after college in May of 1995, I moved to Dallas and began my career in the alcoholic beverage industry (which, by the way, has been wonderful to me some 25 years later). When I moved, I had the clothes in my closet and a good buddy named Brian, and that was it. Brian lived in Arlington and let me sleep on a futon until I could save up enough money to get a place of my own.

Did I mention the futon was right next to the garage? Like, *right* next to it? Didn't matter. The sound of the garage door opening and closing lulled me to sleep, as I remained grateful to have a place to sleep. It wasn't so bad.

I had a car to get me around town - a hot little orange number. That's right, don't be jealous. It was a Mazda RX7 that burned oil so bad that when you pressed on the accelerator, it looked like the mosquito man was flying by you. But hey, that didn't matter either. I had graduated college, landed a job, and moved to Dallas. I was making moves. I wasn't being stagnant, or stuck, or even lost. Goals were being accomplished and my future was wide open and looking bright.

Now, with all that positive momentum came a few twists and turns, and it all centered around the Men's Club of Dallas. I was really into playing softball and had been playing it for years, right up until I moved to Dallas. Some of the guys I had played with prior also played on the Men's Club Coed Team and the Men's Club Men's Team in Dallas. All good guys, and yes, it's just what you would think it would be. Strippers galore to say the least.

Here I'm thinking ... Holy shit, I get to play softball with all these hot ass chicks all summer long? Seriously? Man, I *love* softball. Score! It was like heaven on Earth, my very own Playboy Mansion. Every single one of these girls was absolutely gorgeous. And I mean *all* of them.

I had been playing with Rick and some of the other guys for a while in tournaments, and since I moved to Dallas, I was also going to play with Rick on both Men's Club teams every Sunday. At the very first coed game I played, our pitcher. Rick (RIP buddy), who was also the coach, told me to go play right-center field.

He told me, "Anything hit to the girl next to you in right field? You make sure you field the ball because she sucks. You got it?"

I was like, "Yep, I got it." In my mind, I'm thinking, run over to the hot ass chick. Ya. Fairly sure I've got that covered. Let's do that. Come on batter, batter … swing. Let's hit that shit to right field. As luck would have it, the ball was hit to right field and I could see that the girl in right field didn't know what the fuck she was doing, so I swooped in front of her, fielded the ball, and made the cutoff throw to second base.

She was like, "Hey, cheeseball! Um, thanks, but I would have had that ball." ("Cheeseball," it turned out, was one of her favorite words.) I looked over at her, grinned, and jogged back over to my spot in right-center field.

When my first at-bat came up, I hit a triple and on my way to third base, and made a safe slide. It was a sweet play and all, except for the fact that when I slid in, I damned near took off all the hide on my right shin leaving this huge strawberry-like burnt patch. Now, if you've ever had a strawberry like that, you know damned well that they burn like hell, and it inflames and starts throbbing immediately. Immediately. Then, of course, once you're in the shower and go to clean it up, and the water hits it, you just about want to jump out of your skin. You get to relive the burn all over again, but times ten. And then you get to deal with it as it heals. You know what I mean. It sucks!

After leaving my DNA on the field and scoring, I came into the dugout, took a seat on the bench, and was admiring my new strawberry that was about eight inches long and about three inches wide. The hot girl from right field walked over and surprisingly offered to help me. She had a towel and a bottle of Avian water with her and doctored me up a bit.

She introduced herself as Mia as she poured the water on my leg. I tried to act tough through that very distinctive sting and not let her know how much it burned like hell. I also continued the tough guy act when she used a towel to clean the dirt off it.

Okay, so, it could have been a more grueling experience, I admit it. It wasn't all that difficult to get through the misery because Mia was stunning. She stood at about 5'6", had long brown hair, brown eyes, beautiful Hispanic dark skin, big fake boobs, and a smile to kill for. Just gorgeous. She had this swagger about her, too. She used to wear her hat backwards, and that took sexy to an absolutely new level.

When the next inning was up, I went back out to right field and started chatting with her. I kind of felt that she was flirting with me a little, so I kept the communication going. Remember, this time was easier since the ice had been broken when she cleaned up my leg. I was more comfortable engaging with her now.

After the game, everyone walked together to the parking lot and I saw that Mia had a badass '95 white Corvette convertible with a black top. Man, that car was phat! Now here I was at just 24 years old, had just graduated college the previous week, was sleeping on my buddy's futon, had a piece of shit car, and was broke as hell. What girl wasn't looking for a guy with *those* qualities, right? Shit.

The real question came down to how was I going to be able to get with her, or any of these chicks for that matter, with those shitty credentials?

Despite the odds against me, Mia and I somehow became the best of friends. As it turned out, we did have a lot in common. For starters, we both liked rock-n-roll music and we both liked to drink and party and that was good enough for me at that age. As the summer progressed, so did softball and so did our friendship. We went to concerts all the time, hung out at the touristy Guadalupe River, and constantly went to sporting events with her friends.

I remember during one of our softball games, I was moved to left field and couldn't help but notice that our third baseman Susie and shortstop Paula (who was dating Mickey Tettelton from the Texas Rangers then) were both gorgeous, as well. They were both wearing tiny, little, short-

shorts and as every pitch was tossed, they would both bend over into the "ready" position. Needless to say, that view was to die for, and the rest of my summer was spent playing left field staring at those perfect bodies. From behind. Have I said how much I love softball?

During the day, I was working a full-time job as a merchandiser for Julius Schepps, a liquor distribution company. I wasn't making much and was only bringing home about $500 every two weeks. I needed a second job to survive and save to get my own apartment, and have enough left over to be able to party. So, where else was I to go to get a part-time job? None other than the Men's Club of Dallas, folks. The obvious solution, no?

I was hired to work on Friday and Saturday nights as a floor manager, working from 7 pm to close. I vividly remember my first night on the job like it was just yesterday. I was instructed to watch the floor, protect the girls from the customers, and also make sure that the girls follow the rules.

Now, most of the women that worked at the Men's Club were knockouts. This was back in the day when strip clubs were the shit. Funny how times change, though, isn't it? When I worked there in 1995, the girls weren't allowed to have any visible tattoos. Can you imagine trying to enforce that restriction nowadays? You'd lose more than half your workforce.

On my first night, there were two girls with a customer out by the pool who were not acting within the code. They weren't following the rules and I was told they had to follow the rules, dammit! I reported it to my floor manager, and he immediately went out to the girls, told them to go inside to conduct their business and to either follow the rules or go the fuck home.

The one physically solid chick exchanged some words with him and the next thing I know, she starts walking towards me, glaring at me, all pissed off. She looks me dead in the eye and says, "Thanks, asshole," as she walks off.

I was like, okay, then, I see how things are going to go here. I just stood there and watched "Ice" from the Gladiators go to the dressing room, get her shit, and go home. No money for *you* tonight.

Up until now, I really thought I was the man, let me tell you. I mean, who gets to work at the Men's Club, play softball on the Men's Club softball teams, and hang out with Men's Club girls every week? Me. That's right. Me! And I loved every fucking minute of it. Unfortunately for me, though, all that hype and glory was short-lived. Very short-lived. I quickly learned that I was living a life that was out of my league. Way out of my league.

Funny how small the world can be at times, and it's even funnier how things can happen when you least expect it. I packed up and moved in Dallas to The Village, which is right off Greenville Avenue near Lover's Lane. (Back then, The Village was "the" place to be as all the action in Dallas was nearby.) One day, I recognized a dancer from the Men's Club hanging out at the Village pool, and was like, *Holy shit, it's her. It's fucking her!* She was the tall, tanned, slender dancer with perfect breasts and straight blonde hair and she used to dance to Ozzy Osbourne's "No More Tears" at the Men's Club. She did her thing while surrounded by dry ice and cracking a whip. You know, I think I fell in love with her a little more each time I saw her dance.

Once we made eye contact, I could tell that she recognized me. Once I was sure, I immediately went over to her and began flirting. Why the hell not, right? Tell me what guy wouldn't have at least given it a shot.

Next thing you know, she's sitting on my shoulders in the pool, in her skimpy black string bikini. I was the envy of every dude at the pool for sure. I felt that this was truly a moment in my life that needed to be seized so I came up with a master plan. A plan of all plans. I walked over to the end of the high diving board, with her still on my shoulders, and in front of the 100+ people that were hanging out that day, I jumped. As soon as we hit the water, I felt the pressure of her legs squeezing around my neck. Ah, yes. The thought of drowning wasn't my concern. The thought of needing to surface and breathe didn't get my attention. Nope. It was those thighs around my neck that got priority. That sensation took over all deductive reasoning, rational or not. I was living the desired life. Right. Fucking. Now.

Mia and I started going out and partying it up in Dallas pretty frequently. We would stay out until 3 or 4 am and just get totally sloshed. I had a major crush on her and did the best I could to keep it to myself. I had to keep things relaxed and well, most importantly, open. Why? Well, first of all, there were always plenty of hot girls on the scene, so I didn't want to limit myself there. Not to mention, Mia had just recently separated from her husband Mike, so she was technically still a married woman. I needed to tread lightly there. Mike was a successful businessman who owned a limousine company in Dallas, and Mia was still tied to all of that.

One night, Mia and I were chilling out on the roof at the Green Room in Deep Ellum, looking down on Elm Street right in front of a bar called The Bone, watching a bunch of Harley guys getting all cranked up.

There was one badass bike that was black with lots of blue colors all over it. It totally stood out from all the other bikes. I later find out that it was Mia's naked body that was airbrushed all over the bike, all the way from the front to the back. As we watched the bikes drive off, I remember her saying that the guys on the Harleys were Mike and his buddies, which stunned me for a second. I was like, wait. What? Mike? As in, husband Mike? A few seconds later, that realization that I was way out of my league with this chick struck once again. I can't tell you how many times I had that thought. Didn't matter because it clearly wasn't sinking in fast enough.

As the days rolled on, I somehow maintained that sleeping with our first baseman was a good idea. It made sense, right? Even though I can't remember her name, I do remember that she was built to perfection with boobs the size of grapefruits. She also had a fucking gun for an arm and could hum the ball around the infield better than most of the men on the team, which was kinda hot. She could hit, too, but the best part was watching her boobs bounce when she ran the bases. Hey, don't judge me. I am a man, and it was a beautiful sight to see – brought tears to my eyes, just like the girls in the left field bending over in their short shorts. Man, I love softball!

Mia was still in the picture, and one night we ended back up at her house. As soon as we got there, she ripped off the sheets, grabbed a bottle of baby oil, and poured it all over the mattress. What else were we to do but jump on the bed and start writhing around and getting all slippery, right? Right! We indulged in our very own slip and slide show, ladies and gentlemen, which up until now, I had never fucking experienced anything like that in my life. I was so caught up in the heat of the moment that I didn't remember that I was supposed to meet the first baseman babe in the morning.

As I was leaving Mia's place, she thanked me and said that our night together should last her a couple of weeks. I couldn't believe that I had crafted a plan that potentially provided me an avenue to reap benefits from the best of both worlds – Wow!

It didn't last Mia weeks, though. Soon after that night, the Mia and Britt sexcapade became a regular thing.

One Sunday, I had a pool party at my house and Mia invited several of her friends from the Men's Club to come over and join the party. Some of the girls were waitresses like her and some of the other girls were strippers. Ya. That was the best pool day I ever had. Ever. Watching all those hot bodies barely wearing string bikinis. It was truly a breathtaking moment, forever emblazoned in my brain and in my heart. Spank bank material for sure.

We all went out to party that night in Dallas, and afterward, Mia came back to my place with me to crash. She was always up for doing crazy things, so we decided to go skinny dipping. I remember a security guard walking up on us while we were having sex in the pool and telling us that we had to get out of the pool and get out immediately because the pool was closed.

We decided we had no choice but to exit in style. I climbed the pool steps with her strapped around me, put her down once we were out of the water, and we ran a brisk naked dash across the apartment complex all the way back to my place. We laughed our asses off at ourselves and this kind of behavior quickly became our norm. We always had fun when we were together. Always. And it was always something new.

On another memorable night, Mia and I closed the bars and she asked me if I was up for doing something cool. I accepted her challenge, and we drove up to the Coors Light waterfall billboard on I-35 near downtown Dallas, which is still there today.

Now, this billboard is like no billboard found anywhere else. We parked at the bottom of the hill and had to climb up through brush, through a partial cut of the fence, and even passed a few homeless people along the way. There was a *No Trespassing* sign on the fence, but we ignored it and kept going.

Once we reached the top, the first thing I heard was the sound of water coming from the replication of snow melting off the mountains in Colorado. This is what tied together the whole Coors Light advertising campaign. We climbed down to the front of the waterfall and Mia decided we should go skinny dipping again but under the waterfall this time. She stripped down to her thong panties and jumped under the waterfall.

Like a nervous nerd, it immediately became a discretion call for me. On the one hand, she was smoking hot and distracting, and on the other hand, I couldn't believe I was about to do this illegal thing because we were technically breaking the law by trespassing.

Alright, so the caution phase didn't last very long. The visual of the hot chick totally won out over giving a rat's ass about trespassing. Who the hell was going to hike up here and come get us anyway? The only thing that mattered was what was happening right here, right now (shout out to the VH fans).

I was with one of the hottest chicks on the planet, skinny dipping under the Coors Light billboard, with a killer picturesque view. I still remember that view. You could see the entire west side of downtown Dallas and the passing cars on the freeway below. Once our adrenaline rush was over, we climbed onto a piece of wood that was acting as a bench in front of the billboard. We sat there together, looking out over West Dallas, talking until the sun came up. Once the sun rose in the sky, we climbed down from the hill and Mia suggested that we get a room at the Crescent Hotel. My immediate thought was that I couldn't even afford a drink at that hotel let alone pay for a room. At that time, the Crescent was one of the only 5-star hotels in Dallas. Here we were, walking in at sunrise, in wet clothes, with Mia's long brown hair still wet and tangled. We walked into the hotel and went right up to the front desk. Mia threw down her credit card and asked for 1 room, 2 toothbrushes, and some toothpaste. I could only imagine what the hotel clerk was thinking as he checked us in. As we went up to our room, I recognized that this was my introduction to a 5-star hotel. *This* is how the wealthy folks lived. As the sun rose higher in the sky, we brushed our teeth, closed the curtains, climbed into bed, and passed the fuck out until noon.

As that summer came to an end, so did the softball shenanigans. The only thing that didn't end, however, was the shenanigans with Mia. We fell into a relationship, and I totally fell head over heels in love with her. She was still married but living with a friend in Euless, one of the mid-cities in Dallas-Fort Worth. We went to concerts, partied a lot, and did the things that a couple would normally do together, even though her marriage was always pressing on my mind the entire time.

One night we went to see Bon Jovi and Dokken at the Starplex Amphitheatre. I scored VIP seats through work and the passes came with a parking pass at the back door of the Ice House. The Ice House was the VIP club inside the venue that everyone wanted to get into, but you needed a special ticket or know someone to get in – and we were going. The club only held a few hundred people and only had two bars, but it had clean restrooms and an awesome AC.

We partied it up during the show and after Dokken played, the record label set them up inside the Ice House for their meet and greets. Once I found that out, I was determined to meet Dokken, so Mia and I got in line. When this employee asked us who we were, we lied and said we were the contest winners with the radio station 97.1 The Eagle.

Hey, fuck that! I have loved Dokken since my high school days and George Lynch was one of my favorite guitar players. There was no way in hell I was going to miss out on meeting him. No fucking way. It was now or never. Yep. I'm the contest winner alright. It was all about *now*, and I was seizing the moment.

When we walked in, we immediately saw the band sitting behind two pop-up tables. From left to right, there was Jeff Pilson, George Lynch, Don Dokken, and then Mick Brown. When it was our turn to approach the table and meet the band, I was so pumped! I couldn't believe that I was getting ready to shake hands with George Lynch and Don Dokken! Holy shit, Batman!

Mia was dressed to kill, of course, with cleavage coming out of her top and her ass peeking out of her shorts. From the second George Lynch saw her, his eyes were permanently glued on her. And I mean glued. More like fixated. When I saw this, I felt threatened, sure I did. I mean, what the fuck? I'm going to have to watch George Lynch hitting on my girl now? What the hell do I do then?

George broke my thoughts by directly saying to me, "Hey man, can I borrow your girlfriend?"

I couldn't help but be like, WTF did that fool just ask me?

He then looked to Mia and said, "How about you come meet me on my bus outside, the green one, and we can watch a movie?"

He looked at me and said, "And I didn't say I wanted her boyfriend. I said I wanted his girlfriend." He turned to Mia and made the offer to her again.

I was visibly growing more livid by the passing second, so like a true dick wanting to engage in a pissing match, George turned to Don Dokken and loudly said "Hey man, maybe the other band members want to hang out with him, but I just want to borrow his girlfriend. What do you say, girl?"

He then turned to Mia and slipped a credentials lanyard around her neck. What really pissed me off wasn't the fact that she got one and I didn't. It wasn't even the fact that this punk-ass dude did it right in front of my face, intentionally trying to set me off. What pissed me the fuck off was that Mia was falling for it. All of it. She sure as hell wasn't saying no to him, and I was about to become unglued.

When she finally caught on that all hell was about to break loose, she took my hand and we walked away. Once we were far enough away from the band, I asked her what the hell she was doing. She had the gall to try to convince me that George Lynch just wanted to watch a movie with her and nothing else.

Nothing else. A movie. He wants to watch a fucking movie with her. I wasn't buying it from him and I sure as hell wasn't buying it from her. The whole idea was ridiculous. Ya. A rock star wants to bring back a hot girl to his tour bus to do nothing more than watch a fucking movie. Of course. Watch a movie. Disney style. With glitter and fucking fairies dancing around. It was after I asked her if she was fucking retarded that a fight ensued.

I didn't think for one second that it was me who was in the wrong here, and I couldn't believe what had just actually happened. I mean, I was just publicly douched by one of my favorite guitar players and it was done with the assistance of my own fucking girlfriend. WTF was going on? Was I the only one seeing this, or what?

We grabbed a beer outside of the Ice House and walked to our seats, row 4, far right, not speaking a word to each other. Bon Jovi was already playing, and I still had steam coming off my forehead. Mia knew it, too, and just remained quiet and low-key. After just one song, I reached my limit and couldn't take it anymore. I told Mia I had to take a piss and would be right back.

Now, we all know I didn't get up to go take a piss. And we all know I wasn't coming "right back, either. Who are we kidding here? I marched my ass right back to the Ice House to see if George baby was still there and sure enough, he was still there at the bar with the tour manager.

I walked up with a vengeance and all I could think about was kicking his fucking long-haired rock star girlfriend stealing ass. The thought of MTV News also crossed my mind, and I envisioned Kurt Loder reporting the news that some young, bald, white guy beat the shit out of George Lynch at a Dokken concert in Dallas. As I got closer to them, the tour manager dude saw me coming and instantly tried to cock block me. I told him that I didn't give a fuck who he was because George disrespected me and my girlfriend and that if he wasn't careful, I'd beat *his* ass over it, too.

I never did get to George, which I can now see as a blessing in disguise. I didn't see it at the time that my rage could land me in jail and on MTV News, two very bad things for me, then and in the future. I just wanted to beat George's ass and not think of any repercussions resulting from it. Doesn't matter. The Universe handled it for me and I never got the chance.

A few years later, I told my George Lynch story to a customer who owned Pogo's, a liquor and fine wine store in Dallas. Harris was a passionate guitar player and when I told him the story, he told me he knew George and that it didn't sound like the George he knew. A couple of years later, Harris told me he was going out to see George and was going to tell him my story. When he got back from that trip, Harris relayed to me an apology from George, who wanted to apologize for his behavior. George told Harris that at the time of that show, the tour was the last tour with the original members of Dokken and he was living an out-of-control lifestyle. He said that my story didn't come as a total surprise to him, unfortunately. It felt strangely comforting to get that feedback because at the end of the day, who wouldn't want to have sex with my girlfriend – she was hot. Not to mention George was a bonafide rock star and as I have witnessed firsthand in life, being a rock star can be a powerful thing. I let bygones be bygones at that point, and I continued to rock on. Oh. And I no longer want to kill George Lynch. Total plus.

At this point in time, I was 24, Mia was 29, and her husband Mike was in his 30's. I grew more and more paranoid with each passing day because, in all reality, outside of the Men's Club clan, I didn't exist anywhere else. I was a dirty little secret that no one in Mia's family could ever know about, and certainly, Mike couldn't ever find out about me.

***

One Sunday morning while Mia and I were lying in bed, she broke the news to me that she was pregnant. I had this fierce rush of heat throughout my entire body and the doomsday thought of "Oh Shit" hit me hard.

I just laid there. So, let me get this straight. Mia is pregnant, she's still married, and I don't exist. Wow. That's one fucked up trifecta, and it was my life. My mind swirled so hard it hurt. What the fuck have I just done to myself? To my life? To my chances of ever having a good honest life? My stomach churned. I knew damned well this was more than just a pregnancy; this was a seriously fucked-up situation that had the potential to destroy my life as I knew it. In fact, it was beyond a fucked-up situation. There was no question whose baby it was – we both knew it was mine. I remember sitting up on the side of the bed with both feet on the floor and holding my head in my hands, trying to steady myself. Nothing I did could stop the world from spinning.

Once I managed to speak, my first response to her was to tell her that I would take full responsibility. Yep. I was going to be an adult about an adult situation. I told her that I would do whatever it took to provide for the baby and that I would do everything in my power to be a good father to that baby. Her first response to me? Her first response was about how her parents were going to react and then it was all about how Mike would be utterly crushed by the news. I wasn't even in the picture. Who gave a shit about me, right? I'm just the father, a young father caught up in some serious shit. No. I didn't even factor in to her. It was all about her, *her* family, *her* husband with absolutely no consideration for the legit father of her child. Nope. No joy for this guy. No happiness. No "we." No "we got this" type of reaction.

She looked directly at me and said, "We can't have this baby. There's no way we can have this baby. You don't even make enough money to support us."

Whoa. That hurt. That really hurt. Didn't matter that it was true because I was willing to step up, and I just told her that. Ouch, man. That verbal knife pierced directly into my heart and made me feel like the most worthless man that ever walked the face of the Earth. So, I *was* out of my league this whole time. Game. Set. Match. I'm out of my league, yet now forcibly connected whether I wanted to be or not. I've struck out, yet I can't leave the game. How the hell does that work? Unfortunately for me, I would soon find out.

Mia immediately decided to get an abortion and made me agonizingly aware that there wasn't anything I could do to stop her. I was beyond destroyed inside over the situation. I was raised in the church and was taught that having an abortion was a sin, all by itself, even without adding adultery on top of it. I begged her not to go through with it, but there was nothing I could do to change her mind. She never considered it, not even for a second.

I will never forget that Saturday morning when we pulled up to the abortion clinic on the east side of Ft. Worth. When we got out of the car, we were met by staff workers and protesters at the same time. I was completely overwhelmed as staff workers wrapped Mia up in a blanket, covering most of her body and face. It was like nothing I had ever seen or experienced before in my life.

The staff escorted us quickly inside the building as protesters approached us. I walked behind Mia while protesters waved their handmade signs and chanted "Save Your Kid" over and over and over. Some of them had the gall to get right up in my face and stay there until we reached the front door of the clinic. It was one of the most uncomfortable feelings that I have ever experienced in my life.

Once inside, they took Mia to the back area but first asked her if she was sure about what she was about to do. She said that she was sure about it.

That daddy door closed right on my face. I was left behind to sit all alone in the lobby and just wait. Just sit and wait. I always told myself that if I ever had the chance to be a father, I would never be like how my father was to me; that I would be the best father ever. Yet, here I am, sadly sitting at an abortion clinic waiting for my first child to be aborted, not joyously sitting at a hospital waiting for it to be born. I was experiencing feelings of such hopelessness and such overwhelming feelings of regret that it literally made my entire body shake.

I walked over to the drapes on the window to bring in sunlight to such a dark lobby, and that turned out to be a huge mistake. As soon as I pulled them back, protesters scrambled over to the window and continued their chant of "Save Your Child! Don't let them take it! God loves you!" They all waved their signs with "SIN" written on them and I looked them square in their eyes before closing the drapes. I felt so helpless, so powerless, so futile. So useless. So lost. There was nothing I could do at that moment to change the situation, and I knew I committed a *huge* sin. Even though I wasn't the one having the abortion, and I wasn't the one who was married, in my soul, I was committing the same dreadful acts. I was a major part of all of it. I was right here, in this awful place, waiting for it to take place. I was right there, letting life be taken with my full knowledge of it happening. I was the one who impregnated a married woman. Me. This guy. I'm the reason it happened. I was part of that equation, and it made me sick.

The procedure didn't last very long, and I remember the sight of Mia when the nurses walked her out to me. She seemed so unbelievably fragile and broken, with little to no words to say, which was fine with me. I didn't have anything to say either.

When we walked outside to the car, the protesters were thankfully gone by then. The sun was still shining, and the rays of light were streaming down on us like some sign from God only meant for us.

The ride home was a silent one and when we got to her place, I walked her to her room and we both climbed into bed. I held her close to me for most of that day, but my mind never stopped spinning with the disbelief of what had occurred earlier that day. Of what just happened. Of realizing that as my hands touched Mia's body, there was my child inside that body just a few hours ago, and now it was gone forever, never to be known. What a fucked up, horrible, sad day. For both of us. Actually, for all three of us. And I was one of the people responsible for creating it. A dark day on my soul indeed.

I needed to take a time-out from life as I knew it, and the opportunity presented itself. I moved to Irving to house sit for a guy named Lenny. Lenny was a Men's Club regular and needed someone to watch his house for him while he traveled. He was going to be gone for a while on this trip, so I had to move in and be there daily. The house was cool, complete with a pool in the backyard.

He told me that from time to time, strippers would fly in from LA and stay at his house. I was like ok, cool, no problem there. One afternoon I came home from work, and I noticed there were some purses on the kitchen table and the blinds were open. I looked outside and saw two girls laying out by the pool, so I went to see who they were and when I did, they both looked up and said "Hey, we are Lenny's friends. Hope you don't mind us laying out in the nude."

Um, did she just ask me if I had a problem with that? Without a doubt, that was one of the best perks of living at Lenny's place, especially in the summer. As the winter approached, so did the holidays and my mom came out to stay with me for a little while. I hadn't told her about the abortion yet but that was just a matter of time. This horrible secret was killing me inside and I needed to get it off my chest.

By this time, I had been promoted at work a few times, and on Thanksgiving morning, I needed to stock product at my stores. Mia and my mom both came with me that day and they waited outside of the stores while I did my thing. They were getting along well, but I felt like I was deceiving my mom and it weighed on me like a brick. She had no idea that Mia had an abortion, that she was still married, or that she worked at the Men's Club. She didn't know anything about the real Mia. Not yet anyway.

The first time my mom met Mia, she asked Mia what she did for a living, Mia told her that she worked at Steak-n-Ale, and that's how we left it. We left my mom believing a flat-out lie because I knew my mom would never approve of Mia working at the Men's Club, let alone everything else. It was on this day, out of nowhere, on a day that was seemingly going so well, that I felt it was the right moment to spill the beans.

While my Mom and I were standing in my driveway and Mia was inside, I grew some balls and told her the truth about everything. And I mean everything. My mom was heartbroken by the news, and it hurt her so bad she stood there and cried. All I could do was stand there and hug her while she did. I never felt so ashamed in all my life telling my mom that her first grandchild was aborted, and by a married woman.

I don't remember much after that other than my mom sitting us both down and talking to us about what happened. That was an extremely uncomfortable conversation, to say the least. It was even more difficult to look into my mom's eyes knowing that I was living in complete *sin*. That was hard to own, as a man, as a human being, and as a son. Another shitty trifecta. Merry Fucking Christmas, everybody!

Christmas brought yuletide joy and presents, but it also brought the presence of Mike with it, unfortunately. Mike begged Mia on a daily basis to come back to him and by this time, he knew about me to the point he hired a private investigator to check me out. I will never forget when Mike called my company looking for me.

I mentioned it to Mia, and she coyly told me that she knew Mike had a file on me. Great. Thanks, babe. Thanks for letting me know that. In that file was my home address as a kid in Longview, my old phone number, the names of my family members, and a whole bunch of other shit.

Once I knew that, I found myself constantly looking over my shoulder everywhere I went, wondering if someone was hiding in the bushes tracking my every move.

One day I was driving down I-35 S to Dallas, and I looked out the left window and there was a Mercedes SL 500, which is the type of car that Mike drove. As I looked into that car, sure enough, Mike was looking right back at me. It wasn't long before he sped away, but I think he just wanted me to know that he was watching me. That I couldn't hide from him.

Shortly after the abortion, Mia and I began fighting on a regular basis. Alcohol was a regular practice in our relationship, and it was one of our biggest detriments. When resentment enters an alcohol-fueled relationship, it tends to go to hell rather quickly. Time and time again I begged Mia to divorce Mike and end all the unnecessary madness, but her continued resistance caused me to feel incredibly angry, trapped, and scared.

There I was, in love with a married woman who claimed to love me, who had just aborted my baby but still didn't want to commit to leaving the ghost of a husband to be with the man she loved. Hurt like hell to see her rejecting every facet of me, rejecting me being in her life. As much as I was trying to make the relationship work, it was like she was giving the exact amount of resistance in return to retaliate against it and prevent it. I should have walked away then, but I didn't. Why? Because I'm an asshole led by a dick. That's why.

What didn't help my cause was working at the Men's Club. When you work there, you get more than a job; you also get the roaches of the world that come with that job. My time there as an employee only lasted about two weeks. I had to quit because in Texas, under the TABC rule, you cannot work at a liquor distributor and work at a bar under the same liquor license.

Luckily, I was there long enough to get to know the happy hour crowd on a first name basis. There I was, this 24-year-old kid, broke as a joke, in an environment where some of the guys were in their mid-40s to early 50s, with lots of money, intimidating to me and adding more power to them. Mia was their regular waitress and they always tipped her generously. Well, you know, being super-hot helps with that. Even though these dudes were somewhat nice to my face, I knew they wanted to bang my girl. Join the club. Everyone wanted to bang my girl.

Mia kept a bank bag at home stuffed full of cash tips. Anyone who works on tips knows it's better to keep your tips that way than having it reported on a paycheck – you actually get the whole tip that way. One day she randomly told me she had saved $100,000 in cash, so I'm not talking about some little piggy bank that had coins saved up for a rainy day. These arrogant rich dudes and the whole scene got old with me pretty fast, though, and when I would discuss the intentions of these fools with Mia, she just played it off like "no babe, they are just being nice." Hello, George Lynch take two! Maybe they want to go watch a movie. On a private bus. Hell, with this crew, it could have been a private jet.

I never felt comfortable with this crowd, and I never felt like I was even slightly accepted, or respected, by any of these guys. They didn't give a fuck about me. It was all about Mia and getting her attention. It was all about the Big Swinging Dick Competition, all the time, and who could out-buy who, who could outshine who. It was a really shitty, really impossible situation to be in all the time, especially since I couldn't compete with any of it. Shit. I couldn't even come within distance of it, and everyone else knew it, too.

I remember one Sunday when the 49ers were playing the Cowboys in Dallas. During the '90s, there was a huge rivalry between the two teams, but I need to be clear here. My whole life I have been a Steelers fan, and

I hate the Cowboys passionately, then, and now. Needless to say, for that game I jumped on board with the 49'ers. Mia knew how much I wanted to go to that game, too, but she also knew there was no way in hell I could afford to go. If wishes were horses, right?

Well, *she* ended up going, and not "just" going. She went with one of those Men's Club roaches named Bud. He was such a piece of slimy shit, too. He drove a Pathfinder and wore blue jeans, plaid short-sleeve button-downs, and stupid brown loafers. Just a slimy little MF. You know the type. The kind of guy that makes you want to go wash your hands and scrape off your skin immediately after you meet him. That kind of guy that you would see on a wanted poster.

Mia said he wanted to take her and her friends to the game. But, you know, it was all on the up and up, because it was a group of friends going, not just her. Of course. Only as friends. Everyone's just such good friends. Yes. It's always just as friends. Friends who watch movies or games together, because that's also what Bud had in mind, I'm sure. I knew what his intentions were and had some serious issues with it, but since it was always about *her* since it was always about what was going on in Mia's world, she went anyway. She knew what she was doing and the impact it would have on me, too, and still didn't care, which made that much worse for me.

Okay, admittedly I was a little pussy whipped and it always seemed like my heart hurt for one reason or another, but it's what it was at the time, at that age. Admittedly I didn't have the balls to punt yet, so I sat back like a vagina and took it. Like a wounded little bird, I ended up watching the game at home with an old college roommate, Robert, and had anxiety cramps in my stomach throughout the entire game, to the point I was making myself physically sick. I was consumed with Mia and what she was doing, and who she was with.

I don't remember who won the game, but after the game was long over, Mia still hadn't made it back to my house. In those days, cell phones weren't around yet. We all carried pagers and I paged her several times. Back then, you entered "911" after your number when you needed someone to call you ASAP.

When she finally called, she was shitfaced and hanging out at Humperdink's in Los Colinas. Apparently, they went there after the game and were still there, carrying on little dick Buddy Boy's party. She asked me to come get her and like a fucking spineless moron, I did it. I went all the way to get her drunk ass only to argue with her for the rest of that evening. We both said things that night that cracked open the flood gates, and there was no turning back from it. There was no retracting it. Some major shit was thrown out there, and it was staying out there this time. Or was it?

This behavior had become our norm, and I always made the gutless decision to take it on the chin, which never solved anything for me. All that my inaction did was grow the resentment inside me and provide Mia with the perfect storm to use and abuse me at her will.

On another occasion, she went out with some friends while I stayed at home because, well, I wasn't invited to join them. She called later that night and asked me to come get her, again, but this time at the Crescent Hotel. She added that she would only leave with me if I showed up naked.

I was like, "What?"

She said, "When you pull into the valet you better not have one stitch of clothing on or I'm not getting in the car."

So, what did this pussy-whipped jackass do? Naturally, he thought with his dick the entire time and drove to the Crescent Hotel, naked. Shit. My dick probably drove the car that night. I will never forget the look on the valet's face when he leaned over to me as if I were there to valet my car and saw that I was naked. I just had to smile and say, "Bro, you have no idea."

Right after I said that to him, along came this beautiful woman who jumped into my car, and off we went.

I made it that easy for her. I made it that easy for someone to puppeteer me and my every move. She obviously wasn't going to stop her behavior, and I didn't know how to stop it. Quite frankly, there was a part of me that didn't want it to stop, and that's why it continued. My lack of self-esteem was one of my worst enemies, and it's one that I created myself. I was the only one who had the power to change that, but I didn't understand that yet.

# LOVE AND LOSS

## CHAPTER 4

Christmas was yet again on its way, and Mia decided to drop another one of her Christmas bombs on me. She started off calmly and all sultry to try and lessen the blow of her saying, "Love, Mike wants me to move home with him for one month. Just 30 days. If after 30 days I still want a divorce, he will sign the divorce papers and we can both move on."

I was like, are you kidding me with this shit? She's falling for this utter horseshit from Mike? She's really going to be reeled in by this tactic? Sure, no problem. This coming from the same guy that paid for a billboard across the street from the Men's Club that read "Happy Birthday Mia, Love, Mike"? Oh. *That* guy. The husband. The one that you are still legally married to and have shared your life with. Sure. That's totally fine with me that you go live with him. I mean, what could possibly happen in that situation, right? Give me a fucking break.

Mike isn't the type of guy who is going to simply sign a paper and just walk away. He hasn't done it yet, so why would he do that now? It was so obvious it was an attempt to get her back into his clutches, back into his life, yet, what did she do? Yep. Of course, she did. She sure as hell fucking *did*!

She went back to live with her estranged husband, and what did I do? Of course, I did. I sure as hell fucking *did*! I sat back and watched her do it. I sat back, yet again, like the little sissy boy who took the torture and abuse from this woman at any and all personal costs to himself. I did nothing but agonize and watch her do it. I did nothing to protect myself. I did nothing to plan for my own life, for my own wellbeing. And she couldn't have cared less, just like she never cared about any of it the entire time we were together. She was getting what she wanted, and that's all she cared about. And I pathetically accepted it.

For those 30 days, those horrific 30 days which ended up being a little bit longer, Mia would come by after work in the early evening, have sex with me, and then go back home to Arlington to her husband. You know, Mike, the one she was now living with again? She swore to me that she lay in bed every night next to her husband, but nothing was happening between them. Nothing. He was on his side, and she was on hers. All night, every night. No connections, no interactions. Would you believe that?

That Christmas, she bought me some very expensive gifts, one of which was a new canopy bed. She hated my water bed, so she decided to replace it with this amazing bed. She also bought me a leather 49er's jacket and 4th-row tickets to see Ozzy Osbourne at Reunion Arena in Dallas.

My gift to her was my undying love and my dick wrapped in a bow because I didn't have the money to do anything else. She claimed that she didn't care, but it bothered me. I remember telling my mom about the gifts I received, but she remained unimpressed by any of them. My mom liked Mia enough as a person but hated the fact that she was dating her son, LOL.

I guess that old saying that a mom knows best is true because my mom knew I was dating an immoral woman and the problems that could come from it. She was seeing it firsthand.

As the 30-day house arrest sentence with Mike progressed, I became increasingly angrier and more resentful, and the arguing between Mia and I went beyond the norm. I knew that I loved this woman, but I also hated her just as much for what I was allowing her to do to me. If I were the man back then that I am today, I would have never allowed myself to get involved in such a dysfunctional, stressful, immoral, one-sided situation.

But there I was, my heart broken again, my stomach torched, and I still couldn't bring myself to walk away from this woman no matter how beneficial it would have been for my life. She not only knew that I was stuck, but she also took full fucking advantage of it.

I guess when you're used to taking whatever you can get from a man as your way of earning a living, it also becomes a never-ending lifestyle. Mia was no exception to this. In fact, she was the poster child for it and led the pack by example.

One night I was trying to get a hold of her and couldn't. She didn't answer the home phone and wasn't returning my pages. You would think that I was used to this treatment by now, yet I still couldn't go to sleep without hearing from her. I had this doomed feeling in my gut, so I got up, got dressed, and drove over to her friend's house to see what was going on.

When I turned the corner, there it was. There it fucking was - Mike's Mercedes SL 500. I needed answers. I should have just turned around and left, but I didn't. And of course, with that came the bullshit story that nothing happened, Mike just wanted to talk, and when it got too late, he simply passed out, blah blah blah. Nothing happened. Nothing ever happens. Do you see a cycle here? I wonder what movie they watched.

My blood was boiling, and my already fractured heart was severed further into a million more pieces, but, did I learn? Of course not. I took her back because, you know, I loved her. I loved *her*. Didn't matter how she felt about me, or how she treated me. That's how young and stupid I was at that time in my life. I *loved* her, and as long as I felt that way, the nightmare was never going to end for me. Never. It was just going to keep going on and on and on because I was allowing it to go on, and she was never going to stop. I was the biggest part of the problem but couldn't see that enough to do anything about it. Not even for myself.

Awakening Day finally arrived like a thrown brick to the side of my head. I thought then, and admittedly still often wonder to this day, that this path was God's way of punishing me for an adulterous relationship and an abortion killing of one of his children. By this time, Mia and I were taking things on a day-by-day basis, merely surviving each day. We fought, then we had makeup sex, only to fight again and then have makeup sex again. It was like the movie Groundhog Day … repeat … repeat once more … and then repeat again.

It was now the end of January 1996, and the Cowboys were going to the Superbowl in Arizona to play against my beloved Steelers. Mia asked me if I was okay with her going away for the weekend with some of the girls from the Men's Club. They were all going there to strip at one of the clubs, citing that the money-earning potential would be off the charts amazing that weekend. Here I am again, in that position of WTF and having absolutely no say in the matter. Here she is asking me if it's ok for her to go to the Superbowl in Arizona so she can strip at a club when we both fully knew it didn't matter what I thought. We both knew she wasn't asking for permission. We both knew she already had the whole thing fucking planned already and this was her manipulative way of letting me know about it. Honestly, where was this woman's mind and heart at times? I began to wonder if she had either one, quite frankly.

All hell broke loose, but I won the fucking battle that time. We ended up watching the game at Lenny's house, where I was living at the time. But, of course, victory was short-lived, and nothing came easy when it came to Mia. The night before the Superbowl I cooked shark on the grill so before the game started, I dumped the ashes in the flower bed, thinking it might act as some kind of fertilizer or something. I proceeded to fill up the grill with new charcoal, lit it, and went back into the house to watch the start of the game.

I waited about 10 minutes and when I walked outside to check on the grill, the entire back yard and wooden fence were engulfed in flames. Completely engulfed in flames. I yelled "Call the Fire Department! The fucking backyard is on fire!" The game is on, and my backyard is on fire. Perfect timing. I ran to get the garden hose and began spraying everywhere because the fire had spread into the neighbor's yard.

Luckily, my tenure as a volunteer firefighter was short-lived because the fire department got there damned fast and put out the fire. To them, it was nothing more than a small flame. To me, it was like Chicago burning down.

After it was all said and done, there wasn't a severe level of damage done to Lenny's house or to the neighbor's house, just a few burnt-up bushes and a small section of charred fence. All stuff that could be easily fixed. I felt so stupid, though, but whatever. It happened. It was just another day in my haphazard life.

I remember making that phone call to Lenny and that was pretty much it. "You know, Lenny, it's funny you should ask about the house and yes, I did watch the game, thanks for asking. You're never going to believe this, but…"

I moved out of his house shortly after that. Was I ever going to learn? No. No, I was never going to learn. Never. Apparently, I must have skipped that class.

Summer arrived and Mia and I made the 4-hour drive to New Braunfels, TX, for a family reunion. We were all going to camp out at the Guadalupe River, party hard, and float around on tubes for the weekend.

The party started with us drinking way too much that first night. I must have put down an entire 750ml bottle of Malibu Rum by myself and had a weird dream I can remember vividly. I dreamt that a yellow school bus was heading straight for our tent in a clear path to run us over. In my dream, I was fighting and struggling with that bus, over and over, fighting and struggling, struggling and fighting.

Despite my best efforts, the bus runs over Mia and kills her. I stand up, out of breath, and see everyone running over asking me if everything was alright, and that's where the dream ends.

When I woke up, our tent was in shambles from me swinging and screaming in my sleep.

The next day, Mia and I ended up in another huge fight. It didn't matter where we were or who we were with during those times. We were known to be "that couple," unfortunately. We were "that couple" that always fought and couldn't get along, and we were "that couple" that always ruined everyone else's good time when we were around.

This time, the fight was so bad that we packed up our stuff and headed back to Dallas, only to turn around about an hour into the drive and head back to the party. We were a fucking mess together and survived as a couple day by day because we didn't know how to exist any other way. Our relationship was turning me into an angry, negative, and resentful person, and I was becoming completely broken and hollow inside.

There was nothing left. I was null and void. I was nothing but a big, black void, and Mia was nothing but a conduit to that void, both in its creation and its growth. She was literally draining of every human emotion, every ounce of character, every ounce of humanity and sanity that I had left to give, and I let her do it. I fucking let her take everything from me, and she took every opportunity.

I don't remember the exact time frame, but one night we were out and about in Dallas, drinking it up with Mia's friends in a limo headed to the Iguana Mirage on 75 and Park Lane. Once inside, at the coat check and I saw a guy walking around selling roses. I decided to be a stud and buy a rose for each one of the ladies at my table and sent the guy over to them. When he handed Mia her rose, the stem broke. Hmm. Was that a sign?

I asked the guy to replace the flower, but he wouldn't do it, saying that I bought one flower and I'm stuck with that flower. Sorry. Well, I kind of lost my shit on the guy and found myself being escorted out. Two cops grabbed me, and I tried to explain my situation, but they didn't care.

Once outside, I realized that I forgot to get my jacket, so I walked back towards the door. The cops saw me and asked me where I was going, and I told them that I was just going back to grab my jacket. They wouldn't let me go any further and pushed me backwards down the steps. I didn't fall, but I charged forward and tried to bulldoze by the cops, only to land my ass in jail.

Fuck me, all I wanted to do was get my jacket. I had to piss like a racehorse and the cops didn't care about that either. The more I complained about it, the longer I had to wait. I almost pissed my pants before I finally got to the station.

And speaking of piss. There were numerous times where I would wake up in the middle of the night and find myself lying in Mia's piss. When she got drunk, she would sometimes wet the bed in her sleep and had no clue she had done it. I would have to get her up, pull the sheets off, flip the mattress over, and put clean sheets back on the bed. Now, if that isn't true love, I don't know what is.

Don't tell me I didn't love this crazy bitch. I kept the canopy bed she gave me for Christmas for a few years after we broke up. I had to turn the mattress over to hide the piss stains that were on the mattress. No matter how I cleaned it, they wouldn't lift all the way, and since I couldn't afford to replace such a nice mattress, over it went. Anyway, enough about piss. Back to me going to jail.

This was my second magical trip to the big house. The first journey being the time I was arrested for indecent exposure back in college. When I got to the jail this time, I was locked in a cell with a bunch of other people. The cell was a big square room with a few cots with blue mats and a stainless-steel toilet with a water fountain next to it. How convenient.

As I laid down on one of the cots, my mind wondered what Mia was doing, not about why I was there or what I was going to do next. Nope. It was always about Mia. Man, I was pathetic. I was wondering if she was outside, trying to bail me out, or would she be here waiting on me when they let me out? Is she worried about me? Or shit… is she still out partying with her friends, not thinking about me at all?

The next morning finally came and when I was let out, there was no Mia there to meet me and bring me home. I had to walk to a payphone, page her using the number of the payphone, and wait for her to call me back. I couldn't believe she wasn't waiting for me when I got released.

Once I saw her, I asked her to tell me what she was doing that was so fucking important she couldn't be there for me, and she had the balls to tell me that she was *sleeping*. She was sleeping in her soft comfortable bed because she and her girls stayed out partying all night, naturally.

Are you fucking *kidding* me right now? How many times do I need to be shown that I didn't matter to her? How many fucking times do I actually need to be shown? You guessed it. A few more times, apparently. Ensue another fight, makeup sex, and then pass out until the early afternoon, somehow magically erasing all of the detrimental things that occurred the night before, like always.

It wasn't long after that night I realized I couldn't take it any longer. I really couldn't. I was fucking miserable and sad all the time, and at the end of the day, Mia was still married to Mike. The relationship was causing me to rapidly go downhill personally to the point where my friends didn't even want to be around us anymore.

I realized that I needed to get the evil monkey off my back once and for all for my own wellbeing, so I quit my job, loaded up my shit, and moved back to Longview. I had to escape from this situation to get stable again and get my life back in some form of moral order.

Ya, some might say that I ran away. So, what? I had to do something about my life, so if I had to run, I had to. Okay, so I ran away to Longview, began a new job at Maxwell Distributing, and found out that I couldn't run away from Mia. I had moved in with my best friend from high school, Stewart, and on the weekend before I started my new job, Mia came to town.

That Saturday, we went to a crawfish bowl in Jefferson, TX, where I got hammered on keg beer and was still eating crawfish on the ride back to my place while Mia drove. Our plan was to lay down, take a quick nap, and then meet Stewart out a little bit later, but the next thing I remember, the sun was coming up and it was already the next morning.

Opportunity missed, apparently. I tried to piece together the evening and woke Mia up wondering why we didn't have sex before we went to bed. Well, she called me an asshole because apparently, we *did* have sex and it was the worst sex she ever had in her life. Awesome, because I honestly didn't remember any of it. She went on to tell me how gross and disgusting it was to have sex with me because I had the nastiest crawfish breathe and my fingers were all stained and smelly from the crawfish spices.

She harped on the fact that she was totally disgusted, and my immediate reaction was, "Welcome to my hell, Miss Piss Bed!" Mia stayed with me that Sunday night, and at 5 am the next day, I had to get up and start my new job and start my life over again.

As I left the house that morning, I cried on the way to work thinking I may have made a mistake by moving back there. Mia went back to Dallas, and I knew in my heart that I needed to press on, that I did make the right decision, and that I just needed to keep moving forward. I needed to move forward with my life without Mia in it, without the drama that surrounded being in a relationship with her, and most of all, without the constant fighting. I needed to move forward without bringing any of the negative elements that had been consuming my life with me, but Mia just wouldn't go away that easily.

I only stayed at Maxwell Distributing for about six months before going back to my previous company, Julius Schepps, now renamed the Republic Beverage Company. I finally landed the liquor sales rep position I always wanted. I was finally making decent money and bought a 1994 Corvette that I was so proud to own. It was midnight purple, with a Targa top and a bag phone mounted inside, which was a huge perk as phones were becoming in style. I loved that car and man was it fast.

Mia came to town one night in her white corvette and met my brother and me at a bar. After many drinks and it was time to go, my brother drove my car and Mia drove hers. Once we got on the loop in Longview, the race between the two 'Vettes was on like Donkey Kong!

Right as my brother punched it, a cop car spotted us and made a quick u-turn to come after us. My brother saw that and sped away with the glow of the red and blues flashing in the background behind us. Mia saw it too and stayed back to let the cop follow us. We took a hard right onto the road that led up to Pine Knoll Apartments with some distance between us still. My brother whipped into my complex, hid the car, and we jumped out and hid behind some other cars as we watched the cop searching for us.

When Mia showed up at my place later our hearts were still pounding, no shit. We had just escaped DUI's and most likely having to spend a few nights in jail. The rush was incredible, but not something you want to become habit-forming because eventually, your luck will run out.

\*\*\*

Later that fall, there was a Monday night football game in Dallas with the Cowboys hosting the Eagles. I took my grandfather to that game, and we had a blast. We got home that night around 2 am and as my grandpa drove home, I dozed off because I had to get up early in the morning to go to work.

Stewart always slept in, so I never saw him in the morning, but on that one day, for whatever reason, he didn't. I had just gotten into my truck when I saw him jet out the front door while talking on the phone. He didn't acknowledge me other than a quick wave of his hand as he got into his car, which seemed strange to me, but I went on my way to work and didn't think anything else of it.

That evening, I was back at the house just chilling out, eating dinner, and watching some TV, when I got a call asking if I had heard from Stewart. I hadn't heard from him all day, and the response I received was that no one else had heard from him either. That was extremely odd. Extremely. Stewart was the most social person I knew and for no one to have heard from him all day was totally out of his character, and the search for him began. I stayed at the house and was keeping everyone in the know, but as the clock approached the darkest hours of the evening, the dreaded final call came.

Stewart was found dead at a hotel by Gilmer Rd and Hwy 80. He had committed suicide. He was gone, he was fucking gone just like that, and no one that knew him knew why he was gone. No one. No one even had a clue why he would take his own life.

Time stood still at that moment and even though I heard those words very clearly, it still didn't register to me that he was gone. I couldn't process that my best friend killed himself. I couldn't process that my roommate was never coming home again. I couldn't accept the fact that I didn't even get a chance to say goodbye to him. I was dumbfounded over what just happened.

There were always several cars in our driveway, cars parked on the street, and cars in the lot next door. As I sat there, trying to comprehend the severity of the situation, I heard a car alarm go off and I went outside to check it out. The first car parked in the driveway had the lights flashing and the horn going off. I looked around and there was nobody in sight, no wind, no rain, nothing. Just a perfectly calm night with the stars shining down. I went over to the car and opened the door. The windows were down, and the keys were laying on the floorboard, so I grabbed them, disarmed the alarm, and went back inside.

A few things then crossed my mind, one of which was about Stewart's 5-year-old daughter, Chelsea. She was at her mom's house in Dallas, and she was such a great kid, she really was. I had helped raise her since she was born, and Chelsea and I spent a lot of time together while Stewart and his ex-wife Kelly shared joint custody. Stewart worked late with his car deals and on many occasions, I would take Chelsea to her school and at times, even took her to work with me for the day. I used to jog a lot back then and she would follow along with me on her bike. She wasn't my kid, but I grew to love her as if she were mine.

I was the one who had to notify Stewart's girlfriend, Patty, about his death. I went to pick her up and bring her back to our place. She was utterly heartbroken, just as we all were, and when we got back to our place her parents were there waiting to comfort her.

Once we got inside, that alarm on the same exact car went off again. I was a little freaked out when I went out to turn it off this time because I truly felt that Stewart was nearby like he was setting off the alarm, trying to tell me something. As much as it was unsettling, it was comforting, too. That alarm going off was him letting us know that he was still with us, and I felt like I would welcome any sign from him.

After Patty and her parents left, I got the call to see if I would drive Stewart's parents to Dallas and pick up Kelly and Chelsea, which I agreed to do. I started to get ready, and when I went into Stewart's room,

I noticed there were several of my colored starburst price signs from work taped together with a handwritten note on them. The note said, "I'm sorry, Mommy. Love, Stewart."

I ran over to his closet where I knew he kept his gun, and it was missing. I wondered if I had come back to the house in the late afternoon that maybe I could have seen the note and noticed that the gun was missing, and maybe, just maybe, I could have saved him. I wondered if I could have prevented this from happening.

I called my mom to share the horrifying news with her and told her that I was going to Dallas with Stewart's parents to pick up Chelsea and Kelly. That remains the longest round trip to Dallas I have ever taken in my life. I will never forget that drive until the day I die. I did that for you, buddy. I brought your girls back to your home, which is now theirs.

Hanging in the front hallway of Stewart's house were three small, framed pictures nailed in a diagonal arrangement. When I got back to the house and was walking down the hallway, all three pictures began to sway back and forth, all at the same time in complete synchronicity. It freaked me out so bad that I left and never stayed another night in that house. I even let a day go by before I went back to load up all my stuff, and never went back until about 6 months later when I stopped by to see Kelly and Chelsea one night.

I remember sitting on the couch talking with Kelly when suddenly those same damned three pictures began to sway again. Instantly my skin crawled. I was totally freaked out that the same thing happened again and there's no fucking way I imagined that twice. No fucking way. Kelly said she was used to it because apparently, it happened all the time.

I don't believe in Ghosts but let me tell you something. On those two occasions that I witnessed, I believed, without a doubt, that Stewart was there. Stewart was *there*, man. You could feel him, sense him. It was comforting to know that he was still around, that I could still talk to him.

Shortly after Stewart died, my other best friend, who shall remain nameless, went to prison. These were dark times for me indeed. Two of my best friends had left me and I wasn't sure what to do with myself, so I took the safest route I could think of and moved back home with my mom until I knew what I was going to do.

Unfortunately, the misery of losing Stewart didn't end there. A barrage of debt collectors came knocking on behalf of Stewart, and because my name was associated with several cars, credit cards, jet skis, etc., I was the responsible party left standing to pay them. Stewart's bills were now my bills to pay. It got so bad I had to hire a fucking lawyer and file bankruptcy because I couldn't afford to take on what Stewart left behind for me to have to deal with. I know Stewart had my best interests in mind, but learn something from my mistake here. Keep your shit in your own name and let everyone else do the same with their shit. Bottom line, end of story.

***

Out of the blue one rainy night, Mia called and said she was coming to my mom's because she needed to talk to me. Oh, joy. Another Mia bomb waiting to fucking explode.

When she got there, she looked amazing as always, but I just kept reminding myself that I couldn't get back with her. In no way, shape, or form could I handle any more pain so soon after burying my best friend and having my other best friend sent to prison.

The two of us had a long talk that night, some of which included my mom, discussing the possibility of us getting back together. I'll say again that my mom liked Mia as a person, but in no way wanted me to date her again, let alone talk about marrying her. Mia and my mom were close, and I truly believe they loved each other like family, but my mom just spoke the truth that we were absolutely horrible for each other, that we were downright toxic together, and that our history proved all of it. By this time Mia had gotten her divorce from Mike, but the water under the bridge for us was still at flood levels. We couldn't take back all those horrible names we called each other, all those horrible things we said to each other. We couldn't take back all the horrifying situations that we lived through together. I mean, I loved her and all, but I knew it would truly be a doomed life if we stayed together.

I always felt that God weighed heavily involved in this decision, and I always felt that I was being punished for the abortion and being involved in the adultery of another person. Mia pleaded her case as she always did, and of course, we had sex that night, but I surprisingly stood my ground and said no to getting back together. The need for my own self-worth was greater than my need to be with her for the first time ever. Off she went and I didn't see her again until a good deal of time had passed.

*** 

I went to see Sammy Hagar in Dallas at the Starplex Amphitheatre with my buddy Anthony one night, and guess who was there? Yep. I couldn't believe it. Mia was sitting right in front of us. What are the chances of 19,000 people at that fucking show and here she is, sitting right in front of me! Why God? *Why?*

Mia and I loved concerts and we both loved Van Halen and Sammy was our man. So yes, I always had an inkling feeling that she would be there, but I didn't expect to sit right the fuck behind her. We all drank and partied together at the show, but Anthony and I had to drive back to East Texas right after it ended because we both had to work the next day.

The next thing you know, Mia and I are sitting together in my car, and it didn't take long for the shit show to start up again. We picked up right where we left off, just like how it always has been for us. The love for her was still there but the resentment was right there beside it, and just as strong. Maybe even stronger. Like every other time we drank together, we fought and that's exactly what we ended up doing again.

We checked into a Red Roof Inn in Irving off 183. Not sure why we were in Irving, but we were, and that was the only hotel in the area with availability and within my budget. I think it was $49.99 and the place was a dump, but we were drunk, tired, still arguing, and we needed somewhere to crash. Mia wanted to take a bath and I remember her telling me to never bring her to another dump like this ever again, especially one that had brown stains in the tub.

She was never grateful or appreciative of anything I did for her. Never. Nothing I did was ever good enough or to her fucking standards, no matter how much I tried to do things to make her happy. Everything for her always had to be a 5-star experience and I just couldn't provide that to her, and she always made me feel like shit for it, too. She had that look in her eyes as she always did when she was hammered and that's when she would switch from Jekyll to Hyde in a nanosecond.

When those eyes appeared, Hyde mode took over and there was no turning back. I was instantly reminded of the horrifying hell that comes with this relationship, but like the jackass I am, I apparently didn't get my fill of abuse and misery yet. Not quite yet.

The next day I woke up in a sheer panic, realizing I had to drive two hours to get to work and it was already 8 o'clock. On top of that, I still had to take Mia home. *Fuck!*

I called my boss, and he covered for me until noon when I finally made it back to Longview. As soon as I got back home, I started becoming stir-crazy again. I don't know what the fuck I was thinking. Apparently, my delusional mind was telling me that I couldn't live without her, so I decided I was going to drive to Dallas and ask her to marry me. I was going to put my heart and soul out there, even though I knew damned well that I couldn't afford the type of ring that would suffice as her engagement ring. She made it well known to me in the past that if we were to ever get married, she had to have a Princess cut, 2-carat diamond on top of a gold band laced with even more diamonds. There was no way on earth I could afford that kind of ring.

Regardless of me fully knowing the humiliation I was about to endure, I drove to Dallas, tracked her down, and begged her to marry me. You can say that it was an engagement without a ring. By this time Mia had bought a house and we were seemingly back on track.

One day she went out to run some errands and for some reason, I went into her closet to get something and saw a shoebox on the floor that had tipped over and some pictures had spilled out of it. This is how I discovered that Mike's Harley from back in the day was painted with the image of Mia's naked body. It was Mia to the T, and accurately detailed. I was disturbed by it. I confronted her about it when she came home.

She confirmed that it was her and the nightmare of being in a relationship with her started to reappear. There were also pictures of her Corvette all smashed up and pictures of her with her head covered with blood, so naturally, I asked her what had happened. She told me that someone rear-ended her, and she sustained a head injury and internal bleeding. Oh, and there was one more thing to add to that list of injuries. She then proceeded to callously and coldly tell me that she was also carrying my second child when the accident occurred and that she lost the baby while she was in the hospital. But that's it. That's all that happened to her in the car accident that I never knew happened until I saw the photos. That's it.

Fuck, this woman is such a cold-hearted, self-centered, spiteful bitch it almost made me physically sick. Who does that kind of shit to people? Pregnant again with my child, and she never told me? She just went on with her days and nights with no conscience about it at all? And then she loses the baby, again, and doesn't feel the need to share that with me?

Well, that's what I get. Seriously. That's what I get. I deserved it. I knew better not to keep fucking around with this woman, but I did. I kept on going, kept on hurting myself, kept on setting myself up for failure – and all because *this* woman had some power over me that I gave to her on a silver platter? Dammit!

My thoughts turned to God as I felt the curse of the dark Mia cloud hovering above me, consuming everything about me. I questioned Mia as to why she didn't tell me she was pregnant, and her weak answer was that she tried to tell me. Oh, well, since she tried, that's okay then. She tried? She *tried?* I asked her to clarify exactly when the fuck she tried to tell me, because I really, really wanted to know when that happened. I needed that explained to me, in detail. This time, I really needed to know the reason for her treating me like shit on her shoe, yet again.

She came up with some bullshit story about the rainy night when she showed up at my mom's house. You know, when we were talking with my mom about us getting back together? Ya. That night. Okay. So, I got to thinking back to that night and I told her that there wasn't one split-fucking-second where she tried to tell me something. Not one.

Wait, what was that? Oh, I see, I misunderstood. My mistake, as always. See, she was *going* to tell me, but *only if* we agreed to get back together, and only then. I see. My mistake. I only deserved to know if Mia got what she wanted, and since we *didn't* get back together right then and there, she chose not to tell me at all. Got it. Mia does what Mia wants and doesn't fucking care who it hurts or what she has to do to get it. Got it. Fuck, what was I doing with this manipulative, soulless shell of a woman?? How many games could this woman play? How many times was I going to be secondary, or third, or fourth to her needs and her wants?

The pictures of her naked body on Mike's bike were still bothering me, and I'm not sure why it did, especially since Mia was a stripper and anyone could see everything she owned if the price was right. Shit. I think it was more about the connection between her and Mike that remained and that I felt like I was never as important to her as Mike was to her. Maybe it was that I saw her play with Mike's head and heart like she did mine and it was just too much for me to witness and have to accept that I was just "one more" to her, while she foolishly remained everything to me. I don't know.

I went back to Longview with my head hung between my legs and finally threw in the towel on Mia. I was done for good this time. I was. I really was. I was done. I had to be for my own well-being. I had to because I couldn't take any more. Please, God. No more with her. I give. I do. I've learned, too, God, and I solemnly promise you that I won't ever repeat these mistakes ever again. I promise.

***

My boss at the time, Gary, was a great friend of mine and we became very close. He was a little over a decade older than me and I sincerely looked up to him. I put in for a transfer to get me back to Dallas and my wish was granted in 2000. Gary threw me a going-away party and sent me off with a fondly memorable bang.

It wasn't long afterward that Lloyd, one of the managers on our team, walked over to me with tears in his eyes. I asked him what was wrong. He told me that Gary had passed away the night before in his chair at home from a heart attack. I was devastated and felt paralyzed. Gary had an extreme case of acid reflux and was having a difficult time getting it under control. Apparently, he got out of bed that night to sit up in his chair because when you have acid reflux, sitting upwards helps to keep the acid down. I knew this because I was also dealing with a case of acid reflux from all the stress I was under, and I knew that burn all too well. Gary was supposed to see a different doctor that day but passed away the night before he was to go. Gary was just 44-years old. You were a good man, Gary, and you'll never be forgotten.

***

Fast forward to me moving back to Dallas in 2000. I moved uptown, which was the new up-and-coming spot. I ran into Mia one night and she ended up coming back to my house and yes, we spent the night together. Yes, I'm a dumbass, I know. We actually had a very nice talk and even though some of the negative and hostile feelings reappeared, I won the battle this time within myself, and I stayed away from her after that encounter. I really did this time. I think it was a test, I swear, and I'm so fucking happy that I passed it this time. That was the last time we spent the night together and had sex.

The end of a horribly negative era was finally completed, and I now had the closure that I had been wanting for so very long. I could move on with my life in peace. I would run into Mia from time to time over the next decade, and I even met a couple of her boyfriends along the way, but those encounters never turned into anything further.

I laughed to myself that with each new man in her life the same problems would occur for them as they did for me, the poor bastards! Things remained cordial between us over time, and we joke at times about our relationship and how young and dumb we were back then. The conversations about the loss of the two children and how old they would be if they had lived were the tough discussions. It made me feel the same way I would have felt if there were people throwing stones at me, ripping me apart body part by body part, and I don't think that will ever go away.

***

One night in 2009 at the Ritz Carlton, after a Motley Crue show, I ran into Mia at the bar. Vince Neil was sitting at the table behind us, and Mia walked over and asked Vince to take a picture with me. He agreed to do it, and even though he was smiling in that picture, I had no idea what would transpire in 2016 between me and Vince and that fake smile– but that's another chapter.

One small side note to end this chapter in true Mia fashion. Several years after the breakup, Mia called me and asked me if I would give her my sperm so she could have a baby. Not just any baby. My baby. With no strings attached, naturally. She said that she always wanted a baby, and now she wanted my sperm to make that happen. She kept stressing that it had to be *my* baby.

Well, my first reaction to that was like WTF woman? Are you kidding me? Are you really asking me for this? Here I am, reflecting on the fact that she had conceived two of my babies naturally, and neither child was brought into this world. What's this shit now? What, third time's the charm or some shit? No, I don't think so. Not going down that fucking road again and bringing a kid into it on top of it. I declined the offer on multiple occasions, and she even went so far as to call my mom and ask her to try and convince me. Not sure what she was thinking when she did that because there was no way in hell my Mom would approve of that decision.

Mia never got my sperm again. It had to be that way. It just had to be. To this day, I still believe that God was disappointed in my behavior and my past choices and that I am still living within the walls of karma created by those decisions. I pray for redemption in my soul one day. Until then, I'll be damned if I repeat them. I may not be able to reverse them, but I can damn well never repeat them.

To this day, I will always care about Mia. If she ever, *ever*, needed me, I would be there for her to the best of my ability. My love for her will always be there, but it's now a completely different kind of love. My love for her is an unexplainable, rare, very special kind of love; it's a love that is unique only unto itself and only to our shared circumstances.

Even though our four-year, on-again, off-again relationship was brutal most of the time, I honestly had some of the best times of my life with that woman. I have yet to love another person in the same way, at that same capacity, for that length of time. I don't think it can be done, but I remain open to what life may present me with as my life moves forward. As I've learned, I remain positive, optimistic, and in control of my own life. Guess I learned something after all.

# KRISTY & AMBER

## PART 3

# ADULTHOOD

## CHAPTER 5

**W**hat started as a one-night stand ended up being a lifelong sentence of time, money, and energy not so wisely spent over the years. That fun-loving girl who wore a cowboy hat while riding her cowboy turned out to be the same woman who knocked that cowboy the fuck out in the end, like a true heavyweight. She was the one who slipped a noose around my neck and kept it there for years. That noose was always present, too, always there to remind me of just how fucked up things could get in my life.

After all this time, now I can see the true meaning behind Adam and Eve and that damned apple. Lust will get you in the end, my friends. It will. Trust me. How do I know? What makes me so sure? Bonafide experience.

I remember the day Kristy called me to tell me she was pregnant. As the noose started to tense up, another little tidbit of pressure-releasing news quickly followed. Not only was she pregnant, but she also wasn't all too sure that I was the father.

Ha! I had to let that sink in for a second. I may, or may not, be the father of the baby that is inside the woman. Did that noose just loosen up a tiny bit? I believe it did, in an odd way. I really think it did. The rope is still there scratching my neck, but yes, I think it did loosen a bit.

Anything was possible when it came to this woman and her roller coaster of a life. See, Kristy had a Sugar Daddy, her boyfriend, and then me, and all three of us were Baby Daddy candidates. All of us. So, just in case it *was* me, Kristy wanted to pass this information along so I would be prepared for anything, and she would be sure to let me know when she got confirmation. How considerate. Thank you *so* much for the call, Kristy.

As I hung up that phone, I literally thought I was on my way to becoming temporarily insane. I couldn't process all of my thoughts at once. Am I going to be a Father? A Dad? Me? How do I do that when I've never had a father?

And then the second wave hit me. Holy shit. She was seeing those other two guys and she had a one-night stand with me? I'm one of three? Seriously? What the fuck, am I the next guest on the Maury show for a baby with three potential fathers?

I kept thinking how stupid I was to have slept with that chick. I mean, how did I never once think that this could happen? Pretty fucking easy to prevent it, yet at any minute I might be getting a phone call that could change the future course of my life forever.

After what felt like an eternity and that second call finally came in, I was so nervous I could barely answer the phone. I was already moving in slow motion when paralysis began to set in over my entire body. I didn't even get a chance to croak out "hello" when Kristy blurted out, "You're off the hook."

Whoa. Wait, what? Did I hear that or imagine that? My breathing stopped. I needed to make sure I heard that shit correctly. Now was not the time to make any mistakes or assume any more things when it came to this chick! This time, it needed to be crystal fucking clear in the first round.

Despite the paralysis, I managed to get out a faint, "Wh-what?"

And I heard it again like it was borne on the breath of an angel. "I said, you're off the hook. It's not your kid. Oh, and by the way, I'm dating a guy named Kyle Bennett. He wasn't one of the three daddy candidates, but it doesn't matter. He is going to see me through the pregnancy, and we plan on getting married. So, take care, Britt."

All I could say was, "Okay, good luck," as I hung up the phone.

I heard it. Twice. *Twice.* I heard her say twice that I wasn't the father. I was "off the hook" and the threat of impending responsibility, financial support, headaches, and obligations vanished into thin air. Poof. Bye, bye.

As much as it was liberating, something wasn't sitting right with me. I wasn't enjoying the level of relief that a person would normally be feeling under these circumstances. Those words of freedom were not killing the underlying feeling that a mistake was somehow made in those findings. In fact, the feeling of suspicion only grew stronger. I couldn't explain why I felt I was the father of Kristy's baby. I really couldn't. I still can't explain how I just "knew" I was the biological creator of that baby, but I just did. I just … knew. It was in my soul, not my imagination. It wasn't Kyle, and it wasn't one of the other two candidates, either. It was me. *Me.* It was me, though it didn't matter one bit to anyone *but* me under the circumstances. To the rest of the world, Kyle Bennett was going to be the Dad, and no suspicious feeling was going to stop that from happening. Kyle has been appointed the title of Daddy. Cue to all Baby Daddy candidates. Exit stage left. Run like hell and ring the freedom bell!

I believe that when people and things appear or reappear in your life, it's up to you to decide the longevity of each stay, and this applies to friends, family, or foes. Admittedly, it can be tough to assess some situations when people tend to bring with them their own purpose, individual sets of weaknesses and strengths, and unique paths of either success or destruction into your life.

When you have the power to control your own life and lead your own direction, it's much easier to achieve what you want because there are fewer things getting in your way, plain and simple. If you call the shots, you lead the direction. However, if you lose that guiding power, proceed with caution and protect yourself, that's all I can say. Be careful. Don't become an unwitting pawn in someone else's plan, following *their* direction like I've regrettably done in the past. Be careful when you let someone become an exception to the rules you have set for yourself.

In August 2009, when Facebook was just making its appearance in the world, one of those exceptions entered my life thanks to modern technology. I had all my personal information, including my phone number, listed under the "About" section on my page like everyone else. Go figure. One day, I got a text from an unfamiliar number, but with a familiar area code. The text read: "It must be nice to live the life you do, travel the world, hang around rock stars, have a lovely home, nice cars, and a Harley while us less fortunate have to suffer!"

I had to read the text twice. Maybe even three times, telling myself that I couldn't possibly have just read what I just read. Who the hell is this text from? This had to be sent to the wrong person. But damn. What if it wasn't? What if that *was* meant for me? WTF, that's not cool! Who the hell was that? As I racked my brain, no one came to mind, but it was still bothering me the next day. I just couldn't let it go.

Once I was able to distance myself from the madness a bit, it hit me, and I called the number. Duh. I could find out who it was! Lo and Behold. The voice that answered that call belonged to the one and only Kristy.

Wow. Didn't see that coming, I have to be honest. What an asshole. I mean, I sincerely had no idea where that level of hatred and spite was coming from with her. I didn't do anything to her, and I was willing to step up and be a dad to her baby until she told me I didn't need to. She had no reason to be all pissed off at me. Ah, wait a minute here. You guessed it. I was the dad after all. Fuck. Me. I knew it. I *knew* it!

What a conniving bitch, though, huh? I knew that all of those suspicions and uneasy feelings weren't to be taken in vain. And now I also knew for sure the depths of deception that Kristy would go to in order to get what she wanted. Just like Mia. They were going to play you for as long as you gave them the playground to play you in. The only difference here is, Kristy wanted to have the baby.

Kristy gave birth to a girl and named her Amber. Throughout her young life, Amber only knew Kyle as her Dad. As for me? Other than having to cohabitate with a sick feeling on a daily basis, like some twisted form of moral indigestion, I had no reason to interfere with that relationship. I mean, why? What purpose would that serve? Their relationship wasn't about me, or even about me being her biological dad. It was about Amber having a dad, who was Kyle, and it was about Kyle being allowed to have a relationship with his daughter. It didn't matter if she was technically his stepdaughter. Kyle willingly and effectively stepped up to the plate to be a father figure to a child that wasn't his, and I wasn't going to be that shitty person responsible for ruining a relationship between a positive father figure and a child.

I didn't have a dad growing up and never had that type of essential relationship, so I knew how shitty that felt to have to go through life wanting it. If anything, I envied their relationship, but still didn't feel the need to fuck it up for no other reason than to just fuck it up. Kyle never did anything to me to warrant that type of carnage coming his way, and quite frankly, neither did Amber.

So, as it turned out, I did the right thing in my mind, yet again, by doing nothing at all. More than anything I wanted to know my daughter. More than anything I wanted to give to her what my dad didn't, and couldn't, give to me.

I sat back and did nothing because that's all I could do unless I wanted to send shockwaves through my life and the innocent lives of others. Yet, on the other hand, I didn't want my daughter to ever think that I wasn't interested in her, or that I didn't want anything to do with her, that I was somehow denying her. That was the furthest thing from the truth, yet I didn't know what to do about it, didn't know how to go about relaying that to her. I was torn. All I wanted to do was do the right thing, yet it seemed that everything I thought of doing was the wrong thing in one way or another.

To my credit, it turned out staying silent was the right thing to do after all. The twists and turns of Kristy's own tortured path eventually led to her grandparents taking Amber away from her. The Universe had its own plan, and I was wise to just step back, watch it unfold, and figure out the best time to enter the equation.

Once I knew I was Amber's biological Father, I did want to step up to some degree, though – and I don't mean "step up" like some kind of leotard-wearing Superman Dad with a cape and slicked-back hair or anything. I just wanted to have a presence in her life. I mean, she was my daughter and I wanted to be a human being about it. Sue me. I never had a Dad being there for me growing up and the last thing I wanted was to put that on Amber to suffer through. Shit. I wouldn't put that on *my* kid.

I never wanted her to wonder about me, have questions about me, or make the wrong assumptions about me. I never wanted to be that huge unknown to her. I sincerely wanted to be there so she could witness me firsthand, witness where she came from aside from her mother. I felt there was an opportunity to make a difference here, to try and make it right, and to not be the shitty Dad that mine was to me.

I mean, how could I be the man that I claimed to be if I didn't at least try to do something positive, and act like an actual man? How could I ever claim to be a man if I weren't a willing participant in my own daughter's life? Well, the answer was that I couldn't, and I needed to figure out what to do about it.

I took off for a much-needed boys' weekend, hitting up a Steelers game in Pittsburgh. Even though I have been a huge Steelers fan my entire life, that was my first trip to the Steel City. So monumental in so many ways. I remember standing outside at a local pub, Jack's, talking on the phone to Kristy, telling her that I was going to step up, I was going to do the right thing, and blah blah blah when all of a sudden, there was a major shift in direction. And I mean major.

It took her approximately two seconds to go nuclear and I mean, she went fucking ballistic. She freaked out and started crying so hard that she had to pull her car over to the side of the road for safety. She didn't even have the car in park before pleading for me to stay away, to not do this, to not undo everything she has done. She tried telling me that Amber was in no way, shape, or form able to deal with the lie that would be uncovered. *Kristy's* lie, let's be clear. This wasn't my doing.

Now, tell me again why this crazy bitch reached out to me in the first place if all she was going to do is freak the fuck out and tell me to fuck off? Why the hell would she not be willing to let me do the right thing? Seriously, what was the point of it all?

I took a step back from the moment and thought back to our high school days where Kristy's life was always, always, always full of turmoil and drama. She was a couple of years behind me, but I knew of her enough to know that things didn't change much for her over the years.

Over the next few painstaking weeks, Kristy and I would discuss, in great detail, my position and why I wanted to be a part of my own daughter's life. The conversations bordered on ridiculous most of the time, like some crazy roller coaster, barely holding onto the rails, and not much was getting accomplished. One day it would seem as if we were making progress and then on the next day, Kristy's declaring that she would kill herself if she wasn't a Christian.

Hello, sanity? Can you hear me? Is there anyone out there? Is there a hidden camera somewhere? Please tell me there is because this shit couldn't possibly be real. Can't be. But it was. Oh, but it was. Unfortunately for me, it was all too real, and it was all mine to deal with and accept.

***

From the very beginning, I never wanted to disrespect Kyle or anyone else for that matter. From what I knew, Kyle was always a good dad to Amber and from what I remember, Kyle was always a decent guy, going all the way back to high school. He was two years older than me, and I didn't know him that well then, but knew him well enough to validate that he was a good guy.

In no way did I want to harm Kyle or Amber, nor did I want to become a constantly negative component of their lives. All I wanted was to become a recognized part of the family somehow. All I wanted was to be connected to my daughter somehow, some way.

The game-changer was that I didn't need to work with Kristy on any of this now, and I was more than fine with that turn of events What I needed to do now was to work with the grandparents, Charlotte and Phillip. Eventually, the three of us agreed to work together as best we could to some extent, all for the common good of the little cherub Amber. There was such an innocence about it back then that it's almost comical. My, how that changed.

In April 2010, I decided to move back to Dallas for the sole purpose of being closer to Amber. I even went so far as to hire a financial advisor to prepare me for what lay ahead. I mean, I had to start thinking about things like college, buying a car, insurance, clothes, etc. I wanted to help provide Amber with whatever she needed, but as I looked around at my own life, I realized that in order for me to do that, I would have to let go of a few things. I had to let go of some material possessions. It was time to let go of some of my toys, no matter how beloved they were to me. Amber's needs were more important than, well, basically, my fun.

The first to go was my Harley, followed by the new Lexus I had just bought. The last thing to go was the Hummer, and I loved that damned H2! But I had to act like an adult and let it go. I had to. It was time. I had to prepare myself as a dad and be ready to face the challenges that would ultimately come with that title.

As you can imagine, these overnight changes brought about a certain level of emotional distress to the situation. I needed help in dealing with it all, so I started seeing a shrink. I needed to start sorting things out and talking about the "what if" factors now in my life that would be expanding as we went along. I wondered what I would do if Amber didn't accept me. I also wondered what I would do if she did accept me. What do I do in either of those circumstances? What if I do all this, what if I give it the best that I know how to give, and it isn't good enough? How do you cope with that level of rejection, or even the expectations?

I had to take it one step at a time and see where it all went as it went. In my mind, letting go of the material shit was my first actual step of hope in what would become a long winding staircase of hardship, heartache, and disappointment. But, hey, it was a step, and I didn't know any better at the time.

It was Amber's Junior year in high school while all of this was going on. She was enjoying being the Flag Captain for the football team, which presented the perfect opportunity for me to start easing myself into the scene. I started going to the Friday night games so I could see Amber, even though she had no clue I was there. Shit. She didn't even know that I existed. Didn't matter.

I also went because it gave me the opportunity to speak directly with the grandparents, so there was a dual purpose to it. It allowed me the opportunity to look them both in the eyes and personally reassure them that my intentions were pure; that in no way did I want to become some negative force in Amber's life. The grandparents were open to the suggestion of meeting with me, but with one caveat. One huge exception. I had to cut off anything and everything to do with Kristy. Everything. If I did that, if I went ahead and cut off Kristy, the grandparents would let me see Amber. It was only then that they would allow integration of me into her life, so what else could I do? Exactly. I cut off Kristy without a second's hesitation. Boom. Completely cut her off.

I wanted the opportunity to know my daughter more than anything else, more than wanting, or needing, a relationship with Kristy. I had to. If that door of knowing my daughter completely closed now, I felt that I would never be given that chance again. I had to take the opportunity that was being given to me, right then, right there. There was no time to think about it, no time to weigh the options, especially if that last option were to include Kristy. Nah. No thanks, I'm good there. So, as I said, I cut her off. Snip! Once that was done, an entirely new level of soap opera quality drama ensued, Kristy style.

From that first Friday night game, and as time rolled on, it became quite evident that Grandma Charlotte ran the show. My mother and stepfather Bobby went to that first game with me for moral support, but they sat off in the distance while I pleaded my case to meet Amber.

As we were walking to my mom's car after the game, Charlotte approached me. She reached into her purse and pulled out Amber's school picture. She gave me the picture, gave me a quick hug, and we exchanged phone numbers. The communication between us had begun. As time went on, you couldn't help but notice that Kyle was deathly afraid of Charlotte. It was also hard not to notice that Charlotte gave him very little to no authority when it came to Amber. Made me think about how it was going to be for me, even as the real dad, but I decided to shelve that thought process for the moment and just focus on the fact that I was making progress. Or so I thought.

One Saturday morning, Teri, a mutual friend of Kristy's and mine, reached out to me and told me about a charity mud volleyball game that Amber would be playing in with her daughter. Since Amber and Teri's daughter were best friends, Amber would be riding with them to the game. She suggested that I meet them at the fairgrounds and sit with them, see Amber up close, but still be incognito.

I immediately accepted her offer and went to the game to watch and observe this beautiful, young lady that was my daughter. My daughter. My *daughter!* That experience was both amazing and awkward for me, and it was beyond difficult to comprehend that I was not just watching some young lady play volleyball, but that I was watching my *daughter* play volleyball. Damn! That's really my kid out there. Here I am, having all these feelings and emotions going on about seeing my daughter, yet my daughter had no clue that her biological father was there, in the stands, sitting with her best friend's mom, cheering her on. Ah, life's little surprises.

After the game, the girls came over to sit with us and I was introduced by Teri as a "good friend from high school." It was all a bit numbing to have to be someone else when all you want is to so desperately be yourself. Through the haze I heard the girls saying they were thirsty, so I gratefully took the opportunity for a time out and walked over to the concession stand to buy them Gatorade. When I came back and handed the girls the drinks, I began thinking about how I just handed my *daughter* a Gatorade!

When it was all said and done, though, I was reduced to tears on the drive back to Dallas, yet I somehow felt an odd level of joy mixed in with those tears. From the day I knew Amber was mine, really mine, I had contemplated my first encounter with her. I had no idea how it would go should it ever happen and there was no way of knowing. How can anyone know how something like that is going to go until it's happening, right? Unless you can predict the future, this was totally a figure-it-out-as-you-go type of situation.

Through the tears and the emotional rollercoaster, I remained grateful for the opportunity above all else. It was truly a gift to merely be in the presence of this young stranger who already had my heart and soul, and everything I could give her was hers for the asking. She just didn't know it yet.

***

As time went on, the more I realized that I needed to take matters into my own hands if I wanted to get my desired outcome. In no way, shape, or form did I agree with Charlotte controlling my daughter's life, not to mention I completely disagreed with how she went about doing it. As much as I tried to be like white noise off in the background, laying low and not causing waves became nearly impossible to keep up just for appearance's sake. I tried. I really tried, and I just couldn't keep up the charade. It was much harder for me to endure the constant lie than I thought it would be. I kept telling myself that since it was all for the best for Amber and her wellbeing, I could endure the suffering. But, after some time had passed, I believed that living the lie was worse than anything that may come from the truth.

When I decided that I couldn't do it any longer, when I absolutely had enough of the play-acting bullshit, I hired a lawyer to file a motion to force a DNA test and the grandparents were formally served with the papers. Game On. Needless to say, they were caught off guard when they were served and man, were they fucking *pissed* - and it was awesome.

Charlotte thought she had me in the palm of her hand this entire time and it was a rude awakening for her when she found out she didn't. I remember driving through Highland Park by SMU the day before

Charlotte and Phillip were served. I was actually talking to Phillip on the phone at the time, and he was trying to convince me to wait until Amber got out of school before spilling the beans that I was her real Dad.

Basically, he was like, "Why don't you just let it go … and go away … blah blah blah. Why do you want to do this? You seem like a nice enough guy but, shit, man, go on with your life and let it be already."

Ya, okay, asshole. I'll just walk away from my daughter. Ya, that's what I'll do. She's not important, you're right. I'll just walk away. Asshole. All that did was cause a Cheshire Cat grin on my face as I thought about the nice little surprise they were going to get tomorrow. Wait. Make that a *big* surprise, you fucking asshole. You're going to be served. You're going to be forced to have me recognized. You left me absolutely no choice. I did it your way, and it didn't work. A daughter has the right to know who her father is, dammit!

They weren't just hurting me anymore, they were robbing Amber of a relationship with her biological Dad, and that's the only way I saw it. See you Court. Hasta la vista, baby. Let it go my *ass*! Fuck you, dude. You all brought this on, and now I'm going to finish it.

Day One in court arrived and I honestly had no clue what to expect. I was nervous as hell but not because of anything to do with the grandparents. I wasn't familiar with court proceedings, and I had no idea what to expect from the judge. What if I get denied my motion? Anything was possible now, be it positive or negative. I just had to go with it.

It turned out that just like any other Podunk town and the small-town shenanigans that run rampant in them, this particular Podunk town was no different. The Judge assigned to the case already knew the family. Hell, I had found out that Amber had stayed over at his house on occasion because she was friends with one of his kids. Hmm. Conflict of interest there? Surprise, surprise, right? I wasn't sure if that was a good thing or a bad thing, but it certainly didn't start on a positive note.

The Judge immediately denied my application based on some statute of limitations. Charlotte sat there with this shit-eating grin on her face, and I remember telling myself that there was no way she was going to bully me. There was no way this fucking woman was going to keep me from knowing my daughter. I was not going to give up and walk away so she could fucking grin all she wanted. I wasn't going down without a real fight and if this bitch wanted a war, then I'm going to give her a war alright!

My lawyer went back to the drawing board and a few weeks later, we were back in court. Round 2, Day Two. Fighting for my right to know my own daughter, and Round 2 is being denied. I know judges are supposed to remain impartial and fair, but this Judge was visibly irritated to see me standing before him again like I was wasting his time or something. By the way he looked at me, it was like he thought I was either arrogant or posed some sort of physical threat to him. You know, big, bald, and cocky. This wouldn't be the first time someone had misjudged me so why would this be any different?

Nevertheless, once it was clear that I had no legal remedy available to me, Charlotte's lawyer immediately filed a restraining order against me, and the Judge's gavel made it real. I couldn't believe it. How the fuck did that just happen? I'm the girl's *father*. It made absolutely no sense to me. None of it. I mean, how is a man supposed to step up and do the right thing when he's served with a restraining order that had no real basis behind it?

It was obvious that the Judge was looking at me as the bad guy. Why else would he look me dead in the eye and tell me that by no means could I make any contact with Amber, or he would lock me up? How was I suddenly deemed a threat to Amber? How did requesting a DNA test turn into a restraining order? This is shit you see on The Twilight Zone, not in real courts, right?

Charlotte maintained that shit-eating grin on her face, and it only grew wider after the judge granted the restraining order. When she realized for the very first time in her poisonous life that her control may be taken away from her, she panicked. She couldn't have that, no way. She just absolutely could *not* have that happen. There was no way, in her little pea-sized brain, that she would allow me to step in and take away her control over Amber. It didn't have anything to do with the benefits for her granddaughter. Nope. She was too fucking shallow to see beyond herself. Providing a better, happier life for her granddaughter wasn't even in the picture. It was all about Charlotte and what she wanted for herself. Just like Kristy. Just like Mia. These broads were all the same, and I found myself questioning myself as to why I kept putting myself in these types of situations with these types of women. It wasn't just about the truth being exposed to Amber; it was about wanting a better life for both her and for me.

Sometimes, things are beyond any one person's mortal control and life has a way of making things happen, whether you want them to or not. When things are meant to be, they just are, and they will eventually happen. When the Universe wills it to happen, they *will* happen, and they will happen when they are supposed to happen.

The Universe's plan is far greater than anything else, but I still kept looking for mortal answers to my situation. It just didn't seem fair, but the law protects kids, and that's it. Due to the statute of limitations in my case, it was deemed a closed matter. Done. Over. Paternity apparently comes with a time limit, which is so fucking ridiculous. All I wanted to do was meet my daughter. That's it. I followed all the damned rules and gave my word to the douchey grandparents that I would comply with all their conditions, and I still got denied a simple right of any parent. I remember asking God why this was happening to me in the manner in which it was happening because it was just so cruel. I remember asking for some sort of clarification, some sign, some gesture ... anything ... because I really needed one.

I thought, hell, I should have just been a total douche and walked up to Amber one day and said, "Hi. My name is Britt, and I am your biological father." I mean, damn, it couldn't have turned out any worse than what I was facing now, and I would have saved several thousands of dollars on lawyer fees on top of it. Not to mention, I probably wouldn't have a restraining order against me if I had done it that way. At the very least my kid would know that I existed. Fuck me.

All I could do was hang my head and cry. I felt so hopeless, so defeated. Hard to accept that there are no legal remedies for a biological father to meet his own child. Thousands of men go to jail because they don't want to support their kids and don't want to be a part of their lives, and here I sat, desperately wanting to know my child, and being legally told I wasn't allowed near her. And none of it was a result of me not trying to do the right thing.

Like I've mentioned before, it's no secret that small towns thrive on small talk and big drama. It was just a matter of time before the acidic grapes that made up the local grapevine were passing around their vinegar versions of what was going on with "Amber's family." Didn't take long for the news to reach Amber, either. She got a message on Facebook from a girl whose mom was friends with my mom, starting with "I know your grandma," and so it went from there. Rest assured, within seconds, that message was brought directly to Grandma Charlotte's attention.

Warning! Warning! A breach has been detected! You can only imagine what kind of buzz this created in Charlotte's dysfunctional little beehive. Now she's convinced that I'm this Dr. Evil mastermind behind this evil grand scheme to let Amber know the truth, and she wants me thrown in jail over it. I'm not joking. The bitch wanted me thrown in jail over a post made by a teenager on Facebook.

The drama she created reached a high enough level that it landed all of us right back in Court for Day Three during that first week of January 2012. She was such an ass, always having to stir up drama.

On the days leading up to the hearing date, Kyle was oddly nowhere to be found. My lawyer had been trying to serve him, even going to his house that morning of the hearing, with no luck. The person trying to serve him said he was knocking at the door and could hear people inside the house, but no one would answer the door. It was becoming clear that Kyle wanted no part of Grandma's Round Three at Court.

That morning I walked into the courthouse with my mom. She brought a Bible with her, and we said a prayer on the bottom floor before we went up to the family courtroom. After mom prayed, I truly felt like God was walking beside me that day. I went up the elevator first and my mom stayed behind. I think she was waiting on one of her friends that she saw walking into the Courthouse. When the elevator door opened, Phillip was already waiting there, so we stepped into the elevator together. I held my head mighty high, wearing my new suit and feeling grand. As the doors opened on our floor, he stopped, turned around, and asked me, "Do you know what you are doing, Britt?" I said, "Yes sir, I do. I'm fighting for my daughter." He looked at me totally disgusted and as he walked away, I realized I didn't give him the answer he was expecting.

 To our surprise, Kyle showed up at the Courthouse and sat directly in front of me. Unbeknownst to me at the time, Kyle was completely fed up with Charlotte's nonstop local version of the Jerry Springer Show. Not even the bowels of the Jerry Springer Show could depict the craziness that was in full force and effect here folks, I swear!

During the hearing, you could hear Charlotte raising her voice to her lawyer, totally frustrated, which made me smile and feel all warm and fuzzy inside. During the recess, Charlotte, Phillip, Kristy, and Kyle all went into the room on the side of the courtroom. My party remained in the courtroom and what we heard and saw next completely validated the craziness of dear ol' Grandma.

You could hear this batshit idiot yelling, raising hell, and causing a scene to the point where even Kristy stormed out, not to return. After the recess, my lawyer informed me that Amber would now be called to testify, which is the last thing I wanted. In no way did I want to cause her any more drama than she has already endured in her life. What the hell was I supposed to do now? Be like Charlotte and torture my kid just to serve my own purpose? Hell, no. Fuck that. I absolutely *wouldn't* do that to her. I wasn't going to become involved in her life in that shitty, degrading, awkward public display kind of way.

It was now time for me to act in true parent spirit and put the wellbeing of my daughter before my intentions, or anyone else's for that matter. Right then and there I made the decision to withdraw my lawsuit, but that withdrawal came with one stipulation, and one only. I told my lawyer that I needed to be guaranteed that if Amber ever wanted to contact me, at any time, for any reason, that she would be able to do so without any outside interference. It sucked that it had to be done this way, but there was no more debating it in my mind. I wasn't going to have Amber endure examination, then cross-examination, in front of all of us and a room full of judgmental people. Fuck that. I wasn't going to expose her like that, and I sure as hell wasn't going to emotionally torture her like that.

Unfortunately, and not surprisingly, my caveat was flat-out denied by Charlotte and the family lawyer. Denied. Charlotte was going to try and keep my biological tie to Amber buried forever, and there never was any sound reasoning for it. I was advised to completely walk away and make this nothing more than a bad memory. In my heart and soul, I believe this was Charlotte's plan all along – that she knew I would react this way. She knew I was a good person and would act like a good person, even though for her to do the same was far beyond her twisted character and demented capability. That crusty, nasty, selfish, uneducated piece of white trash bitch was counting on the fact that I would do the right thing. Counting on it.

To this day, no matter what else I've heard or who I've heard it from, I know it was Charlotte's idea to have Amber testify. Just like I knew

Amber was my child, I knew Charlotte went to that sickening extreme just so she would continue to have things done her way. Granted, she took one hell of a douchebag gamble, but in the end, it unjustly worked to her shitbag, white trash favor. How proud she must have been of being solely responsible for keeping a young girl from knowing her biological father.

I mentioned before that the Judge assigned to the case already knew the family. As it turned out, that familiarity was a good thing after all. When Amber was appointed her own lawyer, she told the lawyer that she was downright afraid of her grandmother Charlotte and that she was constantly in fear of being harmed if she didn't do exactly what Charlotte wanted her to do.

The lawyer had no choice but to approach the Judge with the information and for the first time, my side could be better seen and not by my own admission. All the hoops that I had tried to go through, all the "crazy" and unfounded claims that I had been asserting, and all the obstacles that Charlotte created – they were all coming to light for the Judge and from all sides this time. This was the one person, the one entity, who could turn things around. And he did, too. In a friggin' instant. After a closed-door discussion with the two lawyers, the Judge granted custody of Amber to … get ready for this…. Kyle. Yep. Kyle. The judge also stated that Amber had every right to know who I am and by no means could they interfere with her decision to pursue me when she was ready to take that step.

The Judge further decreed that if he found out that there was interference with Amber trying to contact me, he would throw them right into a jail cell.

Boom! Bang the gavel, it's done, baby! Thank you, God. And fuck you, Charlotte.

I remember leaning forward and whispering into Kyle's ear, "Congratulations, man. Now, aren't you glad you came today?" I patted him on his back and leaned back on my bench, smiling, and feeling almost gratified, almost serene.

Kyle was going to walk out of that courtroom with full custody of Amber. My daughter, Amber. Yet, I couldn't help but feel oddly okay with it because I knew the good man that Kyle was, and I knew that he was a good father. I knew that he would not put Amber into any kind of harm's way, and I was grateful for that on behalf of my daughter. I was grateful that she would have a positive male influence in her life. I may not have gotten the recognition that I was looking for at that moment, but it was just as satisfying to watch Charlotte lose what she worked so hard to control.

Amber was moved out of Charlotte's house that day, per order of the court, baby! No resisting that move. Oh, how the tides were changing. What a great January this was turning out to be. What a wonderful way to start a new year.

I remember the encompassing sense of gratification I felt when Charlotte left the courtroom and had to walk right past me in the hallway. She looked at me with her veins sticking out of her neck and grunted out, "I hope you're happy," as she walked by me.

Oh, bet your ass I'm happy, bitch. You're damn right I am happy. Karma is a bitch.

When it was all said and done and the Judge had slammed his gavel down, everyone in that room associated with me felt the presence of God. When I entered that courtroom that day, I was fully expecting to go to jail. Charlotte was willing to put Amber on the stand, only to have Amber betray her and the Judge remove her from her custody. I will never forget the look the Judge gave me after rendering his decision. He didn't have to say a word because that look told me everything. That look told me that he realized that I was a good guy and Charlotte's allegations against me were utter bullshit. I will never forget that exhilarating feeling of having God sit right beside me, protecting me from evil. I may have not gotten exactly what I wanted, but I was able to recognize the gift that was truly given to me. And that gift came in the form of a more secure environment for my daughter.

***

Let's back up to the day that Amber found out about me through the Facebook message. Even though she found out in a way that I did not approve of, I was somewhat relieved that the ice had been broken somehow, and it had not been done by my hands. Shortly after the news had broken, I typed up a lengthy letter to Amber, introducing myself. My mom gave the letter to Meredith (Amber's stepmom), who kindly passed it on to Amber. It read –

*Dear Amber,*

*Hi, my name is Britt Amsler and I believe that I am your biological father. I sincerely apologize for the situation that this has put you in, but know that my intentions are sincere. I would like to share with you the short story of who I am and how this all came about, and hopefully one day real soon, you will let me share the entire story with you.*

*I am 40 years old and was born in Longview at Good Shepherd Hospital in 1971. I grew up on Cheryl St, went to Spring Hill High School, and graduated in 1989. You can see my class picture hanging on the wall in the hallway at the high school. I went to college at Stephen F Austin St University in Nacogdoches and graduated in 1995. Your mom was 2 years behind me, Kyle was 2 years ahead of me and Teri was 3 years behind me (I think I got this right) at SHHS.*

*After college, I moved to Dallas in 1995 and began working for the company I currently work for now called Republic National Distribution Company, which is a liquor and wine distributor. I'm in my 17th year with Republic and have moved around a few times in my career which included time in Longview, Oklahoma, Corpus Christi, and Dallas 3 different times, and where I currently reside today. I have a house just a couple of miles away from downtown Dallas. I have a brother named Aaron Amsler who graduated from Spring Hill in 1993. Aaron lives in Austin, has a beautiful family, a wife named Katie, and 3 kids, Abbie, Bryant, and Allie (ages 11-3). I have a wonderful mom named Joy and a stepdad named Bobby Manning that lives in Hallsville.*

*Let's go back a few years and let me tell you where this all began. Like I said, your mom and I were friends in high school and for several years thereafter. When I found out that your mom was pregnant with you while I was in college, it was never made clear to me that you were mine and I didn't do the right thing by taking the proper steps to get to the truth. I apologize for making that bad decision back then as I am now paying for it. Fast forward 14 years and that is when your mom reached out to me to tell me the truth. I can't tell you how low, horrible and shameful I have felt since and how torn my insides are from the terrible mistake that I made years ago by not finding out the truth. I had several discussions with your mom over the next several months after she reached out to me. I wanted to come forward and I pushed your mom to let me do so, but she only thought it was best that you not know about me, that it would be harmful to you due to the current circumstances. I cowardly backed off but kept in contact with your mom over the course of the next year or so. Over time, I have kept up with you, whether it be by collecting pictures of you from Facebook, from Teri, or your grandma. I've had several discussions with Teri, your mom, dad, and grandparents, and I've come to some of the football this past year. The year my insides were torn to pieces and I could no longer live with my guilt, sadness, and emptiness, I knew that I could not wait/sit back any longer.*

This past summer I began thinking of how to come forward but I wanted to do what was in your best interest; meaning take the proper steps. The night you were crowned Miss Gregg County was it. I picked up my Blackberry and reached out to your mom. That's when I decided that I was coming forward no matter what, that I could no longer live with myself if I didn't. I found out that you were living with your grandparents. I didn't know what exactly to do so I turned back to Teri for help. After several discussions with Teri, I asked her to please reach out to your grandparents and let them know that I am coming forward, what my intentions were, and that I wanted to meet with them as soon as possible. I came to the Homecoming game this past year and realized I was sitting right behind your grandparents. I got up and introduced myself to Phillip and the process began. For the games over the course of several weeks (with the help of Teri), I would sit with and or visit with your grandparents trying to get to know them and for them to get to know me. Each week I would come and watch you perform and several times you would walk right past me not having a clue that I even existed. I wanted to reach out to you so bad so many times, but I told your family that they could trust me and I wouldn't approach you. There were several emails, text messages, and phone calls between your mom, dad, Teri, your grandparents, and me during this period.

Teri did all she could do to help me but look what happened to that relationship between her and your grandma. I feel horrible for that as I feel responsible. Finally, it came to a point where I was tired of waiting, asking, and explaining why you should be told who I am. Everyone in your family knows who I am and has never questioned the fact that I am your biological father. Your mother and grandparents said that I should stay away as it would be harmful for you to know the truth now after 17 years. Therefore, I hired a lawyer and took your mom and grandparents to court, twice now and waiting on a third, trying to find a way to tell you without just springing it on you myself, instead of letting your family do what's right by telling you themselves. Your dad and I have remained civil through this process and we talk or text often, which I am grateful for.

*I want you to know that my intentions are very sincere. I have tried my best to convince your family to tell you about me, only to continue to strikeout. I made it clear from day one to each of them that I would not cause any harm nor try to damage any relationship between you and them. My goal is to bring value to this situation and hope that you will give me a chance for us to develop a relationship over time. I can only imagine how you must feel finding out about me. I want you to know that if you will give me a chance you will not be sorry nor let down. We have missed 17 years of each other's lives and I don't want to miss out on another day. I hope that you will give me a chance when you're ready, reach out to me so we can begin our journey together.*

*The day you played in that mud volleyball game back in Sept. at the fairgrounds, do you remember the man with Teri that brought you guys Gatorade and walked y'all to the car? Well, that was me.*

*Sincerely, Britt*

# MEETING AMBER

## CHAPTER 6

The New Year came and went, and It wasn't until Memorial Day Weekend that I heard from Amber. I was in Denver to see the mighty Van Halen at the Pepsi Center when I got a call from Kyle, telling me that Amber felt she was ready to meet me. I couldn't believe it. My daughter was reaching out to me through Kyle. Wow! I was so excited … and so damned nervous at the same time. I wanted Amber to get to know me. I wanted her to get to know where she came from, get to know that there is a somewhat "sane" side to her family. I spent hours putting a "Book of Family" together for her so she would know her heritage as it related to my side of the family. We met at Kobe, a Japanese restaurant (Amber's favorite) for dinner and she brought her boyfriend with her, which I didn't mind. Hey, if this kid offered her the support she needed while embarking on this new adventure, I was all for it. I was nervous as hell and said a prayer before I walked into the restaurant.

We talked for a while, and at times, it was admittedly a bit uncomfortable for all of us because we were at such an odd place at that moment in time. Here I am with the daughter I never knew but wanted to know. Here was Amber, with her biological father that she never knew, but seemingly wanted to know.

After that dinner, three months went by without one peep from Amber. Nothing. To add insult to injury, I was told that the "Book of Family" I put together didn't go over very well for some unknown reason. Because of that book, Amber didn't want anything to do with me or my family ever again. I don't know if I was surprised, shocked, hurt, or what. I sure as hell wasn't expecting a complete shut out, and especially not because of the book I labored over putting together for her, but that's exactly what I got in return for my efforts. A big Fuck You. I've told myself, at times, that life gives you limited things, and that's it. No more, no less. I couldn't help but wonder if this is what I truly was meant to get from all this. Time would tell, and only time, because that's all I had. There is no book to read on this, there are no published manuals, no guidelines. And if there is? I sure as hell didn't know where to find them. I was winging this and battling the tears and emotional scars while doing it. I had to just man up, go with my heart, and hope for the best, no matter how difficult it was to do. I put so much time, love, and pride into that book for her you have no idea how crushing it was to find out Amber deemed it trash. Even more devastating that she deemed it to be a way out of getting to know her father. Do you have any idea how that made me feel as a man? As a fucking human being? I'll tell you how it feels. It's like walking around with an open wound that always causes you pain and never heals. Ever.

***

Fast forward to Labor Day weekend. I got a call from Kyle, Amber's "Dad." He told me that Amber was going to be coming to Dallas because she needed to do some high-end shopping for a dress for the Miss Gregg County Pageant. Amber had won the crown the year before and was going to be handing off her crown to this year's winner. I was grateful to be included in what was going on and appreciated getting even a small sense that I was a part of Amber's life. Kyle and I arranged for me to have lunch with Amber, and then take it from there.

Before lunch, Kyle brought Amber to my house, and this was the first time that we had some time alone. I walked her through my house and took her up to my office where I proudly showed her my rock-n-roll collection of guitars, drum sticks, photos, memorabilia, etc. I had stuff all over the walls and in a large wooden trophy case. As she looked around, she said, "This is cool" and that her new boyfriend would love it. I thought this was a great start to the day.

We had lunch at Terilli's, my favorite restaurant in Dallas. Lunch went seemingly well, and there wasn't as much tension as I had anticipated, which was fucking awesome. Minimal stress meant that we could actually have a relaxed conversation and catch up the best we could.

We went to meet Kyle at the dress shop. Amber picked out a green number for the pageant for which Kyle and I split the cost, and then she found a blue gown for Homecoming. Kyle reminded Amber that they came to Dallas to only get one dress for the Miss Gregg County pageant, not two. I could tell in Amber's eyes that she really wanted that blue dress, so I asked Kyle if it would be alright with him if I bought that blue dress for her. He agreed, so I bought the blue dress, and Amber left the shop smiling with both dresses in hand. I remember feeling so incredibly happy that I could put a smile on her face. I made that happen. I made something positive happen for my daughter, and I'll take it.

It seemed as if things were finally getting on the right path, and the time we were spending together felt like good, quality time. I was extremely grateful for not only the time and the opportunity, but I was so thankful for my ability to buy those dresses for Amber's events. It wasn't about the amount of money that was spent, either. It was more than that. It was about being a provider. That's what a father does. He provides. He supports, he cares, and he provides. He's the rock. He's that one person that you can go to when you need something, when you need help with something.

I felt included. I felt needed. It felt more than good, but those good, warm fuzzy feelings didn't last very long. Not long at all, and neither did the connection with Amber. Her interest in me ended as soon as I signed the credit card receipts for those fucking false hope-creating dresses. It made me question whether her smile was for spending time with me, or if it was because she just scored two dresses. I didn't want to believe that my little girl was devious like that, like she was becoming a product of her environment and becoming of the same cut of cloth as Kristy or Mia. I didn't want to believe that, but, unfortunately for me, that's how it turned out to be with her in this situation.

The deep levels of hurt and disrespect that I constantly faced at the hands of my own daughter became unbearable at times for me, and all I could do was sit back and live with it. Thanks, Kristy. Thanks a lot for creating this situation, for fucking it all up not only for me but for your own daughter, as well.

I continued to attend every football game so I could watch Amber perform at halftime and I only missed one game that season. I left Dallas every Friday afternoon, for nine out of 10 weeks, and traveled to whatever city the football game was being played in just so I could support my daughter. I sat in the stands with the other parents, with the other family members, with the other friends, cheering on the home team. The only difference for me was that I was just about the only person there who didn't get publicly recognized by anyone participating on the field.

At first, no one knew why I was there. No one noticed me enough to the point where I stood out. No one on that field ever came up to me to hug me, acknowledge me, or say how happy they were to see me there. There was never any connection between me and Amber, or to anyone else there, except for the small number of folks who were in on the dirty little secret of who I really was, and who I was there to see play.

The shitty part was that Amber knew I was there, each and every time, yet she never came up to me once. She never let me know that it meant something to her to have me there, and she also never let me know that she *didn't* want me there. Not once. She chose to make me nonexistent. She never even looked in my direction, never cared to acknowledge how painful her actions were to me, and never thought about what it took for me to be there every Friday.

She didn't care, she wasn't going to care, yet I continued to go to the games, up to and including the Homecoming Game, like a true glutton for punishment. I wasn't ready to give up on her although she had clearly, and completely, given up on me well before now. As the weeks rolled on, I interacted with essentially every damned person attending those games, yet never once interacted with my own daughter. Not once. And she couldn't have cared less.

How I managed to be deemed such an unworthy, useless, disposable person to Amber I'll never know. I can only assume that the associated drama with Kristy and Charlotte was at the epicenter of it all, but I couldn't do anything about the damage that was already done.

No matter how hard I tried, Amber didn't want to know her own father and it continually crushed me more than words can express. So many men flee the responsibility of being a parent and here I am begging for it, and get treated as a total outcast, like a bad situation that just needs to go away.

The final kick in the nuts was when everyone, and I literally mean *everyone*, was called down to the field to take a picture while Amber was being crowned Homecoming Queen. I wasn't allowed to go onto the field. That's right. I wasn't allowed. You see, I wasn't "family." I wasn't anyone according to Charlotte and since Amber didn't care enough to say otherwise, I didn't get to be on the field and a part of the photo, a part of the memory. I didn't exist. I had to stand there like some loner onlooker asshole while everyone else was participating in the reason why we were all there in the first place.

I wasn't allowed to be in the snapshot where Amber was wearing the dress that I bought for her, the one that Kyle told her it wasn't my place to buy, yet I did, for her. I wasn't good enough or worthy enough to share the event with her, to support her, to be a part of the moment. Nope. My part ended with signing the credit card receipt, and that was good enough for her.

Fuck, that hurt. You know, it's my own fault, though. I really am an asshole for allowing myself to believe that I mattered to her, for allowing myself to maintain such false hope that I would be able to have a relationship with my daughter.

I felt such an aching, consuming emptiness that I can't quite explain it even to this day, but I can still think of that moment and feel it as hard as I did on that day. I can tell you that it hurt like nothing I've ever experienced, though. More like it burned, and just kept burning.

As I walked away from that field and everyone there, the whole situation made me too sad to be angry. Disbelief? Yes, that was also there. Did that really happen? Yes. Yes, it did. It all happened. My Homecoming memory now came with the image of a fist with the middle finger extended high above the rest, pointing directly at me. Sucker punched. Right in the fucking gut.

Actually, it was more like getting hit in the heart because it hurts more than getting punched in the gut. The pain doesn't last as long, either, when you get socked in the gut. You feel it, you lean over, wait a minute or two, straighten back up, and you're good. You get punched in the heart and that shit hurts for years at a time, no matter if you lean, stand, sit, or crawl. It just hurts, more at times than others, but it's always there. Always.

I cried most of the way home to Dallas and I was growing tired of being in tears over and over again. I was growing fucking tired of the same bad situation repeating itself and destroying my life, over and over again. I was tired of setting myself up for the failure and regret that only I felt.

***

Charlotte was hell-bent on keeping the anti-Britt movement going in her favor, so her next move was to start threatening to kill herself. I'm serious when I say that she would literally do just about anything to keep the focus on her. Psycho bitch. Honestly, at this point, I didn't care if the hag offed herself or not, but her antics did have a severe influence over Kristy, Kyle, and Amber. Just like she wanted.

The whole ordeal was in full force mode by the time Amber's graduation came around. Like the hopeless believer asshole that I claim to be, I still went to the graduation, and I didn't care what anyone else thought about it, I was going. I was going to see my daughter graduate and I especially didn't give a flying fuck if Charlotte chose to use my being there as her platform for suicide. Fine. I'd take my chances on that one, thanks.

This was only going to happen once for her, and I wasn't going to miss it. My mom, Bobby, and I sat in the upper level and could barely see what was going on, but it didn't matter. We were there and we weren't leaving.

Regrettably, the whole experience was nothing short of an exact, precise flashback to the Homecoming game when I wasn't allowed to be in any photos because I wasn't "family." I don't know what I was thinking when I decided to put myself out there again. I don't know how I even remotely thought that the same rules wouldn't still apply here at graduation. I couldn't believe this bullshit was happening again, with the same ending of me getting shit on and tossed out like trash. Dammit! I couldn't believe I *allowed* it to happen again. But it did. It so fucking happened again.

When was I going to learn? When? What was it going to take for me to wake the fuck up and realize that I was not wanted? How long was it going to take until I would acknowledge that I wasn't respected, and never would be?

If this happened to anyone I know, my advice to them would have been to call a cease-fire on themselves a long fucking time ago and walk away with whatever sanity they had left. By all means, wave the white flag, turn around, and step away from the edge before it's too late. You see, this edge was like no other edge for once you fell off it, you miraculously didn't die from your injuries. Instead, you are placed back on the ledge, wounded, left to fall over and over again. That's all you do. You keep falling over and over again, and you keep getting hurt, over and over again with the pain increasing with each fall.

For me, as usual, it became obvious that I'll never learn, under any circumstances and I wasn't going to start now, not here. Enter the perfect setup for the next sucker punch, the next fall off the edge, and a new set of emotional injuries.

When I became aware of Amber's college plans, I completely understood why she wanted to go far away from home. I did, and I wholeheartedly supported it. She deserved the chance to lead her own life, on her own terms. She deserved to have a life without her mother or grandmother tugging at her at all times, trying to manipulate everything she did so that they got what they wanted, not what she wanted for her own life.

She was accepted into Mississippi State, started there in the fall of 2013, and was given the opportunity to join a sorority, which she said she wanted to join. Great for her, but she was told by her family that they could not afford the membership fees and there was no way that she would be able to join the sorority. I told Kyle that if she wanted to join a sorority, that she should go for it ... that I "got this."

For anyone who has kids in college or who is a student themselves, you are painfully aware that things aren't free nor cheap at college – especially joining a sorority. Just to join came at a cost of $600+ per month. How the hell is a student going to pay that, come on now! It's like an exorbitant HOA fee or something.

Nonetheless, I offered to cover the cost so Amber could become a part of something she wanted included as a part of her college experience. I had the fees directly billed to my credit card every month to make sure that there wouldn't be any interruption or issues with the sorority getting their money. I never received a thank you ... never received any token of appreciation or gratitude for helping with the college costs from her family other than from Kyle. He appreciated it.

The whole thing just sucked because I didn't do it for the accolades. I didn't do it so I could do a show and tell with the credit card receipts to show how great I am. I thought I was doing what a parent does to make sure their kid has the right tools they need to grow up and be a responsible, decent human being. I thought I was doing something good, something to help my child that could not have been done for her otherwise. I kept telling myself it was the parental, unselfish thing to do, no matter how unrewarding, upsetting, costly, and unsettling it all was for me. All that mattered was that my daughter was in college and that she was happy. I was looking out for *her* wellbeing, not mine.

I was lucky enough to be given one small crumb of worth tossed my way when I was invited to visit Amber at her university for one weekend to watch Mississippi State play Alabama. Whoop-de-doo, right? Well, it was something, and I was still excited at the thought of getting to meet Amber at her school and meet her friends. I flew to Jackson, MS from Dallas, rented a car, and made the 2+ hour drive up to Starkville to meet Amber and her new boyfriend for dinner. We had an easy, enjoyable time at dinner, and then I drove to my hotel, 20 miles away.

The next morning, I patiently waited for a text from Amber giving me details so I could meet up with her, spend the day together, meet her friends, and see her sorority house as we had discussed at dinner. There I sat in my hotel room for most of the day, waiting for that text. Waiting.

When I finally did get her text, she told me to meet her outside the dorm, and then we could go to the game together. By the time we got to the stadium, it was already game time. I bought our tickets and we enjoyed sitting at the game together, even though Mississippi State lost. When the game was over, so was our time together.

I drove back to my hotel empty-hearted as I've done every time. As much as I enjoyed seeing Amber, I was engulfed in sadness and self-loathing yet again and burdened with an overwhelming sense of regret for putting myself through it time and time again. I had envisioned spending the entire day together, meeting Amber's friends, visiting the sorority, and getting to know one another. I envisioned a relationship forming, understanding being built, and mutual respect between a parent and a child starting to form. None of that happened, nor did it seem that it would ever happen.

It wasn't until after our time together during this trip that I realized she wasn't ready for any of that to happen yet. I called my mom the next day, just friggin drowning in a wide range of emotions. I just couldn't fucking understand why my daughter didn't want to know me. I could understand why my daughter couldn't see my efforts to get to know her, to become a part of her life and her a part of mine. I couldn't understand what could have possibly transpired to make her dislike me so much, to look at me and treat me like some contagious disease.

As was customary, there was always a final kick in the nuts just to add insult to injury. This time, when I drove back to the Jackson airport, I arrived too late and missed my flight. Ah, the perfect fuck you ending to another "fuck you, take what you get and like it" weekend.

*** 

It wasn't until June of 2014 that I interacted with Amber again, and that interaction only happened because I invited her to Cabo for a 4-day vacation. I was never going to learn. No matter how much I was tortured, ridiculed, belittled, and disrespected, she was my daughter, and I wasn't going to give up on her. I wasn't going to be the dad who just threw his hands up in the air and walked away.

Much to my surprise, she accepted the incognito invitation (Grandma Pain In the Ass didn't know about this, naturally), and she and her now-fiancé Jack agreed to join me in Cabo. Since I was the one who arranged for the hotel room, I made sure that their room had two beds. Yep. Once a dad, always a dad, even a new one who isn't acknowledged and just trying to figure things out.

I enjoyed my time with Amber and Jack, even though I always felt our interaction was being kept at a safe distance. I didn't want to do anything to dampen the spirit of our time in Cabo, so I took what was being offered and didn't push for anything more.

There's a painting on the wall at the Mango Deck of the two of us, and it's still there to this day. Sadly, I think that may be the only memento of that trip. No other photos were taken, no joy or enjoyment was given to me by Amber, and she never gave me any indication that perhaps this trip was something to remember. To top it off, I have not seen Amber since that trip. Once again, Amber took what benefitted her, at my expense, and then kicked me to the curb. Again. What number sucker punch are we on now? What is that saying that just because someone is your family doesn't mean that they are good for you?

I moved to Vegas right after that trip, and the next two holiday seasons were more than disappointing. Amber and I didn't spend any time together as we had discussed. Not surprising. I don't even know why I believed getting together over the Holidays was ever a true possibility. You see, Grandma was still wreaking havoc and she made sure that this was not going to happen, even if Amber wanted it to, which I'm not convinced of either. If Amber really wanted to spend time with me, she wouldn't just sit back and let Charlotte off her leash. Charlotte caused such an uproar that she completely cannibalized our plans.

I remember Christmas in 2014. I started crying as soon as I got a text telling me of the all-of-a-sudden cancellation of our holiday plans. I was sitting at my mom's house, feeling all excited about seeing Amber, and had even purchased a large suitcase just to transport all the gifts that I bought for her from her Christmas list.

I wasn't allowed to give her these gifts, so a few days later, Amber went to my mom's to pick them up. This was only the third meeting with Amber and my Mom, and the only thing that Amber said to her grandmother was, "He always buys the best gifts. Everything on my list."

And that was it. She took the material things and left like it was nothing more to her than a "cha-ching" of getting what she wanted.

*** 

As late as the Summer of 2017, I had never posted any pictures of Amber and me, but on this particular day, I decided to post one of the rare pics of us to Facebook. My sole intention was to send a positive message because I knew she would hear about it. I wanted her to see that I was proud of being in her life and proud of being her dad. I wanted her to see that our time together meant something to me, that it was important enough to me to share with the world that knew me.

A month later, I posted another picture. This time, within two seconds flat, I got an email from Kristy, asking me to delete the photo because it was "distressing" to Amber. Distressing? Are you fucking kidding me right now? Are you sure it's Amber that is distressed by it?

Kristy also told me that I would destroy their relationship with the Almighty Charlotte because she had been lied to about the Cabo trip and if Charlotte saw the picture, she would know the truth. According to Kristy, that trip never happened, and it had to stay that way.

I had unfriended Kristy and Kyle on Facebook a while back, but I was still connected to Amber's boyfriend (Amber had blocked me from having a connection to her). However, after the second picture went up, Amber's boyfriend deleted me, too. I have yet to figure out how and why these photos were distressing for them. How is having a man who always tried to do the right thing, who owned up to having a daughter and being a father, be distressing? How can a trip in Cabo with a father and daughter, and her boyfriend, distress anyone on any level? Someone, *please* explain that to me. Please. I'm all ears.

Like a masochist, I kept trying to form a relationship with my daughter. Why I kept trying like I did, I'm not exactly sure. Even to this day, I'm not sure why I kept setting myself up as many times as I did. It took my Mom telling me, "No more, you're done!" at Christmastime in 2015 for me to finally put a stop to some things.

After having Thanksgiving plans canceled, after having birthday plans canceled, and after now having holiday plans canceled for the second year in a row, enough was enough. At least to my Mom, it was, and I had to agree with her. Finally, I really had to agree and comply. I had to be done. No slight fraction of being done, but really done. For my own well-being, I had to be done. It was no longer a choice; it was no longer an option. The time had come for me to wave the white flag. I needed to walk away before all I could do was crawl. I had to stop hurting myself.

My mom and I both felt that if Amber couldn't genuinely be a part of our family, on even the smallest level, then she shouldn't be entitled to the family funding. I wasn't a bank, I wasn't an ATM, and I was tired of being looked at like a pinata.

There's a give and take to things in life, and whether she intended to be this way or not, it didn't matter anymore. She was old enough to know right from wrong, and she was old enough to know the difference between respect and disrespect. She was also old enough to know when she was using someone for her personal gain. All she did was take, and take, and take some more, which, unfortunately, was my fault for allowing that to happen repeatedly. I was an enabler. I was a supplier. There was no emotion to it, no feeling to it from Amber, so this was on me to stop. After all the cancellations, after the constant displays of disrespect, after the constant willingness to accept material possessions and monetary assistance with absolutely no gratitude or acknowledgment given in return, the Britt supply chain finally went dry, and it would remain dry until things drastically changed.

***

I was aware that Amber had moved to Michigan to attend law school and had gotten engaged to Jack. Mind you, I found this all out second-hand. Will I get invited to the wedding? Probably not. If I do? I don't know what I will do. Do I care? I'm not sure at this point.

On one hand, I would love to at my daughter's wedding, but I won't know until, and if, that situation happens. I know that I'm not going to push for an invite.

On the other hand, I sure as hell don't want an invite extended to me just so a good wedding gift is given. You know, it's truly a tragedy as most men run away from this type of situation. I chose to take it head-on and with open arms and the results didn't work out in anyone's real favor. My mom and I are the ones who have all lost out on so much. Way too much has been taken from us as the victims of selfishness from Kristy and from her family. All I can do now is pray that one day, Amber will come around. As I told her in our last communication, I love you and my family loves you. You are always welcome to be a part of our lives. The door will always be open, and we will be there waiting with open arms. I am still waiting for her to walk through that open door.

To this day, I still have every email and text that I ever received leading up to the day of my coming forward – even the ones I got when going through the court battling days. The messages are from every member of Amber's family – Charlotte, Phillip, Kyle, Kristy, Amber's stepmom Meredith, and Teri. I have them all printed out, sorted by person, date, and time, and all layered in a notebook flagged by each person.

One day I plan on giving this to Amber, so she can read it and see how the true story really went, how everything *really* unfolded. Everything she will ever need to know to learn the truth is in this notebook. Everything. From her devious, plotting grandma attempting to falsify Amber's DNA during the court days, all the way to the grandma's betrayal of Kristy, her own daughter, and grandma's senseless backstabbing of Kyle. All the craziness is clearly documented, with all responsible parties in clear, legible print. All the lies that Amber and I were dealt are encapsulated for the world to see. And if they stay buried there, I think that's okay by me, too.

I will say this, though. No matter the hurt, anger, sadness, and despair that has been placed on me, I am Amber's father, and I will always be her father. I will always welcome the chance of a relationship with my daughter, and I will probably dream of having one with her until the day I die.

Why? Because she is a part of me, and that will never change. Because I was the other half of the equation that created her, and for that, I will never be willing to just walk away. If Amber chooses to do that, well, I can't stop her. That's her choice to never know her real father. I do hold onto the hope that someday, all the negativity will be put behind us and we can focus on what the future holds as father and daughter. If it never happens, at least I'll know it wasn't for the lack of me trying or caring.

I will end this chapter as an open note to my daughter.

*Amber,*

*No matter where you are in life, no matter where you may roam, no matter the situations you may find yourself in, I will always be proud to be your father. I will always be there for you if you ever need me. One day, I hope to know you as a father should know his daughter. Until then, I wish the best for you in whatever paths you take. Stay strong, stay smart, and stay grounded. Take care, baby girl.*

*Love, Dad.*

# VINCE

## PART 4

# IDOL

## CHAPTER 7

From the beginning of time, I was a hard-core fan of Motley Crue, idolizing the shit out of Vince Neil in particular. In my attempt to identify with his bleached-blonde, leather-wearing, screeching glory, I was no different than every other teenage headbanger who believed in the way of the rocker back in the mid to late 1980s. I totally rocked out the whole theme, too. I wore the crazy clothes, sported a then-in-style 80's mullet, and I knew every word to every Crue song. I only wore the most recently issued concert t-shirts, always screamed at the top of my lungs whether I knew all the lyrics or not, and I was either throwing my fists or waving lighters in the air at every single show I ever attended. Man, when I say that I rocked that shit with a vengeance, I mean I *rocked* that shit! What a cool time in my life that was for me.

It was such a rare opportunity that allowed me to *live* in the intersection of fantasy and reality of my life. Some things were no longer part of a dream; some things were now tangible. It was a small window of time in my life where nothing was what it appeared to be and because of that, it was also a cherished period in my life when ignorance was pure fucking bliss. All the joy, excitement, and soulful connections that I felt during that sliver of time of my life sure as hell didn't end with the same sentiments they began, unfortunately.

After years and years of self-imposed buildup, after all the fanatical hype, after all of the unadulterated adoration, after everything that happened in between, the bubble burst, leaving me let down not only by the experience but by the majority of the people who played parts in that experience. I was left to feel utterly disappointed, completely let down, unsure, and well, just really, really pissed off and bitter. Now, as with most experiences in life, I'm sure there was a hard lesson to be learned in there somewhere, however painful it was for me to fucking learn it. It was there, I'm sure of it. The question that remains, however, is whether or not I happen to know what that particular lesson was that I had supposedly already learned. I mean, did I *really* learn it? All I can say is that I sure as hell hope so because it's not one that I ever care to repeat. Ever.

The first time I met Vince Neil was back in 2003 at a Christmas party at the Westin Hotel at the Galleria in Dallas. Of course, since Vince was somehow involved, needless to say, worst-looking it wasn't some ordinary, Ho Ho Humdrum Christmas party. Oh, hell no. This was a Christmas party being thrown by a stripper in support of her favorite charity. Completely on the up-and-up, not to worry.

Now, to the credit of some people who actually deserve it, it was a legit event supporting a legit cause. A promoter I knew from the Men's Club of Dallas was behind the event, and he was the one who invited me. He told me that Vince and Kip Winger were going to perform that night and were also going to be infiltrating the party as hired guests, so my buddies and I decided to be merry and engage in some holiday spirit, rocker style. Why the hell not. We bought a table, rented tuxedos, and set out to have a rockin' evening.

As soon as we get to the hotel, the first thing we see is Vinnie Paul and Dimebag Darrell from Pantera at the bar getting a drink, with Dime wearing this solid purple suit like he was some walking Crown Royal billboard. What a fucking awesome way to start an evening!

We grabbed our drinks and made it inside the ballroom only to find that our table was right next to Vince's table. Wow. Rocker Miracle #2 for the night, which was turning out to be the compensation for the unexpected disappointment over the less than mediocre strippers that were at the event. Not to be disrespectful, but the best-looking girl there couldn't compete with the worst looking girl back home, and that's no exaggeration. It was a major, major letdown, but thankfully there were other fun, festive things for us to focus on. Kip Winger performed an acoustical set, which was the official Bummer #2 for us that evening that kind of left a big black shit mark on the "rock it" scale, but whatever. You couldn't stay too mad about it for too long because Kip sounded awesome. The guy can really sing, I won't lie, and even though it was acoustical, he still rocked it.

When it came time for me to break my seal, I found myself standing next to Vince at the urinals, of all places. As I was standing there taking a piss, I nonchalantly looked over to my right, looked down, and yep, there he was, all 5 foot nothing of him, haha. I immediately got all cluster fucked in my own head like some star struck little kid who just met Batman, with rapid thoughts flying back and forth between 'holy shit, Vince Neil is right next to me' to 'holy shit, Vince Neil is a *wee* fucking little man.' I couldn't decide which one to focus on more. What to do, what to do. I mean, do I say something? Do I look away? Do I just keep pissing until maybe *he* looks over to me and says something? Shit.

I really wasn't sure what the protocol was for this sort of thing, so I decided to just oddly blurt out, "Hey Vince, how are you, man?"

He blew me off like he didn't hear me, even though I know he did. I mean, shit. I was standing right next to the fucking guy. But you know me, I'm a dumbass. Since I wasn't going to give up so easily, I just kept fucking going, making sure that I spoke loud enough for him to hear me this time.

"I hear you guys are going out on a farewell tour and have a movie in the works. That's cool."

No reply from him again. So, I kept going. At this point I wasn't sure *why* I kept going, I just did. It just felt like the right thing to do at the time, what can I say?

"KISS went on a farewell tour and didn't retire so are you guys kind of looking to do the same thing?"

I know he sure as shit heard me *that* time, and as he turned to look at me with these beady, little, intoxicated, fucked up, dark eyes, he managed to muster under his breath, "We're not KISS, asshole. You can go see the show, go see the movie, I really don't give a fuck what you do."

As he walked away zipping up his fly, I watched him go while thinking "what a fucking asshole." Wow. Fucking little troll, thinking he's all big and badass. At that point, I no longer cared who he was or what he may have meant to me in the past. Right now, in current time, he was nothing more than an egomaniac fucking rude little prick who needed to learn some respect. Time for that rock star puppy to get his arrogant little ass housebroken.

Honestly, I was so pissed walking back to my table, veins were sticking out of my neck like I was some deranged Frankenstein. On speed. On a bad day. I mean, fuckin' wow, really? That *really* just happened. I found out that the *one* person I have idolized for pretty much my entire life was nothing more than a bona fide douchebag in his real-time fat little hobbit life. Such a letdown. Dammit!

As I was telling my friends what happened, they thought I was making it up until they saw me get more and more pissed as I talked about it. When I was able to stop the rage long enough to seriously mull it over a bit, I cast disappointment aside and came up with a great idea. Correction. I came up with a brilliant idea. Arrogant little prick. Nope. I wasn't going to let it go. I couldn't. Not in my nature to just walk away like that after *that*.

To my credit, I did manage to keep my focus long enough to decide to still take the higher road alternative, and, as such, slightly altered my initial plan. I called the waiter over and asked him to send Vince a bottle of whatever he was drinking and put it on my tab. I intently watched as Vince was presented with the bottle, watched the waiter point to me, and then we all watched that arrogant asshole refuse the bottle.

*Now* I was mad. The time allotted for taking the high road had just ended. Game over. Vince was treating everyone there at the party that night like shit, not just me, but that didn't matter much to me and didn't do anything to console me or calm me down. I mean, he was being a dick to the waiters, being a dick to the staff, being an uptight asshole to everyone there. The worst of it was that he was intentionally being a dickhead for no other reason than just to be one, and everyone caught onto that pretty quickly. It wasn't "cool," and there was no reason for it.

As we were walking out, I caught the waiter just outside the ballroom and I asked him if he was willing to deliver a message to someone for me, even though this message was for sure going to utterly piss off the person who read it. He wasn't sure about it until I told him that the person was Vince.

He coyly smiled at me and said, "It would be my pleasure, sir. He's been an asshole to me all night."

I whipped out a pen and scrawled out a nice little love note on a napkin that said: "Vince, Fuck You! You Fucking Asshole!" The finishing artistic touch was signing the message "from KISS."

I was literally giggling like a schoolgirl as I was writing it out and even more while my buddies and I watched the waiter deliver the napkin to Vince. Man, it was like having Christmas come early.

We watched as Vince took the napkin, we watched as he read it, and we laughed as we walked away, just as his tantrum was beginning. It was awesome. I can't tell you how enjoyable it was knowing that I ruined that little cocksucker's night. Fuck him. He ruined the night for practically everyone else there and he had it coming to him, in more ways than one.

I fantasized about what happened to him that night after we all left. Needless to say, when I ran into the promoter the following week at the Men's Club, I couldn't ask him fast enough about the party. His reaction was priceless, too. No, it was beyond priceless.

He tells me, "Bro. For real. You're not gonna believe this. Someone sent Vince a message on a napkin and he, like, blew up. I mean, he *blew* up. Lost his shit blew up. He was so pissed off he refused to sing, and he left the party. He fucking left, dude."

It truly, truly was an award-winning performance on my part to act totally clueless about any of it as I extended my deepest sympathies over his ruined party. But, deep down inside? Yeah, that's right. Boom, baby! Boom! Mission accomplished. Fuck you, little Vince Neil. Fuck. You.

***

There was a second ill-fated time that I ran into Vince, this time in Oklahoma City on April 12, 2005 for a work-related event. Skky Bar was one of my main accounts at the time, and it was "the place to be" back then. The top executive brass of Skky Bar approached me about co-hosting a party after a Motley Crue show and since I was still a Crue fan, even after the showdown of my first time meeting Vince, I was willing to put the animosity behind me and positively engage in the opportunity being presented to me.

My boss bore the burden of signing off on every aspect of the party, which included a $10,000 fee to secure Vince's appearance, so the pressure was on to get it done, and get it done right. We headed over to the party immediately after the Crue show and Skky Bar was already a complete and utter shit show. And I mean ... Shit. Show. Was every single person in that arena trying to get into the party? Seriously. The place was beyond packed.

After a few unpleasant minutes of battling the crowd to get inside, the first thing I saw was the unpleasant look of sheer disappointment plastered all over my boss's face. Fuck! Not a good way to start off to say the least. There were so many things going wrong that it was hard to take them all in at once. For starters, the DJ wasn't doing the proper shout outs as he was instructed and hired to do, Skyy Vodka and Jack Daniels weren't at all visible anywhere in the bar, and of course, Vince was running later than late.

What did that all mean? Well, it meant that the entire purpose for the party wasn't visible or known to anyone who was there. We were supposed to be promoting our brand and not one person at that party would be able to identify it. Epic failure.

By the time Vince did show up, he was barely functional and could barely stumble through the door on his own. He was downright shitfaced and had three hard-looking blonde strippers in tow. Now, let's be honest here. There wasn't *one* person in that room who was surprised that he was shitfaced; that was to be expected. As for the three strippers who were hanging all over him and groping all over him? It wasn't cool to be out in public acting that way, not even for a known "rock star." His douche-ness went beyond the "image" bullshit and I'm pretty sure his new wife would have been more than just a little pissed off and upset that he was publicly acting like some damned fool who was getting laid for the first time.

Once he managed to get to his table, he didn't move from that spot. And I mean, he didn't budge. He basically just sat there like a blonde lump. He didn't talk to anyone, he didn't move, he didn't sign, he didn't react to anything. Basically, he didn't do any of the things he contractually agreed to do that night – things which he was paid in advance to do. He did none of it.

The only thing he did manage to do was grovel all over the third-tier strippers he showed up with and ignore everyone and everything else. Man, I knew my boss was pissed about it, too, and why wouldn't he be? I mean, I convinced him to spend $10k on Vince's appearance, and the only return on that investment was having talent too wasted to engage, at a shitty party, where no one knew why they were there or who was putting on the party. The evening was turning out to be an absolute embarrassment. An expensive *corporate* embarrassment that I personally brought to the table. Not cool.

To add insult to injury, as if that were at all possible, I brought a few photos for Vince to personalize and sign for me. I wanted to give them to some friends, family and customers who would appreciate the gesture because they didn't know Vince and could still be Crue fans.

As I walked over to Vince's table with the photos in my hand, his humongous bodyguard with absolutely no personality stared at me for a few seconds and then finally said, "What do you want?"

I calmly and nicely let him know I was the one sponsoring the party and that I had a few photos for Vince to sign. He told me to leave the photos and a Sharpie on the table and he would have Vince sign them. Easy enough, right? Right.

I leave the stuff on the table with an amazingly simple list of five names to put on the photos, walk away, and see the big dude handing them to Vince, who, to my surprise, starts signing them. Wow, okay.

When Vince was done signing, the big dude waved me over. I walked over to get the pics. I said thank you, and as I'm walking away, I noticed that every name on the photos was misspelled. Every. Fucking. Name. Stupid asshole, for real. I mean, shit man. The names were written on a piece of paper and there were only five names. All he had to do was copy them.

I went back to the table and the big dude still had his attitude, put his hands up to me and told me to "step away." I told him all the names were spelled wrong and all he could say was, "Sorry, man, now step away."

I was one pissed off Texan. Since all I could do at that point was walk away, I threw the Sharpie down on the table, turned away to head back to my table. I didn't see my one-in-a-million chance jackpot shot made possible by hitting a one-in-a-million chance angle. Apparently, the Sharpie ricocheted off the table and hit Vince square in the middle of his chest with perfect precision. It was totally random and accidental, and I couldn't do that again if I tried, but, oh, the huge drama that immediately ensued.

The fragile little rock Princess was acting like I speared him or something and he needed emergency surgery to repair some gaping wound. Aw, he got pegged with a Sharpie. Boo hoo, little Vincie Vince. It's a fucking *Sharpie,* dude Fuck, it even had the cap on so it's not like he even got an ink spot on his clothes from it. The level of ridiculousness escalated to the point where I was asked to leave the venue. Yep. Me. I was asked to leave my own party!

A security guy walked up to our table and said to me, "You have to leave."

I was like, "What? Why the hell do I have to leave?"

The guard looked at me and said, "You threw a Sharpie at Vince. You gotta go. Now."

Talk about shit icing on a shit cake of an evening.

When I finally got that dreaded call from my boss, the one that I knew was coming, I couldn't fucking believe it when he told me that Skky Bar was pissed … about the Sharpie! Not about the party being a bust. Not about the main event showing up late and then just being a mound of soggy incoherent shit at his table. Nope. They were pissed about a fucking Sharpie bouncing off a table and flicking off a grown ass man's chest. This wasn't a joke, either. The guys at Skky Bar were pissed and they were threatening to pull our brands over it.

Thank God a Guardian Angel was watching over me and I was miraculously given the chance to make it right with our vendor. My boss made it crystal fucking clear, too, that he didn't care how I did it, I just had to do it and do it now. I had to make it right, not just for my boss, but for myself. I was grateful to be given the opportunity to turn things around, and I immediately set out with that exact game plan. I didn't waste one second.

The next day, I set the appointment to meet with the manager of Skky Bar. On top of my verbal, diarrhea-like spewing apology that would be done in person, I arranged for gifts to be sent to him, as well, which was a case of Skyy Vodka and a case of Jack Daniel's 1.0's. Nice fucking gifts, right? (Here's a quick little liquor lesson for you. There are 12 bottles in a case, 33.8 ounces per bottle. When you break that down into cocktails, divide a bottle by 1.5 ounces (average pour per cocktail) = 22.5 cocktails per bottle x 24 bottles x 2 cases = 540 cocktails at $6 each = $3,240.00 straight profit.)

Anyway, I'll say it again, I brought some nice fucking gifts to pad my apology and came with my tail tucked between my legs. Luckily for me, the manager ended up being pretty cool and quite reasonable about all of it. He thanked me for the cases. The rest was forgotten, and since the relationship continued with Skyy, my boss could then let it go, too. Funny how life works, though.

***

Fast forward a few years. I ran into that big dude bodyguard at a Jagermeister tour in Corpus Christi, TX. I was there representing my brand, which happened to be Jagermeister, and he recognized me right away, saying out loud to me that I looked familiar. When I reminded him of who I was and what went down that night at the Skky Bar, he admitted to me that he knew Vince was acting like a dick that night and apologized for having to do his job and defend the little fuck. I high fived him, and we laughed it off.

Random as it was, that interaction justified a few things for me. For one, I knew I needed to look at things differently moving forward, especially when it came to interacting with Vince Neil on any level. And two, no matter what you do in your life, no matter what actions and paths you might choose for yourself or even just want for yourself, if the Universe has other ideas for you, prepare yourself for a bumpy ride if you go by way of the path of resistance. Trust me on that one.

***

In August of 2014, at the Red Rock Casino in Vegas, I'm with this guy, Bob Hewko. Bob and Vince were good friends at the time and Bob wanted to introduce me to Vince to talk about some business opportunities. Of course, I was a bit stressed wondering how *this* introduction was going to go, praying that history doesn't repeat itself, but as it turned out, none of it mattered. Not only did Bob not know the history between me and Vince, Vince had absolutely no fucking clue who I was even as I stood right in front of him and shook his hand. It was like he was meeting me for the first time, so I just went along with it.

Our conversation started out with me talking about the liquor industry and how I could help Vince with his Tatuado Tequila and Tatuado Vodka, you know, keeping his interests because it was about him, and then we eventually turned to discussing the birth of the Las Vegas Outlaws. The Outlaws was an indoor arena football team within the AFL (Arena Football League), and notice I say "was," but that's later in the story.

Truthfully, I had never once watched an AFL game, but the concept for the creation of a Las Vegas team sounded pretty cool and something that I really thought I wanted to be involved in.

It was at that moment in my life when I should have paid more attention to what was going on around me. It was at that moment in my life that I needed to wipe the stars out of my eyes and pay attention to how things were being done, who was doing them, and why they were doing them, but I didn't. Like, for instance, the time that I should have seized the opportunity to walk away from engaging in any "business" the first time I was subjected to the deep dark depths of Vince's drinking problem, and everything that went along with it. Shit.

On a Sunday, drinks for him were being poured with the start of the 10am NFL games and by the time the 1pm games rolled around, he would have moved through multiple bottles of wine or champagne followed by an onslaught of never-ending Grey Goose on the rocks. Doubles. Naturally. Oh. And with four lemons. It had to be *four* lemons. Got that? Not three, not two, not five lemons. Four lemons! If the waitstaff brought any less than four fucking lemons, Vince would get pissed off to a point where you were embarrassed for him over his over-the-top rude reaction. Heaven forbid the puffy red faced crispy-fried-blonde leprechaun throwing a tantrum didn't get his exact number of little fruity gold pieces for his magic elixir.

Seriously, he could be such a tool at times. The running joke with the crew was that Vince left his body like alcohol vapors after Drink #6 and then the new Vince materialized, whether you were ready for him or not. Sad as it was, it was absolutely a spot-on accurate assessment. That Drink #7 broke the demonic-inducing barrier that instantly turned little Jekyll into big Hyde. Well, okay. A bigger Hyde than usual.

One random day, I invited a waitress who I had met earlier in the week to stop by and join us for the second game that afternoon. She wasn't impressed by Vince at all, and after she was there for about an hour, she said something to him that clearly didn't go over too well. She was done and wanted to leave, and she asked me to walk her out. She didn't care to say goodbye to Vince or to Bob, and after I walked her to the entrance and said goodbye, I never saw her again.

When I got back to the table, I made some comment to the guys about not giving a shit that she took off because I wasn't looking to hook up with her anyway.

Vince looked at me and said, "Bro. Get fucking real. She's a hooker, man. She ain't no waitress, trust me."

Now, I have to admit, I was taken off guard and was even a little bit offended, but then thought, ya, okay, it's Vegas, totally possible for something like that to happen and was ready to just let it go, but it didn't end there. It's what that delusional little shit said to me next that made my jaw drop.

He looked up at me and said, "And you know what? It doesn't matter if she is or isn't. Doesn't fucking matter if you don't like her. *I* don't fucking like her. That's what matters. I gotta approve of any girl you want to invite to this table. Got it?"

At first, I thought he was joking around, you know, just busting my balls like guys do, but he wasn't. He was serious. Dead serious. He was that self-absorbed and he actually believed, in his alcohol flooded mind, that I was going to follow his commands or some shit. It was a total fucking joke. I blew it off so I could enjoy my Sunday funday, but the irritation over it never left me. Not for a second.

When the last game started shortly after 5pm, Vince was already beyond the point of shitfaced and Bob was not too far behind him. For the rest of the NFL season, the weekends always ended with the same result, a drunken shit show because of one person's actions, and that person wasn't me.

I did take away one sobering thing, though, and it's called reality. Famous people appear to be on top of the world, you know, really seem to have it all, right there in the palm of their hands. Everything is ready for their taking, readily there for the asking, and all of that may be valid to some degree, but it isn't always what it appears. The seedy truth behind the celebrity façade is that these "human idols" we put on pedestals still face the same issues that regular, everyday people face, people just like you and me, and the well-known front man for Motley Crue was no exception.

During one of our football Sundays, one of the casino waitresses came over to join us. She was a cool looking chick, with Elvira-like black hair, and you could see right away that there was something going on between her and Vince. It didn't take long before Bob left to get a room for Vince and Elvira, under a different name, naturally. Made me laugh thinking about Wing Nut trying to have sex while he's that fucked up, but whatever. Sink or swim, it was on his dime, not mine.

He and Elvira left to go up to the room and get busy and I noticed that he left his credit card on the table. I decided to do the decent thing, if that can apply in this type of situation, and sent him a text. He immediately called me and said he was "sending the broad down to get it," which literally made me laugh out loud. I also had to laugh out loud when this girl just nonchalantly took the card from my hand and was like, "Thank you," like she was taking a piece of gum as she went off to handle her business. As I watched her walk away, it dawned on me that Dip Shit probably doesn't ever take into consideration that renting a room in another person's name yet paying for it with your own credit card doesn't really give you anonymity. Honestly, I don't know how he handled this kind of shit. I didn't care then, and I don't care now, but it did make me laugh out loud thinking of his credit card statement with a charge of: "Elvira's Traveling Plumbing Services – Emergency service call: blocked pipes."

# NO LIMITS

## CHAPTER 8

Throughout the entire block of time that I hung out with this jerkoff motley mooching crew, I never let Vince or anyone else out-step me for the tab. Not once. I always made sure to pay my own way, and then some, but I also knew my limits and I stuck to them, too. I'm thankful that I had the discipline to do that, and also grateful that this discipline didn't end with my finances.

It seemed to me that limits were something Vince never learned. Shit, he didn't even know what the word meant, and, well, honestly, he should have, but too little too late by the time I came into the picture.

One time at T-Bones restaurant, he ditched a girl, Amanda. He spent all evening getting shitfaced just so he could go hook up with this other group of attractive 40-year old women that came into the bar. And when I say ditched, I mean *ditched*. His plan? He got up from the table, said he had to hit the men's room, and told Amanda to go with him. He told me to go, too, and wait for him outside. Then while she was in the ladies' room, this motherfucker sneaked out of the men's room, waved me over, and made me hide behind pillars with him so she couldn't find him when she came out of the restroom.

Now, I get what you're thinking, and yes, it actually *was* that easy to pull off because she was so shitfaced, and the mission was accomplished in record breaking time, too. She came stumbling out of the ladies' room, frantically looked around in all directions for about a minute or two, got discouraged and further disoriented, and well, just wandered off.

As soon as she was out of sight, Vince looked at me and said, "Good. Now I'm gonna go fuck those chicks at the bar!" Sure shit enough, within minutes after us going back to our table, the three 40-year-old cougars prowled right over.

Vince loved being the center of attention and he needed that attention at all times. All times. He literally couldn't handle it if he wasn't, even for a split second. The women were flirting with both of us, not just him, with a couple of them grabbing my bi-ceps and rubbing my chest, and I immediately sensed that The Attention Whore was not at all happy about the attention that I was getting. I could feel the tension in the air growing with every passing second. The funny thing, though? I wasn't attracted to *any* of these ladies. I mean, they were nice enough people to talk to and socialize with, but they were clearly gold diggers or hookers looking to make their score off some rich drunk dudes. No, thanks.

Didn't take much time before Vince was an absolute train wreck and had singled out the brunette who was playing him like a fucking fiddle to the point where it was hard to watch. Once her antics got boring, Mark (who you will learn more of later) and I basically told to her to either fuck him or move on for the night.

She looked at Vince and said, "Let's go," and we were more than happy to leave. Someone had to put an end to the pathetic public display of dysfunction and addiction. Someone had to do something to spare all the other patrons and the staff working at the restaurant that night.

While all of us were waiting at the valet with our delightful drunken duo, Vince decided to jump into this chick's white convertible Mercedes.

Mark looks at me, says, "You drive the Rolls, I'll drive your Denali," and off we went. Not really a big deal, except for the fact that I had never driven a Rolls Royce before, and it's not like driving just any other car. Seriously, I had flashbacks to Anthony Michael Hall in *Sixteen Candles*, only I didn't have a drunk blonde chick in my Rolls. I was chasing a drunk blonde dude and a gold-digging slut. Close enough.

Thank God Mark knew what the "flicker stick" was so I could get the fucking thing started. Funny. As soon as it started, an Elton John song came on the radio at top volume and I was like "Seriously, Vince? Elton John? Wow. Go figure."

We were no more than a few miles down the road when Vince's hands flew up in the air and the white Mercedes made a hard, quick left into the turning lane, darted into a parking lot, and came to a harsh stop. I pulled in right behind them to see what the fuck was going on, and next thing you know, Vince jumps out of the car, screaming like a fucking madman, and slams the door shut. He was pissed!

I knew all about these temper tantrums of his, not only because they were infamously publicized, but because I saw them for myself time and time again. He just stood there, screaming, "Fuck you, fuck you!"

The chick did her best to get him to calm down, and somehow, some way managed to get him to agree to meet her at her house, but the caveat was that he was going to go there in his own car. WTF?

He looked at me and said, "Follow that whore!" I'm not joking either. That's exactly what he said. As I looked into his eyes, I saw that deranged, empty, soulless, whacked-out, vacant look I saw the very first time we stood next to each other at the urinals in that bathroom back in Dallas a few years ago.

Well, I took off after "the whore" and had no clue where we were going. Not to mention, the thought of getting a DUI was stuck in the forefront of my mind and to say that I was nervous as hell driving is an understatement.

When I stopped at a red light instead of blowing through it like a drunken idiot would, Vince, a true drunken idiot, looked at me and said, "Can't you keep up with that bitch?"

Jesus! I looked over at him and came to the sobering realization that this situation had the potential to get ugly. Real ugly. Real quick. From the moment Vince got into the Rolls, he just rode my ass, relentlessly poking an already irritated pissed off bear.

I caught up to "the whore" while Mark managed to stay close behind.

As we were waiting at the guard station entrance to "the whore's" house, the guard looked into the Rolls and said, "Hey, you're that rock star!"

Vince the Eternal Prick manages to slur out, "Ya, it's me, and this fucking moron doesn't know how to fucking drive."

 I think I stopped breathing for a moment. I was like this stupid MF just called *me* a moron. Me? I'm the moron? Oh, hell no!

To keep escalating the situation in his traditional form, out of nowhere and for no reason, Vince shouts out "Fuck this whore. Get me the fuck out of here and take me home. Now."

I was already just a centimeter away from completely losing my shit on him and those notorious Frankenstein veins were starting to pop out of my head again. As he insisted that I get on the freeway, he continued to mouth off, "You don't think I know where the fuck I live? Only been here for 20 years. I think I know where the fuck I am going, now get on the fucking freeway, man!"

And that, my friends, was the final straw. I was done. Done. You know the saying about the proverbial straw that broke the bleach blonde camel's back? Well, it went beyond that. Beyond. I came *unglued*. And I mean, 100% unhinged.

I don't think I've ever wanted to physically fuck someone up so much in my life. And I mean, I wanted to inflict some serious physical pain on this little arrogant fuck. I wanted to *hurt* this loud-mouthed, arrogant little prick. I slammed on the brakes, right there in the middle of the street, and with both hands still on the wheel and veins now sticking out of my arms and neck, I looked over at him, into his dark, soulless beady little bloodshot eyes and met him with a dead stare in my eyes that he had never seen before.

The rage just went off inside my head. "I will drag your tiny, shitfaced, spoiled rotten, arrogant little leather pants ass right out of this fucking car and beat you fucking stupid right here on the side of the fucking road. You got me? And I'll leave your fucking ass there. You got me? Huh? You got me this time, bro? Dammit man. Nothin' but a fucking ungrateful piece of shit you are! Done with it. Fuck you, Vince! For real!"

After about 7 seconds of awkward silence, a deadlocked stare, and my death grip on the steering wheel that was turning my knuckles white, he got my point without me having to verbalize the murderous thoughts in my head. Oh, he got it alright, even as shitfaced as he was. He got my point. He got the point that he was about to become paralyzed and left on the side of the road. And he also knew he deserved it, too. Such reality can become quite sobering when it needs to be, don't you think? Too bad it didn't happen to him more often.

As I did my best to stifle the adrenalin rush and prepare myself to keep driving, I made myself a promise right then and there. I told myself that if this little MF tries to sucker punch me while I was driving, oh, no, no, no. If that happened, it was on. Oh, yes, it was gonna be on like fucking Donkey Kong, baby, and there wasn't anyone there to save him this time!

Once he realized he was about two seconds from getting his face punched in, he smartened up, sunk down into his seat like a scolded little kid, and re-evaluated his approach. With his hands on his thighs and head hanging forward, he all of a sudden became very polite while he quietly said, "Um, exit here, take a left, then take the second entry on your right. My gate clicker is in the left lower door panel. Click it right when we get to the gate."

I was amazed at how quickly he could readjust himself when it became life threatening. As we pulled the Rolls into the driveway, Mark parked my car on the street. As I got out of the car, I looked straight at Mark and there was no need for us to exchange any words. He knew. Body language said all that needed to be said.

As I'm standing there, Vince stumbles over to me, gives me a hug, and then tells me he wants to show me the cars in his garage. Even though I was still fuming and ready to make him into a human punching bag, curiosity did get the best of me. What the hell. I mean, I was already here, and I really did want to check out the cars.

He had a Ferrari, a Lambo, and an old white car that was a convertible with no top, brown seats and big 'ol headlights. I'm not sure what kind of car it was or how much it was worth, but I do know it was ugly as hell. He also had a yellow H2 Hummer sitting outside with flames on it, which was tacky as hell, and I couldn't help but wonder if he needed to take a running start to be able to jump into it. Shit. Did he drive it with blocks tied to his feet so he could reach the pedals?

After our car tour, Vince was so drunk he didn't close the garage door and Mark and I were like "fuck it" and left it open. Shit. Wasn't our garage!

Mark looked at me, said, "Welcome to the club," and we both laughed. Mark told me that Vince would never, ever, ever apologize for anything, so he told me to never expect it and I won't ever be let down. What he will do is become a slobbering kiss-ass the next day as his form of an apology. He guaranteed that just as much as that Drink #7 change was guaranteed. Come to find, that's exactly what he does, too. Sadly, predictable as hell.

The next day was football Sunday and there Vince was, promptly at 9am, sitting in his booth, ready to place his bets and watch the game like nothing ever happened. As I sat down, I wondered if he remembered anything about the night before and wondered how much of his life he truly just doesn't remember at all.

Mark was there, Dave showed up, and it became our typical day of Sunday Football. Dave was the husband to Kelle and was Vince's best friend. Kelle was the personal assistant to Vince's ex-wife for many years and she did a lot for Vince as well. Both of them were extremely close to Vince.

Vince bought me breakfast and lunch that day, and became quite the storyteller once his buzz kicked in. I must admit that a lot of his stories were highly entertaining. It was rare for Vince to warm up to me like that because he never really took me into his trusted "inner circle" discussions. It was like there was always something missing between us, but more on that later. His stories eventually led to stories about hookers (go figure), and the fact that he had deduced over the years that it costs him too much money to pick girls out of the stands. Well, there you have it, folks. Finance 101.

He was like, "I always arrange for a hooker."

So, of course I had to ask him why. I had to know. He said, "Girls in the stands will sue you. Hookers? Hookers don't sue. You pay them their fee, they do what you pay them to do, and then they fucking leave. It's perfect. Much easier. Much cheaper that way."

Hmm. Okay, I can see how there may be something to that logic, especially on a rock star sized scale.

Vince proceeded to take out his phone and showed me a picture of a hot chick. Ya, she was "inviting," … but she also came with a price tag of $1,500. Hello. He looks at me with this wild-eyed excitement and says,

"You want one, bro?"

Now, first and foremost, there was no fucking way I would pay $1,500 for sex, even though that girl in the photo was *hot* - nor was I into hookers, which was the bigger deterrent. Not judging anyone, just not for me.

We then moved onto the next topic of Playboy models, and Vince gloriously relived memories from back in the 80's and 90's when Playboy Magazine was like an open buffet to musicians. He told us how he would skim the magazine, pick out a girl they wanted, make a call, and boom. That girl would magically appear, just like that. Poof! Instant Playboy Pussy at their literal fingertips ... and other tips.

He told me about one girl he wanted when Crue was out on the road with Aerosmith. He made his request, a few days went by, and lo and behold, the fucking girl shows up with her suitcase in hand. She stayed out on the road with Vince for a little while until one day, he couldn't find her. Made me laugh thinking about that girl Amanda he ditched when she went to the ladies' room. Reverse timing Karma.

Anyway, when he did find her, she was with Steven Tyler! He went back to his bus, threw all of her shit out onto the ground, and left her ass there. Classic. Made me think of the 80's music videos on MTV.

I remember Vince telling me that day when his alcohol consumption was in full force that his girlfriend, Rain, left him. She apparently caught him having sex with one of the girls that they had had a threesome with one evening. Yes, you read that correctly. As it turns out, that chick was one of Tiger Woods' former girlfriends. Ha!

Oddly enough, Vince actually seemed genuinely down about it, like he had some form of a heart and feelings and shit like a normal person. Hard to believe, I know, which is why it took me by surprise. He admitted that he loved her and said he didn't think she was coming back this time.

Why? Because this time, he broke the rules. Like, he *really* broke the rules.

Throughout their relationship, he said Rain picked the girls to bring into their bedroom, but there would not be any "cheating" of any kind allowed. You see, it was considered to be cheating if Vince had sex with other girls when Rain wasn't also there participating in the activities. Hmm, okay. I thought to myself, well, shit, that's simple enough. Just be monogamous. But I knew that was never going to happen. Not with Vince. Nothing with Vince was ever simple.

As we walked to the valet, the customary battle of getting Vince's car keys from him ensued, as it always did. He usually talked shit to the valet guys when they brought out his car and onlookers couldn't help but cringe as they watched it unfold. He would pour himself into his car like liquid lard and drive away, completely shitfaced, with no concern over what could potentially happen driving in such an impaired condition.

It's sad to watch someone with fame become lost in that fame, to watch them become so delusional, so unapproachable in their own minds. It's even more sad to watch it unfold in situations where other people, innocent people, can involuntarily be put at risk and possibly harmed because of it. Perhaps the saddest part of it all was that he just didn't give a fuck about anyone but himself, on any level, no matter the situation, no matter the person, no matter the relationship. That's just who he was, and no one was ever going to change that about him. No one. Not even himself. He didn't want to, and that was that.

As I was becoming more and more acquainted with Vince's inner circle, I was given the Golden Rule of Vince that he insisted I adhere to: We don't talk to the other band members. Yes, he meant the Crue. I was told that I am now on "Team Vince," and this is how it worked for everyone. There was such levels of animosity and turmoil all around the band, and I had no idea what a legitimate shit show it really was until I was seeing it unfold right in front of me.

Vince had told me that he couldn't stand Mick and would never speak to him again after the tour because Mick brought his lawyer to the filming of the country version remake of "Home Sweet Home." I don't recall exactly what he told me, but, whatever it was, the bottom line was that he was done with Mick.

He openly said he thought Tommy was a shitty drummer and that anyone could play his rollercoaster solo – boom boom bish, boom bish, boom bish! When I heard that I was like, "Whoa, slow down there, dude, Tommy Lee's awesome!" As he kept on the Tommy rant train, he threw in the claim that he fucked Pam Anderson before Tommy did. I wondered about that one, but, again, whatever. It didn't matter to me what the hell he did, not then or now, nor did it matter with whom he did it with.

The only person he never had anything negative to say about was Nikki, but I honestly believe that was out of pure fear. Why? Because Nikki controlled Crue. Bottom line.

Okay, so, no talking to other band members. Gotcha. I flew home the weekend Crue was playing in Bossier City, LA on Oct 12, 2014, about an hour away from where I grew up. Vince told me to give him a call in the afternoon on the day of the show and we would meet up. Later that day, Vince let me know his bus was running late and that we would have to catch up backstage. He told me he left my credentials for me at Will Call and I must admit, I was surprised to find there was actually an envelope left for me when I got there. Kinda cool, though, giving me a full access pass like I was a crew member. Imagine that.

By the time Vince arrived, I was already standing backstage. He came and got me, and we headed to his dressing room to check out the Sunday night NFL game. The Dolphins were Vince's team and had lost to the Packers earlier in the day so not a good start for him, I guess. At first, he wasn't very talkative, and it was a bit awkward, almost on the verge of being uncomfortable, but once we started chatting about the AstroTurf for the Outlaws field the conversation came to life a little bit.

It was no secret that Vince was a big drinker, so when he started pacing around the dressing room, I knew something was up. Someone very close to Vince (I will leave this person anonymous) had tipped me off that Vince was prohibited from consuming any alcohol on the day of the show or the band would fine him $50,000. My unnamed source said that since Vince wasn't an actual member of the band and was more like a contractor, this was the avenue of control that management took to guarantee that a sober Vince would be present for each show.

While we were sitting on the couch, Vince's personal assistant walked in with a guitar and asked Vince to sign it. As I checked out the guitar, I noticed the signatures from the other guys in the band and realized I never saw any of them the entire time I was backstage.

When Vince's PA knocked on the door to tell Vince it was time for him to start getting ready, Vince had to literally *force* himself to put on the rocker outfit that was hanging in the armoire and go do his rocker thing.

We agreed to meet after the show and off I went to the side of the stage to catch what was left of Alice Cooper's gig. What a cool spot, too. I got to witness the behind-the-scenes production for an extremely theatrical show, complete with walking monsters and a medieval times scene when Alice gets his head chopped off. It was so cool. I saw it all.

After the Alice set, I ventured out into the crowd and caught up with some friends that I hadn't seen in a long time. Even my Mom and Bobby were there - their very first Crue show. I was so proud. I remember thinking how cool it was that my Mom took me to my first Crue show in 1987 and sat outside waiting for me, and here we were doing it again, in modern day, in the same city, at the same venue, but this time, my Mom was inside with me enjoying the show and not waiting in the car. Funny how certain things in your life have a way of coming back to you. The lights went out, the Crue show began, and another memory was about to be made.

After the show, I went back to Vince's dressing room and waited outside for a few minutes while he cleaned up the after-show grime. Mick walked by once, but there were still no signs of Nikki or Tommy that night other than them performing on stage. I thanked Vince for the VIP pass and told him I'd see him back in Vegas. As I was walking away, I heard Vince asking two girls if they wanted to join him on his bus for a drink, and I just had to laugh.

See, here's the thing about those "drinks on the bus" scenarios. Whatever liquor Vince didn't consume while out on the road, he took home as his personal stash. Might not sound like a lot for one show but think of how many shows there are when the band is touring and start doing the math. It adds up, believe me. At the end of one tour, Vince took so much booze home that it almost didn't all fit on the plane. I'm not kidding. With that one tour alone, Vince copped enough booze to fill up one side of his garage. After every show, *every fucking show,* there were 2 bottles of Grey Goose, 2 bottles of Santa Margherita Pinot Grigio, 2 bottles of Silver Oak, and 2 bottles of Veuve Clicquot Champagne for the taking, waiting for him on the bus, after every show. It doesn't take a mathematician to realize that amounts to a lot of fucking booze. I don't care how much you like to drink and party, there's going to be excess.

Vince was a connoisseur of drinking alcohol, and at this point he was making attempts to turn being a lush into becoming an entrepreneur and start manufacturing the alcohol. Okay, okay, bullshit called out right now on what he was actually doing and what he *said* he was doing. Let's be clear here. He *endorsed* the products; he didn't make them. He was like a pickled, walking billboard anyway, so it made sense on some level, right?

He did have two alcohol products out on the market at the time, both named *Tatuado*. One was an 80-proof vodka and the other was an 80-proof silver tequila, but it wasn't a 100% agave tequila. The vodka bottle had his picture on the front of it, and the tequila bottle had his name running across the middle of the bottle and nothing else. Both bottles came with a screw cap and a shrink-wrapped label over a plain, generic glass bottle, and the vodka bottle had some teeny tiny print on it, like "Distilled From Grain & 5 X Filtered" and some information on the bottling plants, blah blah blah. That was it. No story, no heritage, no tagline, no slogan, no catch, no connection. Nothing. Just two shrink-wrapped bottles with either his face or his name on it. That's it.

Bob had mentioned to me several times that Vince wanted to take this brand to new distribution levels across the country and that he obviously needed my help in pulling it off. No shit. So, one day I offered to help Vince. To this day, I'm not exactly sure why I offered to help him, but I did. Maybe I was still mesmerized that he left the backstage passes for me, I'm not sure. I told him that I'd invest an entire day with him, give him a legit presentation on the industry, and give him the tools and the information he needed to improve the marketing and the sales of his brand. You know, truly educate him on what I knew as gospel in the industry, which were the primary things he needed to know and understand. If he was going to be an actual player in the liquor industry, he needed to develop some awareness on both categories of the liquor type, the competitive set, pricing, packaging, markets, etc. Everything. I was willing to share everything I could with him for nothing more in return than to make his brands better. I was offering a legit education that cost him nothing more than his time.

We set a date on the calendar for December 22nd, right before I left to go home for Christmas. In the meantime, I did my part and put in about 12 hours researching his brand and creating this all-inclusive presentation that was being made for his sole benefit. We met at Kona Grill in Summerlin, a location that set a perfect example of a bar where I could explain how "on premise" works, and it was conveniently located right next to a Lee's Liquor Store and a Total Wine outlet. I figured I could show him the presentation over lunch, discuss the back bar, POS System, and menu print at Kona Grill, and then we could walk over to both liquor stores so I could further explain how the retail side works to him. Simple enough, right? Yeah, sure.

As soon as we sat down at Kona, he let me know that his girlfriend, Rain, was going to join us. That immediately told me I had limited time on his attention span, and I was now going to have to fly through all this shit before she got there. Dammit! Not cool. Not what I had in mind at all. This wasn't something I wanted to rush through and just gloss over. This was something that I wanted to explain so that it was understood at a deeper level.

I had no alternative but to quickly show him some Nevada sales data for the categories of vodka and tequila where his brand wasn't just on the low end of the scale, it didn't even register. I used that example to stress the importance of marketing, packaging, and the impact that it all had on consumers. I talked about his target audience. Who are they? How did they relate to him as a brand? He had no clue what I was talking about. None.

I was like, "Dude, I know who you are, but the generations below us don't have a clue who you are or even how to pronounce your brand!" I tried to relate living examples to him by explaining how going out on a solo tour with a black drop curtain with nothing but the word "Tatuado" on it didn't provide much benefit when no one in the audience knew what the hell it meant. Now add the fact that his brand was only sold in Nevada, so advertising a brand in a state where the product wasn't even sold made no sense at all either.

When I asked him where the distillery was, he said he didn't know. "Somewhere in Las Vegas." Okay. When I decided to go another route and asked him what the production capabilities were, he said he didn't know. When I asked him what the plan was to get his product sold in the other 49 states, he said he didn't know. Hmm. Wow. Okay then. He needed more of an education on this than I thought. When he says he "doesn't know," he means he doesn't know about anything at all, even with his own brand. So much for my presentation and insight and making them relatable.

I finally asked him if he was ready, willing, and able to follow the example of Sammy Hagar promoting his Cabo Wabo brand, meaning, put on a suit and bounce around the US to meet with distributors and sales forces. Just when I began to wonder if anything that I was saying was sinking in, he looked at me and told me he would hire me to do all this *for* him and give me 40% of the profits. I flatly, and quickly, refused that offer, telling him there would have to be drastic changes made for me to consider it even remotely. Just then, Rain shows up to the table and the business conversation abruptly ended.

After lunch, I told them I wanted to take them over to Total Wine to check out the vodka shelves. I already knew where Tatuado was located in the store, but when we stepped through the door, I looked at Vince and told him, "Go find your brand."

After a few minutes, I had to point it out to him. I started talking about shelf presence and pricing versus the competitive set. It seemed like it was starting to sink in a little bit, so we walked over to Lee's to keep the momentum going. At this store, his stuff was on the bottom shelf and at close out pricing below $20.

I looked at him and said, "Vince, you drive a Rolls Royce and yet your products are on the bottom shelf at a commodity price. Your brand needs to be like a Rolls Royce, man. Super premium kind of price to appeal to consumers, not priced under $20 bucks and on the bottom shelf collecting dust bunnies."

That was the comparison he seemingly could relate to finally. When we were done, we shook hands, he said, "Thank you," and we never discussed it again. Not once. Not even a hint. Not even a *mention*. He still managed to walk away from all of that enlightenment and education with the steadfast misguided belief that all he needed was his face to sell his brand. Any brand. Just like he did with our football team, but that's another part of the story. Ah, hindsight; at times you are, for sure, a kick in the ass when you are finally recognized.

Now, at this point in our relationship, I felt as if we had reached a higher ground, a true development of some sort of trust between Vince and me in both our personal and professional dealings. Man, was I fucking wrong. So wrong. In fact, I couldn't have been more wrong. Over the holidays when the NFL playoffs were in full swing, we did our customary table at a casino to watch the games. Rain came into The Palm one afternoon while we were all there and told Vince she wanted to play blackjack and asked him for some money. So, in the customary Pimpin' Sugar Daddy role he always played for her, he pulled out a $100 bill and handed it to her.

I made a quick, off the cuff comment that I loved to play blackjack, so Rain turned to me and said, "Britt, do you want to come to the table with me?"

Not thinking anything beyond going to play cards, I was like, "Sure, let's go!"

Trust me when I tell you that I had no interest or attraction to Rain, nor did I have any intention of making a pass at her or interacting with her on any inappropriate level. First of all, she was my friend's girlfriend. Secondly, and in full disclosure, the thought of hooking up with a chick that had sex with Vince Neil made me want to shower and take some penicillin.

Anyway, as Rain and I walked around the corner, some dude she knew was walking towards us and before he could say anything, Rain said, "It's cool, he's Vince's buddy. It's fine." Hmm. That was fucking weird, not to mention uncalled for in my opinion.

We got to the table and I made sure to leave one seat between us to avoid any accusations or give anyone any reason to think otherwise. Now, keep in mind, we were sitting at a table literally around the corner from the Sportsbook, maybe 75 yards away from the boys. Next thing you know,

Rain's phone starts to ring. She showed me her phone and it was Vince calling. She gave me that look, and guys, you know the look.

I was like, no fucking way this asshole thinks I'm hitting on his girlfriend. For anyone who gambles, you know that you cannot answer your phone when sitting at a table. It's not a joke, either. He called her immediately, and when she didn't answer, the texts started rolling in. She showed me one text that read: *Is Britt trying to pick you up?????????*

I was like, are you fucking kidding me right now? Man, I was so disgusted. I was almost physically sick. I mean, what a fucking douchebag! Once I saw that, I was so worked up I couldn't focus on the cards, so I just told Rain I was done. Card game over.

We walked back to where the guys were still sitting, and both Rain and I were clearly annoyed. As we turned the corner, there he sat. Little Mr. Rock Star, all butt-hurt and pouting like he just broke his favorite toy, sitting in his little red highchair, swinging his feet with no one to play with him. He and Rain exchanged some relatively quiet words and she walked away from him, letting him sit there alone pouting and all pissed off.

I walked over to his chair, took one knee so he could look me in the eye, and said, "Bro, you being serious right now? You can't possibly think it was like that."

He came back with, "What do you expect me to fucking think? You walked off with my girl!"

I was immediately vaulted back in time, all the way back to high school in a flash. Only this time, I wasn't this shy gangly kid who was afraid of getting his ass kicked. This time I was one of the bigger kids who made people afraid of getting their ass kicked. Oh, how the tides have turned.

I said, "Let me tell you something bro. I'm not one of your band mates ,and I'm sure as hell not trying to bang your girl. I don't do that to my friends. When Rain is with me and you are not around? She is in the safest place as she could be because I got you."

Dumb ass. He reacted just like a little high school boy would react and said, "Ooooookay," and shook my hand.

I was utterly annoyed and was going to leave, but something told me to stay and I'm glad I did. I got to meet Todd Haley, the OC from the Steelers, who showed up with his wife Crissy about an hour later. It was beyond cool for me to be able to have a few drinks with them at the bar and then have more drinks with them at the Cosmo. I had the pleasure of staying in touch with them and sent them a case of booze for the holidays each year for the next few years. When the Steelers played the Cowboys in Pittsburgh in 2016, Crissy got me tickets from the Steelers office and even though we lost, we had a blast at the game. It was an introduction and experiences worthy of enduring Vince's sophomoric shit, let me tell you. Go Steelers!

February 15, 2015, brought the Superbowl with the Seahawks playing the Patriots and Vince throwing a Super Bowl party at his so-called restaurant/bar. My good friend Robert Olivares had flown in for the weekend, which was a helluva good start to the weekend and it was also comforting to know that I had a true friend in my corner. At the bar, Vince had a roped off area with a table for all of us and everyone else had to stay behind the rope. It was cool, though, because I got to meet Michael Godard, an extremely talented and creative artist known as the "Rockstar of the Art World." (Most of his paintings showcase animated olives and strawberries believe it or not.)

Kickoff was still a few hours away and for some reason, I had this eerie gut feeling that a major shit storm was brewing and that it was going to touch ground at any given moment. Dave was there that day and he was a huge Seahawks fan, so needless to say he was pumped for the game. Vince told me that he had a replica Super Bowl ring and that he was going to surprise Dave with it as a gift. He showed me the ring, and it was really nicely done. It was an identical replica of the Seahawks' ring earned the year before when they beat the Broncos.

When he gave it to Dave, the guy was genuinely blown away. And I mean, totally, authentically, blown away. He got, like, all emotional and shit -- that kind of blown away. It was a nice gesture and a pretty cool one at that. Vince loved jewelry. He was always wearing rings and necklaces, and always had on a nice watch. That much I have to give the guy.

Anyways, Vince was getting warmed up in his usual ways as the restaurant started to fill up with fans, all of which wanted a picture or autograph with Vince. Now, remember Vince didn't own the place. His name was on the door and his memorabilia inside, but he received comps in return for that name usage. That's it. That's what he told me. And I'm not sure who wrote the ad as it had improper grammar, bad punctuation, and false narrative. Here's the ad so you can see it for yourself:

*"Vince Neil to host Superbowl party in Vegas and you are invited.*

*On February 1ˢᵗ, experience Super Bowl Sunday at Vince Neil's Tatuado Eat Drink Party Restaurant & bar, situated inside Circus Circus Hotel and Casino in Las Vegas, Nevada.*

*Hosted by Motley Crue vocalist Vince Neil himself, advance wristbands are available for $35 each, including buffet and entry; they will be $40 at the door. Kids are priced at $25 each, and $20 beer buckets will be on offer. Raffle prizes of signed Vince Neil memorabilia are also up from grabs. Doors open at 1pm. Come on down to Tatuado and party with Vince and the Las Vegas Outlaws Posse. For reservations call 702-691-5991 (long distance charges may apply).*

*Vince Neil's Tatuado Eat Drink Party features two large video walls, projection screens and 22 HD flat screens, with an emphasis on a fun and exciting party like environment. The mouth-watering menu offers up signature burgers, burritos and more to tantalize guests' taste buds. The dining room bar allows guests to pair their meal with a cold beer, lavish cocktail or one of the rocker's very own premium brands."*

What was the false narrative, you might ask? Well, let me put it this way, there was no way in hell that Vince was going to intermingle with the fans at that party. No fucking way. None. That wasn't his style, and it didn't matter to him that it was his fans' loyalty and money that provided him with his lifestyle. He didn't care. He wasn't going to do it and that was that.

During the entire first half of the game, fans would come up to the red rope which was directly behind our chairs in hopes of getting to shake his hand, get an autograph, maybe a picture, or any type of interaction they could get with him. Some folks even brought their kids over with them to just be left standing there. The ad said that Vince was the host and to come "party with Vince," right? Wrong. Vince had no intention of making any dreams come true for anyone else other than himself.

It wasn't until Vince went to the restroom that his "alter ego" mood kicked into gear. Ah, there it was, the shit storm I sensed was near, and it was about to rain like diarrhea.

When he came back to the table, he was bitching about how he just wanted to be able to take a piss without being bothered by "some fucking guy" interrupting him. He came back in a fucking mood, and it just escalated from there.

Katie Perry played the halftime show and when it was over, Vince sat there, giving two thumbs down shouting, "Boo, boo! Boo! That was fucking terrible!"

While that was going on, another group of fans walked up, one of which was a very persistent woman. When she called Vince out for ignoring her, that's when it started to get ugly. I don't know how that confrontation ended because Robert and I got the fuck out of there as soon as it started to go down. Fuck that scene. I couldn't watch that shit go down anymore. I always felt sorry for the fans because if they only knew what I knew, they would have never showed up in the first place, and they would sure as hell stop spending their hard-earned money on him.

Ah, hindsight, you slick motherfucker. You were there the whole time, and I just didn't see you. If I did, maybe I would have taken heed of my own warnings before engaging in a business venture with Vince down the road. I think the Universe was trying to tell me something then, and I think it tried to tell me on several occasions. Shit. Well, I wasn't listening, okay? I admit it. Unfortunately for me, I just wasn't listening when I should have been listening to every fucking word. Lesson here learned, and learned the hard way.

Opening Night – Bob Hewko, Carrot Top & Vince Neil

Opening Weekend – Sunday Funday at Vinnie Paul's House in Vegas – Bobby Manning, Vinnie Paul, & JMAC

Robert Olivares – Las Vegas Outlaws Game – Las Vegas, NV

Gene Simmons – LA KISS Game - Las Vegas, NV

Mike Shanahan – Outlaws Game - Las Vegas, NV

Paul Shortino – Outlaws Game/National Anthem Day – Las Vegas, NV

Ron Jeremy - Rainbow Bar & Grill - Hollywood, CA

Vince Neil- Outlaws Practice – Las Vegas, NV

Sunday Funday @ Vinnie Paul's House - Arlington, TX

Dennis Huff, JMAC, Tom Maxwell, Vinnie Paul, & Jamie Sexton - Vinnie's Tour Bus - San Diego, CA

Steve Levy & Bob Hewko – Red Rock Casino Las Vegas, NV

JB Bernstein, Bob Hewko & Coach Aaron Garcia – Party in the Park – May 1, 2015 Las Vegas, NV

Bob Hewko, Vince Neil & Mark Daniel's – Shots of Tatuado Tequila – Official Launch Party @ Circus Circus Casino – Las Vegas, NV

Bob Hewko, Todd Haley & Vince Neil @ The Palms Casino – Las Vegas, NV

Tanner Varner (DB) & JJ Raterink (QB)

John Corabi & JMAC @ The W Hotel – Dallas, TX

Vince Neil, Dave Hein & Kelle Stang – Outlaws Pregame Opening Night – Las Vegas, NV

Dave Hein & Vince Neil - Superbowl Party @ Tatuado Restaurant – Circus Circus Casino – Las Vegas, NV

Mark Daniels , Vince Neil  & Bob Hewko – Outlaws Game – Las Vegas, NV

Paul Shortino, Carlos Cavazo, Dave Alford & Jeremy Green - Green Room at the Whisky a Go Go – West Hollywood, CA

Steve Levy & JOD @ Outlaws Game Opening Night – Las Vegas, NV

Dave Hein, Michael Politz, Bob Hewko, Vince Neil & Mark Daniels - Sunday Funday @ Red Rocks Casino Las Vegas, NV

Vinnie Paul, Bob Hewko , Carrot Top, Jamie Sexton, Bri Dog Jones, Jeff Molitz & Chelsey Yeager - Backstage at Carrot Top Show@ The Luxor Casino Las Vegas, NV

AVN Awards – Hard Rock Casino & Hotel – Las Vegas, NV

Shannon (Playboy Playmate) Las Vegas Motor Speedway

Carlos Cavazo & David Alford – NAMM Show - Los Angeles, CA

Robert Olivares, Carrot Top, DJ Ashba & Paul Shortino – Las Vegas, NV

Mom & Vince Neil – Outlaws Game Las Vegas, NV

Vinnie Paul @ DFW Flying Back To Las Vegas

I'll be damn !! Look who's on the same flight back to Vegas with me!!! BRITT!!

Doug Aldrich - W Hotel in Dallas, TX

Ozzy Osbourne – Whisky a Go Go – West Hollywood, CA

Vince Neil - Ritz Carlton, Dallas, TX

JB Bernstein, Michael Politz, Vince Neil, Bob Hewko, Sohrob, Mark Daniel's, Coach Aaron Garcia, Carrot Top & The AFL Commissioner - Outlaws Kickoff - Freemont St Las Vegas, NV

Bob Hewko, & Vince Neil – T-Bones Steakhouse Red Rock Casino – Las Vegas, NV

Jon Gruden, Bob Hewko, Dave Hein & Johnny– STK Steakhouse Cosmopolitan Casino Las Vegas, NV

Loni (Playboy), Paul & Carmen Shortino & Daniela, Doug & Ryder Adrich

Kelle Stang & Dave Hein – Las Vegas, NV

My Papa Lero Sanders, Family & Friends – Vince Neil Pre-Concert Party – Tyler, TX

Mom - Freemont St – Las Vegas, NV

Mikayla Ice Skating @ Cosmopolitan Casino – Las Vegas, NV

Anthony Baker, Screech & Bob Hewko – Saved By The Bell Party – Las Vegas, NV

Mom & Dad – 1971 at my grandparents house in Henderson, TX

High School Graduation 1989

Amber – Cabo San Lucas, MX

Mom and I – April 1971

Christine Scott – Day 1 of Writing the Book – Hard Rock Casino Las Vegas, NV

Lola – Looking over the Las Vegas Strip

Dog The Bounty Hunter – Carrot Top's 50th Birthday – Paris Casino – Las Vegas, NV

50th Birthday – Cabo San Lucas, MX

Jerry Natividad – Baja Brewing Co – Cabo San Lucas, MX

# HELLO, LAS VEGAS!

## PART 5

N ever in my wildest dreams did I ever think I would find myself living in Las Vegas. Ever. Out of all the times I had visited there, more times than not I couldn't wait to get the hell out of there after just a few days.

The decision to become a Sin City resident was a fast and furious one, spontaneously spawned during my last days at Republic National Distributing Company. Once it hit me that my career, and the potential there, had run its course after 19 years, the winds of change blew through my soul. It was time to shift sails. Though my days at RNDC were some of my finest, I accomplished all that I was going to be able to accomplish there and there weren't any options available to keep going further. I had come to a dead end. If I wanted to grow and move forward on my career path in a substantial way, I needed more experience to get me there. Bottom line was that it was time to move on.

Once I acknowledged that decision, I also acknowledged with it that I needed to put a plan into action, like *now,* and not when the time was right. Delaying the decision wouldn't make the decision better in any way. I needed to act at a time when I was still young enough, and still crazy enough, to just pull the plug and look for a new outlet somewhere. Time to shit or get off the pot as they say.

Well, what else could I do, but take the shit and go for it? Now the next question I had to answer was -- Where the fuck do I go now? The answer to that was going to require a tad bit more research and soul searching, but the answer did come.

The final push came from a chain of events that were triggered in June of 2014, and it began with me sending a simple email to a long-time friend while I was sitting by myself at lunch one day. *Gerry, do you have some time to chat?*

He immediately replied and told me to give him a call. Once I got back to my office, I closed my door and my heart started beating at an accelerated pace as if it knew that something was going to happen, something that I didn't yet know.

Gerry was the VP of the Central Division at William Grant & Sons and he had tried to hire me back in the day. We were always close, and I had a tremendous amount of respect for him. When I told him I was leaving Republic, he told me about a State manager's position that would be available in 60 days, *in Nevada*, and then asked me if I would consider moving to Las Vegas.

My first reaction, "Hmm. Sounds interesting. Let me get back to you."

The following week, when I took my daughter Amber and her boyfriend to Cabo, the thought of moving to Las Vegas consumed me the entire time we were there. And I mean *consumed* me. No matter what I tried to do to occupy my mind on other things, I couldn't shake it. I couldn't silence the inner voices of pure excitement over the chance for a fresh start, a new job, a different company, a new life. I couldn't help but view Las Vegas as the land of opportunity, and one where I would be given the air space to spread my folded wings to reach that success I was going after. I mean, if I could succeed in Las Vegas, that would absolutely slingshot me into the next career level. Without a doubt.

As I was checking in at the Cabo airport for my return to Dallas, Gerry called me and offered me the job, right there, right on the spot. Apparently, I didn't have any more to debate about. It was time to make the move, and I had to give him an answer the next day. I thought more and more about it during the entire flight home, all that evening at home and a little bit more that next morning, until I called Gerry and said, "I'm in. I'll move to Las Vegas." Decision made.

My next step was to fly out to Vegas for a few days and find a place to live. Gerry recommended living near the Strip, but I already knew that wasn't the direction I wanted to go in. All I heard from the people at my last job was how I would fail regardless of where I lived because of my lifestyle and that the temptation of what Vegas offered was going to do me in. I knew enough about Las Vegas to know that I wasn't going to put added pressure on myself by having Sin City's best debauchery establishments as my next-door neighbors. Nope. My mission of finding a home was of an entirely different caliber. I wanted an actual home, not just someplace to sleep and shower, like a hotel room.

I was able to connect with an amazing realtor, Sahara, who was recommended by my brother's college roommate Seth who lived in Vegas at the time, and she recommended an area called Summerlin. Summerlin was the nicest part of town on the west side of Las Vegas with a Las Vegas address. When I met with Sahara, she showed me five homes she had in mind to visit, all of which fit the requirements I had laid out - stucco, minimal grass, lots of rock – and they were all within gated communities with surrounding privacy walls. The first house I walked into I immediately knew it was home. Search over.

I loved that house. The best part was the view it had of the Las Vegas Strip from the patio deck, which was nicely located off the master bedroom. But most importantly was the feeling that I got from being there. It just felt… right. It felt like *home.* I still checked out the other houses Sahara had picked out, but when it was all said and done, I asked her to take me back to the first house.

When I walked through the doors to that house a second time, I had to say out loud, like I was claiming it. "This is it. This is home."

I signed the lease right then and there, put down the deposits, and then hopped on a flight back to Dallas to prepare for the upcoming move. I had about three weeks, which is a decent amount of time, but the packing began immediately. The next thing I did was sell my Jeep Wrangler so I could get a more comfortable ride to Vegas, loaded up all my stuff into Pods with the help of my buddy Anthony, and then arranged for the Pods to be shipped out. It was like I was set on autopilot. Things were just happening, seemingly on their own. It was *really* happening. I was moving to Las Vegas!

New beginnings that are sparked by a stale present are risky because they have the power to manipulate your past into appearing desirable if you're not careful. I felt as if I was approaching everything correctly, looking at everything properly, and I just kept moving. My company threw me the obligatory farewell party on my last day, and it was nice to see so many of my colleagues stop by to have one last cocktail with me and to wish me luck.

As much as I was ready to take on a new future in an entirely new direction, as much as I was fucking stoked about what lay ahead of me, I cried like a bitch in the hall after saying goodbye to so many good people. Ya, I did, and I'm not ashamed to admit it, either. Not one damned bit. I spent nearly 20 years of my life with those people, with that one company, and throughout that entire time I never once imagined that I would resign from there and move out of Dallas again. I rode the emotional waves as they hit and kept reminding myself why this was all happening in the first place.

I kept my focus on the fact that it was time for a new challenge, that it was time to grow, that it was time to leave my comfort zone. I told myself, *It's time to fucking move on, Britt.* I needed a 180-degree change in my life, personally and professionally, and it was fucking time to make that all happen. I knew in my heart and soul that if I didn't take control of my life, right now, and take necessary and immediate action, right now, that I would have to accept the fact that I never would. Period. I would have to accept the slide back into mediocrity, at best, and lead a life of *what if* from that point forward. No, thanks. Not this time. I wasn't going back. I was only going to go forward. And I sure as hell was done living with regret over opportunities missed.

In continuing with the farewells, that Friday night my mom threw a party for me in Dallas at Christie's Sports Bar. Christie's is a cool uptown bar and the party was a blast. Many of my friends showed up and we partied into the wee hours, taking shots, getting silly, and taking lots of pictures to remember it all.

Amidst the fun and activities, though, reality creeped in once again, and it hit me harder than it had before. Boom. The severity of the flip side of the situation was grotesquely dancing in front of me, front and fucking center. The awareness had become relative on a personal level now. I was about to move to the west side of the country, to this strange land called Las Vegas, to a world of complete unknowns. I was leaving my comfort zone of family, friends, and a job that I had loved for the last 20 years. Shit. What the hell did I just do? Double Shit! Was it too late to undo what I had just done?

Deep down inside, I didn't want to *not* go to Las Vegas, and I knew that. I tried to readjust my focus from the fear onto why I was leaving, reminding myself of the land of miraged success that awaited me. I knew I wasn't staying in Dallas, but I was still nervous as hell about it.

That night, I stayed with my best friends, Anthony and Melissa, and couldn't sleep to save my life, so I was up and at 'em and already behind the wheel shortly after 5:00 a.m. I loaded the coordinates into the GPS. *Las Vegas 1,060 miles, est. 19 hours* popped up on the display, and away I went. As August 2014 ended, so did my life in Dallas.

As the still dark, awakening downtown Dallas skyline appeared in my rearview mirror (*shout out to any Pearl Jam fans!*). It was difficult to depart from this city that I loved for so long. Tears ran down my face, taking with them the already fading memories of my past life. Take care, Dallas. Thanks for the amazing memories and for all the love. Until we meet again, this is my official peace out. May it not be too long before we see each other again, and may it be under good circumstances. Amen.

***

I made it all the way to Albuquerque, NM, on the first day, checked into a Marriott, and hit up a Jason's Deli for dinner. As I sat there and ate, I felt very much alone, questioning everything I just did to myself and to my life, totally mindfucking myself throughout the entire night. Oh, and it didn't end there. Seriously, *why* make it easy on myself? I never have before, so, why start now, right?

That next morning, as I crossed over the Hoover Dam from Arizona into Nevada, I had gotten myself so worked up that an anxiety attack was in full swing. It wasn't until I topped that last hill just outside of Las Vegas that a calming effect began to creep in with the madness. Even though I was teetering on full panic mode, there it was, all laid out like a mismatched Legoland of Adult Mayhem. There it *was*, the original City of Sin. Sin City, to be exact, and the skyline was fucking magical. Right in front of me lay an entirely new, uncharted world, mystically surrounded by staunch mountains and filled with unbridled dreams.

I was feeling better as I checked into a Marriott near Summerlin, got a good night's sleep, and geared up for getting the keys to my new house the next day. It took me two days to get everything out of those damned Pods and into the house, even with the help of movers.

Since this marked my first official weekend in the new house, my good buddy Robert Olivares and one of his buddies flew out to kick off the occasion with me. My stuff was strewn all over the house, but the beds were set up in the guest bedrooms and that's all that we needed at that moment in time. The rest of the unpacking was put on a temporary hold and the Christening of my Las Vegas Life officially began.

We immediately got on Tinder and began swiping away, checking out the local talent pool of single girls. Seth wanted to take us out for dinner and then to this strip club called the Crazy Horse III, but I wasn't into that whole strip club scene anymore. Been there, done that, and to a maximum, but, whatever. Boys will be boys and we went anyway. Fuck it. It was a party, right?

As soon as I walked into the club, who did I see? My realtor! Haha. Apparently, Sahara was a part-time realtor/part-time stripper and apparently it's no big deal to have that kind of setup out here. Didn't take me long to understand that *this was Vegas*, and people do whatever they need to do to make a buck out here, and no one really cares. And I do mean, do whatever.

Now, before anyone from Vegas gets their panties in a bunch over my statement, I'm not trying to stereotype every single person living in Las Vegas as being like this, so relax. No one can deny the well-known truth of the matter, and it's out there for all to see and to enjoy. End of discussion. The money-making industry in Vegas is the "service industry," and levels of that "service" can range from making you a cocktail to giving you a blow job, perhaps even making you a cocktail *while* giving you a blow job. With a steak on the side. The options are truly endless.

If you have money, you can get whatever you want in Vegas. It's all put out there for the sole purpose of being found. And I do mean *whatever* you want is put out there. Supply and demand, baby. Supply and demand. There are no rules, no boundaries, no judgment, and all of it comes with a price tag. If you have the right kind of money to spend, you can make any fantasy you have come true and even come up with a few new ones in the process.

Day two was about me and the guys hanging out at Caesar's Palace where Robert's buddy hooked us up at the private topless pool. We ordered a bottle of vodka, which naturally and quickly turned into two, and *of course*, we overspent on everything. The pool was crowded, but not what I had expected. We all wanted to meet some hot girls, but, alas, it was not meant to be on that day. It wasn't a total loss, though.

Redemption for the lack of hot young women came via a comedic interlude provided by a bony, way too tanned, 70ish-year-old lady in a yellow string bikini. Yes. Go ahead. Allow that visual to sink in for a moment. She was there with her husband, too, who just sat off in the shade, watching her flirt with all the younger dudes. As the day and the alcohol consumption simultaneously progressed, that old lady took her flirting to an entirely new level, one like I've never seen before, which is saying something believe me. Man, she targeted this one poor bastard who must have only been in his late 20's, at best. He was there with a bunch of other young dudes, and like most tourists who come to Vegas, was taking the motto of "what happens in Vegas stays in Vegas" way too seriously.

Next thing you know, He and Old Yeller start making out. Yes, making out. I mean, arms wrapped around each other, full-blown tongue swapping spit action going on. And yes, it was quite revolting to witness. Everyone watched in total disbelief, like when you look at the wreck you just passed on the highway.

Unfortunately, the group of shocked bystanders included this lady's husband who, at this point, was now standing at the edge of the pool asking his wife to stop messing around and get out of the pool. What might have been funny at first had now gone way too far.

I couldn't imagine what was going to go through that kid's mind once he sobered up a bit and realized what the fuck he just did. Bleh! Now, I realize that making crazy memories with your buddies while in Vegas is a main objective, preferably with the element of getting laid added into the equation, but this was not the kind of experience I could imagine anyone ever wanting. Ever. No matter how drunk or fucked up you got, not even by Vegas standards.

While the friends of that kid kept cheering him on, the husband finally managed to pull his drunk bag o' bones out of the water, and it was then that the worst imaginable thing happened. As Old Yeller was coming out of the water, her bikini bottom stuck to the side of her thigh, and yes, you guessed it. There it was. Full-blown 70+-year-old vagina right there. All of it. All for the world to see.

And get ready for this added level of grotesque. It was bald as bald could be, too. I shit you not. There wasn't any hair to help cover up that pruned mess, so it was all hanging out. Fuck! I think I vomited in my mouth a little when I saw it.

Anyway, the husband got her out of the pool, covered her up in a towel, and they walked off, returning to whatever bizarre life they lead together. What did I take away from that experience? Well, I will always remember thinking that no matter how old a person gets, the potential for a spouse or loved one to crush their soul exists until death. That risk never ends, not even with marriage. Sad, shitty, and frightening all at the same time. Wow.

Later that night, after the horrid memory of Bologna Flaps was fading into the background, we met up with a guy named Bob Hewko at Cabo Wabo over at Planet Hollywood. I originally met Bob through my buddy JMAC, and on the introductory call we had while I was still in Dallas, he immediately dropped the, "Hey! I'm good friends with Vince Neil and we need help getting his Tatuado tequila and vodka placed in distributor houses around the country. Reach out to me when you get to Vegas and let's do business."

I was like, "Fuck ya! Vince Neil! I'm in!" Fucking shame, though, that at the time I didn't know was how much of a total scammer and con artist piece of shit this guy was in all facets of life. The unfortunate part was that he unknowingly got me over-excited about that kind of opportunity, too. Dammit! Anyway, after dinner, we took in the Carrot Top show, got to meet Jeff Molitz, Carrot Top's personal assistant, and then also got to meet Carrot Top (Scott Thompson). We were already shitfaced but continued to have more cocktails and great conversation with him. Scott is a very down-to-earth, incredibly talented individual, and he is *extremely* funny.

So far, it was a great start to my new life. When the weekend buzz died down and the boys' weekend fun was over, Robert and his buddy flew back home to return to their normal lives. I remember sitting in my house realizing that this wasn't just a weekend party with the boys anymore - this was my daily life. I could do this kind of shit every day, seven days a week, if I wanted. Wow, what a change from Dallas. This was home now, so I told myself to get used to it and make the most of it. Time to get going on what I came here to do. Time to leave my mark.

The following week, my mom, stepdad, and Marie, my Mom's best friend from Portland, all came out to help me get completely settled. You know, give my place that "home" vibe. My mom and Marie did a great job doing the shopping and pairing up the bedrooms with my office and both living areas, while Bobby provided all the manual labor, putting everything together. I helped out when I got home from work, but they had done pretty much everything.

Once they left, I felt the true permanency of the move. I had no friends here other than Seth, and I knew from prior moves that it would take me at least six months or so to make new friends.

By the time I rolled through my first six months, I established good working relationships with my distributor, Wirtz Beverage, and in August of 2015, that hard work paid off. My buddy Steve from Brown

Forman and I were nominated for Supplier of the Year on behalf of the Wirtz Beverage Co. My blood was flowing through my veins like a freight train as I heard "And the winner is…..Britt Amsler!"

The applause broke out as my name appeared on the screen and when I got up to claim my award, it was one of the most remarkable feelings I have ever had in my career. My heart was filled with joy and the first thing that popped in my head was a big *I did it* directed at the folks back home who said I would fail in Vegas.

That moment helped define a lot for me, actually. It gave me that confidence, that added little push to move forward with my new life. It made me feel like I was starting to make my mark, legitimately leaving my imprint on Vegas. And it felt amazing.

Fast forward to Halloween 2014 when some of my former coworkers and a former boss, Charles Britton from RNDC, came out to Vegas for a supplier incentive trip. We all went out for dinner and then hit the Chandelier Bar at the Cosmopolitan, my favorite casino in Vegas at the time. It had everything from fine restaurants, great gambling, and some of the best premium bars found on the Strip, one of which was the Chandelier Bar. It was a classy bar, constantly stocked with gifted bartenders who consistently poured great cocktails. Oh, and there were hot chicks there all the time, too.

On this particular All Hallows Eve night, I experienced the dreaded sting that only the dark side of Las Vegas gambling can bring. I lost $2,000.00 in under 30 minutes. I was so disgusted, so pissed, I can't even tell you. It wasn't just about losing the money. It was more about the *fuck you* that came with it. You see, I had won $3,500.00 at the Golden Nugget the weekend before and now I just gave most of it right back to the damned casino. Talk about taking the wind out of your fucking sails. Damn.

Chris and I decided to regroup back at the Chandelier Bar, throw back some shots of Ancho Reyes Liqueur, and return to the scene of the crime, right back to the same table that took my money. I brought a sacrificial $500.00, and luck was with me this time. I won back what I had lost. All of it.

A celebratory return to the Chandelier Bar ensued, of course, when I got this wild hair up my ass and decided I was "feeling hot" and decided to go back to the table. That damned table. I was up, I was down, and in a mere hour's time, I lost it all. Again. The insult this time was that I gave the casino more than what I lost the first time around. *This* time, I lost $2,500.00, not just $2,000.00.

After I drunkenly told Chris that I was going to the ATM, he called me a stupid motherfucker, we laughed, hugged, and he left me to my own demise. I still had an accessible $200.00 on my $700.00 limited ATM card, so what did I do? Yep, I sure did. I grabbed that fucking $200.00 and went right back to the same damned table, and I sat in the same damned chair. Fuck superstition.

I didn't start too well and lost seven hands in a row, leaving me down to my last $25.00 chip when the miracle happened. The tides turned, the angels started singing, and the magic began to flow. Once I had won all my money back, I shifted gears and started betting $500.00 a hand, then $1,000.00 a hand, feeling like I was utterly unstoppable. Before I knew it, I had amassed about $19,000.00, and, by the Grace of God, recognized that I wanted to keep those winnings this time and not give it back to the damned casino.

With that awareness, combined with losing the next three hands, I was able to tell my drunk ass to get the hell out of there while I was still ahead.

I tipped the cab driver $50.00 on a $50.00 ride, left Chris a message, and then blacked out in my bed. I honestly didn't remember how much I had won until the next morning when I counted it. $16,545.00! Not bad for one night's work. I had one other good night at the Tropicana while there to see the show Raiding the Rock Vault, but other than that, my luck turned south, way south, and I learned the cold hard truth that the casinos weren't built by paying out to winners. I learned that if you play long enough, they will beat you. And they will beat you badly if you don't know when to quit, know when to walk away.

I'll say it again for y'all out there, so let it sink in now and prevent problems down the road. Vegas wasn't built on winners. The sooner you realize that the better you will be for it in the long run. Trust me. *Especially* if you ever plan on living here. There's your Vegas 101.

# FUN AND FRUSTRATION

## CHAPTER 10

Things in Vegas weren't always bad and negative, though. I did have my share of fun times, too, I must admit, and those fun times will last with me forever. Like the one night we hit up the KISS show at The Joint, partied deep into the night, and had to engage in the well-known practice of "hair of the dog" just to feel human enough just to show up for Sunday football at Red Rock.

As usual, it was the normal diehard crew of me, Vince, Dave, Kelle, and Bob, at the same sportsbook, at our customary VIP table. However, since the crowd was much bigger than usual as Anthony and Melissa had flown out, we moved over to an adjacent table. Once Carrot Top showed up, Vince started ordering shots of fireball for everyone at the tables, but when the shots came to the table, it became awkwardly obvious that Vince ordered shots for everyone at the two tables, everyone except for Anthony and Melissa, that is. I can't say anyone was surprised by it, though. Vince and his childish dick moves were more expected than they were surprises to anyone at this point, but it was still baffling how someone could just so openly be a dick and for no real reason other than to just be one. Anyway, I told them not to take it personally, just as I've said to so many others in the past, and by the time the second round of games was starting, we moved to the Circle Bar and none of us were feeling any pain at that point. The only one who didn't carry over with us was Carrot Top because he had to prepare for his show that night

A pretty bartender was working at the Circle Bar that night (who I will call "Mikayla" and not use her real name) and I already knew that Vince liked her. He claimed her the first time I met her and introduced her to me as "his girl," Mikayla, like that was supposed to act as some warning label that was now stamped on her friggin forehead or something.

As was also common practice, Vince got too fucked up to get himself home, so Dave and I had to take care of his drunk ass. Now, to be fair and give credit where credit is due, Vince *always* paid his portion of any tab and then some. He never once stiffed anyone on a tab, a practice that Bob never followed. Shit, he didn't even understand the concept. As soon as any check was laid on the table, Bob's arms instantaneously shrunk up like those of a T-Rex to make it impossible for him to reach for his wallet. And I mean, *every fucking time.*

On this one particular night, Vince was beyond fucked up and simply forgot to pay before leaving, so I happily picked up the tab for him, and Bob happily watched me do it. Just the type of wormy guy he was to the core. After all the tabs that Vince had covered for him, he didn't even offer to *help* cover one tab for Vince. Just gross. He would never step up to help Vince when it put him out any, but he was always much too happy and willing to step up and be a mouthpiece for Vince. Why not, air is free, right? Especially hot air and Bob was full of it. The idiot could fill a Macy's Day Parade float by just blowing into it, I guarantee it.

Once Vince was safely tucked away at home like the child he was and we adults got back to the bar, it was brought to my attention that Mikayla was interested in me. Yeah, baby! As soon as Bob saw my face light up at the news, he acted like the Vince-wanna-be-dick he always was and stoically took it upon himself to remind me that Vince said she was off-limits because of his own interest in her.

Deciding at that moment that I was a grown ass man, and also deciding that Mikayla was hot and I wanted a date with her, I promptly told Bob, in no certain terms, that I didn't give a rat's ass what Vince thought about it. And just in case it wasn't sinking in with Bob, I added that I also wasn't asking permission from anyone to take her out. I knew it would take Bob a whole 30 seconds before relaying that information to Vince, and I didn't care.

The following Sunday, while at Red Rock doing our customary Sunday thing, I stepped away from the group to saunter over to the Circle Bar to wish Mikayla a happy birthday and earn some brownie points by dropping off a birthday card with my wishes. Inside that birthday card I wrote, *Happy Birthday – will you go on a date with me?*

When I went back later that afternoon to hopefully get an answer, she looked up at me over some customers and said, "Yes!"

Cool! We set a date for the following week around her work schedule and even though my mom was going to be in town then, I was not going to delay or completely miss this opportunity. My Mom would totally understand, so I wasn't worried about it. If anything, my Mom would be the one to encourage me to go.

Date night with Mikayla arrived, and when I knocked on her door to pick her up, nobody answered. I was immediately like, *Oh fuck, here we go again with another flake! Got played again.* When I tried calling her cell, and when she didn't answer, I turned to leave.

She finally opened the door, and she looked beautiful. I can't tell you how relieved I was to see she wasn't the traditional flake. A rare find. I took her to Crush, one of my favorite restaurants inside the MGM, and we had a great time. The conversation was consistently pleasant and easily flowed, and it made for an awesome first date. Mikayla was a single mom with two young kids and when I asked her about the Dad, she told me they never married but did try to make it work. He was a party guy with not much motivation to work or provide for his family, so it just didn't work out for them as a couple. My immediate reaction was *Perfect, I can swoop in and save the day, save her,* because, you know, I couldn't just date her. I had to *save* her.

When we got back to her house, we were greeted by two rowdy dogs and a pig, which was a first for me. Man, let me tell you, though. She let those animals run rampant all over that house and if there's one thing that can kill any type of romantic mood is the lingering smell of urine, and it was throughout the entire house. I did my best to ignore it and focus on the Pussy Prize, but all we ended up doing that night was make out on the couch. It felt like we were teenagers, sitting on Mom and Dad's couch, and it gets all hot and heavy but doesn't lead to anything.

As the night wore on, I never got her cue to stay, so I went home. That's it. Nothing ever came of it. Ever. We would always end up at her house, on the couch, and I was never asked to stay over, and I never asked her to stay at my place. There was only one time she came to my place and we climbed into bed together, but, again, nothing happened. After an hour or so of lying there with her, she said she had to go home and left.

It started to make sense after a while. Bob was regularly a visitor at her bar and although I never confirmed it, my suspicion is that he was the wedge that developed between us, in one way or another. And it wouldn't surprise me if he were not only saying shit about me to her but that he was manipulating her by dropping the almighty Vince card that he so often liked to play when he tried to control things. There's no other explanation. It just got too weird, too fast with her, for no reason.

The last time I spent any time with Mikayla was when she came to pick me up at the airport after one of my Dallas trips. She always looked pretty, but this time she was wearing pajamas and some weird animal-like house shoes. We went directly to her house, sat on the couch, made out, she asked me about any long-term plans of staying in Vegas, I dropped a hint about any life-changing experience influencing those plans, we made out some more, got hot and heavy some more, and yeah, then she tells me it's time to take me home. It was starting to come off as more than odd that I never got to stay over at this chick's place, that I never got to be in her bed.

I drove her car to my place, we made out some more in my driveway, I asked her to stay, she said no, and off she went. I couldn't figure her out. I kept thinking that there *had* to be some other dude in the picture, like maybe an ex who was still in the picture. I gave it one final shot when I asked her out for the following Thursday night, a night when she didn't have her kids with her. I didn't hear from her all day to confirm, yet I still bought some flowers to bring to her. Just as I was getting in my Denali to go pick her up, she texts me to cancel. I replied with a picture of the flowers I had bought for her, and never got a reply from her.

I got pissed at myself then, because I've put myself in this type of situation too many times in my life. I should know better, but I always continue on the destructive path. Even after the icy silence over the picture of the flowers, we began texting a few days later and I was now asking her for an explanation.

New Year's was later that week, and I had a trip booked to go to Cabo on January 2nd. I asked her if she wanted to go with me, and she said she did, but that she needed to clear it with work and make sure her Mom could watch her kids while she was away. When she asked me how much the ticket was, I told her not to worry about it because I had it covered. She insisted she pay, so I told a white lie and said that I was using points to book the tickets just to get her to agree to go and not feel guilty about it.

Her lack of commitment was driving me insane, so when Robert flew into town to go to Tao's NYE party with me, I figured we could stop by Red Rock before hitting the Strip and I could give it one last attempt to lure Mikayla into committing to go to Cabo. I figured, why not. We were wearing suits and looking sharp. She poured our drinks, bought us some shots, and told me to meet her by the parking garage after she got off work. Like an idiot, that's exactly what I did.

When she walked up to her car I was already there, we got in the car, kissed, and Cabo came up one last time. Again, she said she would love to go but still needed to check with her Mom. She told me to give her an hour, and she would get back to me with an answer. Well, my phone never rang, nor did I get a text from her, and let it ruin my night at Tao, like a jackass.

Kyle, my daughter Amber's stepdad, was in town and I invited him to join me and Robert. I had a table with comped bottle service and due to my current situation that was eating me alive, I was a terrible host and had an absolutely shitty, shitty time. Snoop was slated to perform at midnight to roll in the new year, and instead of staying there, enjoying New Year's Eve, enjoying Snoop, I jetted home, all depressed, and left Robert and Kyle there to salvage what was left of the evening. I was such a dumbass to allow this woman to ruin my night, but I did.

I woke up at 6 am the next morning with a notion that an explanation from her was there waiting for me and I did something that I have never done before in my life. I went to her house. And when I did, my explanation was there for me, right there in plain view when I turned the corner. There sat an old truck, just like the truck that she described to me as the one that her ex drove. It justified a lot of things for me, and it also justified that I was done with her.

I only saw her one more time because Vince called a meeting at the Circle Bar to discuss merchandise for the Outlaws. When I walked up to meet Vince, Bob, and JB Bernstein, she was there behind the bar, and I was instantly uncomfortable. As we sat around the table discussing the merchandise options, Mikayla came over to take a drink order, and that was the end of any conversation.

After the meeting was over, I walked up to the bar to break the ice, but she didn't respond to me, so I just turned and walked away. That was the last time I ever spoke to Mikayla and to this day, I'll bet that it was Bob who interfered, and cock blocked me with her. Well, that and the fact that her ex was apparently still in the picture. No regrets, though. I gave it a shot, enjoyed her company for a bit, and that's all she wrote about "Vince's girl, Mikayla." Honestly? In hindsight, they're perfect for each other.

During the few months that I was hanging out with Mikayla, Bob repeatedly took it upon himself to remind me that she was Vince's girl. It got beyond ridiculous. Each time he felt the need to deliver his warning-laced message, I'd tell him to fuck off, remind him that I didn't give a shit what Vince thought. And each time I did that, I knew he was going to run off and tattle to Vince like the whiny little bitch that he was.

I was also well aware that it was just a matter of time before the shitstorm of Vince's backlash was going to strike. Bob was nothing but a full-blown drunk, he was always completely and utterly broke, an absolute scam artist, a shameless taker, a compulsive and habitual liar, and did nothing but 100% kiss Vince's ass. Vince was his meal ticket, and we all knew what he was doing. We *all* saw it. We all knew he was playing Vince, yet, somehow, the only one who didn't catch on was, sadly, Vince. Bob lived the gypsy lifestyle and spent his days seeking out free hotel rooms, always having to bounce from casino to casino because he had to rotate any comps, which occasionally put him staying at the Red Rock. But, more on that later. Back to finishing out our Sunday afternoon with Anthony and Mikayla joining the crew.

So, Dave and I drove Vince home, took him inside so he could delve into his alcohol coma, and went back to the Circle Bar where Anthony, Melissa, and Bob were still hanging out. Once we got there, Bob announced that his buddy, the TV actor who portrayed Mr. Belding, was in town for a *Saved By The Bell*-themed party and that he could get us in as VIP if we all wanted to go. I can't remember what casino the party was being held at, but Bob was pushing for us to go with him. It wasn't such an easy sell for him because we were all out of gas at that point having pushed the envelope all weekend long. We were all running on fumes and couldn't fathom ingesting any more alcohol, but once Melissa and Anthony chimed in with "What the hell, let's go," we were all in to go check it out.

As soon as we arrived at the party, Mr. Belding and Screech both appeared and we rolled down the red carpet with them, took the mandatory and expected pictures, and entered as a group to a packed house in the club. We were escorted to a roped-off VIP table, promptly took our places on the couch, and the bottles of vodka began to flow. Once we were all past that first cocktail, we were back in action. I ended up sitting next to Screech, who had given up drinking to get his life back into order. He was married now and living in Wisconsin, staying out of trouble and out of the spotlight.

Fast forward to a few weeks later where I read he stabbed someone in a bar and was headed to jail. Go figure. The Mr. Belding guy was a cool enough dude, but was kind of a creepy, overweight womanizer who liked to hit on all the young girls. We all stayed to have a few drinks, nothing crazy. Anthony and Melissa went back to Dallas the next day.

Before we knew it, Thanksgiving was once again upon us and what should have been a day of giving thanks, having fun, and enjoying the company of those you loved, was nothing short of a complete fucking disaster. Kelle, Dave, Bob and a few other friends were coming over, and Vince never responded to my invite and was giving me the silent treatment. When I asked Kelle what she thought was going on with that, she told me that Vince always hosts Thanksgiving at his place every year and that he was probably butt hurt over the competition of having people over at my place. Whatever. I wasn't going to let it bother me or ruin *my* Thanksgiving. There was an absolute feast awaiting us, and dammit, I was going to enjoy it.

Kelle, Dave, and I split the cost of the food, and since I was in the industry, I made sure that we had a stocked bar. It was a nice crowd of people. Bob came over, my roommate George was there, and a good friend, David, who was in town with his girlfriend Karen, two people that I had decades of history with going back to my RNDC days. Everyone was there to have a good time, enjoy the Holiday, and keep the booze flowing.

After the Cowboys game, David and Karen took a taxi back to the Strip, only to be replaced a little later by a woman named Sam who was accompanied by her new boyfriend.

Sam was a very cool and interesting lady, one that I would describe as an aging beauty. She was a retired prostitute who wanted to escape her career at the Bunny Ranch and find a new beginning in Las Vegas. Her boyfriend was a cool enough guy, but he had no idea of her background as the rest of us did. Whatever. That wasn't anyone's business but theirs. Honestly, I sincerely wished peace and happiness for Sam and who was anyone, really, to try and sabotage that for her. Not me. By the time she showed up, though, everyone was pretty buzzed, and Bob was wound tight and more lit than the rest of us. A deadly combination.

At this point, which was only a few months into this so-called "friendship" with Bob, I managed to learn that if Bob was drunk and you varied in opinion with him during any type of conversation with him, be prepared for an oncoming explosion. It's going to happen. It happened every time.

Now, truth be told, I had been making these lethal espresso martinis and maybe should have stopped making them sooner than I did for this particular crowd, but, whatever. I didn't. George was passed out for the second time that day because he wasn't really a drinker and Kelle, a wine drinker, was attempting to hold her own in the liquor department with Bob. Next thing you know, Bob was getting loud with Kelle, then turned to Sam, and then back at Kelle again. Bob never had any boundaries with anyone, and he never cared whom he insulted or whom he hurt, or why. He was that much of an asshole that he truly, truly didn't care what he said to people or how it affected them, and alcohol only took that evilness a step further.

Now, because of whatever he said to the girls, the house was divided. It was no longer a friendly, loving Holiday gathering amongst friends. Once Bob started taking personal jabs at Kelle, I stepped in and told Bob that it was time for him to go home. I let this asshole know that he needed to call a cab and that he was no longer welcome in my home. I was pissed at myself for being involved with this clown in the first place.

After bitching about the difficulty of having to get a cab from my house, I offered to drive him to Red Rock where he could easily get a cab at a casino. Like the self-centered prick he was, he tried insisting that I drive him all the way to the Strip. He didn't care that I was legally drunk and that I was already uncomfortable about driving him down the street to Red Rock. Nah. Wasn't his problem as long as he got to where he needed to go. And what an arrogant prick to boot. He insults the women guests in my home and is now demanding limo service to and from the meal and cocktails he just freeloaded

When I pulled into Red Rock, this POS started cussing me out and really testing my patience. I snapped. I turned to him and said, "Fuck you, you piece of shit! Get the fuck out of my car before I beat the fucking shit out of you!"

And all this pathetic excuse of a man could retort with was, "My brother is a lawyer and if you touch me I'll sue you!"

I couldn't help but laugh in his face. Once I told him that he could either get out of the car or I would remove him from the car, he got out, looked at me and said, "Bro, you have T Rex eyes," and closed the door.

I was so glad to get that asshole out of my car and be on my way back home. When I got back to my house, I apologized to everyone for Bob's behavior. No one could believe what they just witnessed, and no one had any explanation for why it happened in the first place. There was no mystery to it, though. It was evident that the man had a black heart, no soul, was nothing more than a broke ass drunk with no barriers who thrived on conflict. Just a truly, truly vile excuse of a human being. Just *not* a good dude, someone worth avoiding, at all costs.

Now, onto a more fun memory. For those of you who do not know anything about the AVN Awards, they encompass basically the biggest night in the adult film industry, toting the industry's highest honors, and it's been held every year in Vegas for about three decades. The show is basically a full-blown celebration of outstanding achievements in "the business of pleasure," handing out about 100 awards. There's always the standard red-carpet pre-show and a host of Grammy award winning musicians performing, too.

This year, I was invited to go to the Awards ceremony and to two other parties during that week of January 24, 2015. And yes, of course I went, come on now. The first party was at Dre's Nightclub and I got hooked into going that night because of this shyster named Johnny who insisted that Dave, and Bob, and I go with him to this party. He enticed us with saying he had two tables reserved, free bottle service, and an atmosphere boasting about 25 porn stars.

We all met at the Cromwell and threw back a few drinks before heading into the party, and the entire time I had this gut feeling that the whole thing was going to be nothing but a waste of fucking time. Johnny was this little Italian dude who maybe stood at 5'5" on a good day, always wore some goofy ass hat, and he prided himself on being a self-proclaimed boxer "back in the day." Even knowing he was full of shit most of the time, we went to the party with him anyways. What the hell.

We got to the party at about 10pm and the party was dead. And I mean, fucking d-e-a-d. Now, in all fairness, clubs in Vegas don't even get going until Midnight or so, but we were already there. Johnny wasn't getting in touch with his hookup and had been trying for over an hour with no response, which only confirmed my hunch about the direction the evening was going to go in.

Once the stars began to arrive, it was just as you imagined it would be - women so scantily dressed they may as well not have had anything on. Bob decided to go over and start shooting the shit with a few of them, and I told Johnny to get over there, introduce himself to at least one of the guys in the group, and let's get on with the party. He just stood there, holding his phone, looking like a dumbass because his hookup left him out to dry. I walked over to go join the group Bob was talking to, and the next thing I hear is one of the porn dudes tell Bob, "Get your fucking ass out of here before I beat the shit out of you dude."

Ah, and there was the shitshow cue that it was time for me to leave and go play some blackjack at the Cromwell. Bob came with me to play cards, unfortunately, and he always liked to play red chips and stack them as high as he could when he bet. He got on a hot streak and had at least 20 of the $5 chips stacked on the bet circle.

When the dealer asked him to color up and not stack the chips so high, Bob acted the dick he always was and just ignored her. When she politely asked him again, he blew up, insulted her, and next thing you know, the pit boss was on his way over to the table. He was always so embarrassing to be with, and it never mattered where you were. He just didn't care. It's like he was this social moron that came with a guarantee to fuck up any situation he was in, along with anyone he was with at the time.

Because I never learn, Bob and I went to the second party the next night at the 35 Steakhouse inside the Hard Rock. For that entire week, the Hard Rock was filled with people associated with the AVN Awards. Bob turned to me and told me that there's a party going on in one of the VIP suites and he had an idea on how to get into that party.

As we approached the guy with the clipboard and he asks us for our names, Bob blurts out that we were friends of Don, the President of the Hard Rock, and that we were two of the Owners of the Las Vegas Outlaws – you know, the team with Vince Neil as one of the Owners? Yep. The clipboard man stood aside and opened the door for us.

First thing I noticed were the hot chicks pouring drinks behind a huge bar, and I went directly to one of them to get a vodka, water, and lime. As I sipped on my cocktail and took in the surroundings, it didn't take much time to realize that most of the people in that room were pretty much naked. There was so much cocaine and other drugs readily available, I couldn't believe it. There was more in that room, in one place, than I had ever seen. Everywhere you looked there were shitfaced, naked people. I just kind of blended into the background and watched, took it all in for a little bit, and then went home. All I could do was shake my head as I left. I was truly, truly blown away by what I just saw going on at that party.

During this period of time, the person who handled Vince Neil's social media was a gal named Kristy, and she invited a few of us to go to the Award show. Apparently, one of her clients was a blonde named Holly Madison, and she was expected to win an award. Honestly? I had to Google her to find out who she was, and once I did, it was clear as to *why* I didn't know who she was.

I figured it would make for an awesome people watching extravaganza, so I showed up at the Hard Rock ready to mingle. The Hard Rock had a red carpet that swept through the entire casino, right up to the front door of The Joint where the Awards were being held. I had to cross over that red carpet to get to the 35 Steakhouse, and I swear, there were so many creepy people hanging out that it actually made me feel uncomfortable. It really did. I remember saying to myself, "I hope Jesus doesn't come back tonight while I'm at the AVN Awards."

Once I managed to get through the sea of creeps and make it inside the steakhouse, I saw Bob already there sitting with Don, the President of the Hard Rock. I had met Don a few times before in connection with the Outlaws' game days at the Hard Rock. Don also dated Vince's ex-girlfriend, you know, the one who had a restraining order against Vince. Such a soap opera in full motion, I swear.

Anyway, that Holly Madison chick apparently didn't have enough tickets left to get us all into the party, so Bob and I told Kristy that we would just hang out at the bar with Don. No problem. Kristy told us to meet her after the awards show at the Center Bar, and she would bring her friend Holly with her, another one of her clients, and that we could all just hang out and party. Cool.

As we were sitting there with Don, he asked Bob and me if we wanted to go to his suite at The Joint and catch some of the Awards ceremony.

Umm… wait. Let us think on that one. I mean, hell yes, we want to go to a suite that the President has. Seriously? Don picked up the tab at the bar, and off we went.

Now, let me tell you about the location of this suite. It was dead center, second level, and offered perfect viewing. Just as I walked in, I glanced at the wording on the screen behind the stage as the presenter was announcing the candidates for "Best Anal Scene." I was like, wow, okay. Rock and roll, right? The next award was for "Best Female Performer," and when the winner was being announced, I witnessed something so unusual to me, so foreign, that it was almost to the point of it being taboo. As the winner took the mic at center stage, you would have thought she had just won a Grammy or something. She thanked her Mom and her husband who were sitting right there in front, cheering her on.

And get this. The next award was "Best Male Actor," and you'll *never* guess who won that category. Yup, the husband. I was totally blown the fuck away. Truly. I'm not exactly sure why, but I instantly felt dirty and felt like the devil was standing nearby. I remember saying to myself, again, that I hope Jesus doesn't come back tonight while I am at the AVN Awards. Weird. Simply a weird experience.

After the show, we all met at the Circle Bar as planned. Kristy walked up, introduced us to Holly and a young lady who was with Holly, who, apparently, was just getting into the business. I shook their hands, said, "Hello," and went back to drinking my cocktail.

The wannabe pornstar came over to me, started flirting with me, and then the "Hey, she likes you" started with Holly and Kristy. The girl asked me where I was staying, and when I told her I lived in Vegas, she kept mentioning that she had a room at the Hardrock and began to rub up on me. Don't get me wrong. By no means was this girl ugly, it's just that she wasn't really attractive to me either. All of a sudden, she grabbed my face and licked it from bottom to the top, with this fucked up look in her eye and a dirty grin.

At that point, I knew it was time for me to leave. I told her that I had to go use the restroom and would be right back. And then I promptly walked straight out of that casino, jumped in a cab, and went the fuck home. With no disrespect to anyone, truth be told, I have never felt dirtier in my life than I did that night at the AVN Awards. Not something I ever need to do again in my life. Once was enough. Again, no disrespect to anyone – just not my comfort zone.

A few weeks later when we were into February, Bob called and said to meet him over at the Cosmopolitan. Apparently, his buddy, the original owners of Hooters, was in town along with Jon Gruden. So, naturally, Dave, Johnny, and I went over and met up with Bob in the lobby downstairs. We hit up STK Steakhouse where Jon, his son, and Bob's buddy from Hooters were sitting at a table. They were in town for Jon's son's 21st birthday.

You talk about a cool dude, that would be Jon. He is the same in person as you see on TV. He looked at me and said, "Man, you are a big dude. How did you get so big?" Then he punched on me and made that chucky face. He let me put on his Super Bowl ring and took a picture with me wearing it. So cool!

We told Jon we had to leave to hit the Carrot Top show, and he told us that he would love to meet him. We told him that we would have to make that happen someday and left.

We met up with Jon and the Hooter dude one more time that week over at Javier's restaurant. Talk about awkward, though. So, the Hooters Dude was wearing these Hooters Fantasy Football Rings that looked like actual Super Bowl rings. Carrot Top had one and Bob had one, but Bob wore his every day, flashing it around Vegas like it was some actual Super Bowl ring or some shit. Man, he was such a douchebag. Funny thing, though, was that it was embarrassing for everyone but him. Anyway, I offered to take Jon and the Hooters Dude back to their hotel and during that trip, Jon sat in the middle back seat, punching on my arm asking me, "How did you get so big?" Fucking awesome memory.

The month of February also brings with it birthdays for Vince, Dave, and Carrot Top. Vince's was on February 8th, Dave's was on the 10th, and CT's was on the 25th. Kelle and Dave arranged a dinner at Echo & Rig later in the month to celebrate Dave and Vince's birthdays, complete with a nice table out on the balcony upstairs. This place was awesome. I had eaten there a few times and on one occasion, Dee Snider was also enjoying a meal out on the patio. I told Vince that and he said, "Oh yeah? I fucked his wife once." It made me laugh out loud. Okay, then.

Once we ordered our drinks, I handed Vince his gift, and he said, "Wait, bro. Let's wait a bit." My first reaction was *Wow, what a dick*, but okay, it's his birthday. Whatever.

When dinner was being ordered, that's when it was time to pass gifts to Dave and Vince. I don't remember off hand what I gave to Dave, but I gave Vince an allocated, numbered bottle of Milagro Unico II, which for those of you who don't know, is a $300 bottle and only 1,200 bottles produced for the United States. He seemed to like it, but, then again, it was alcohol, so there was never a genuine concern over it.

Carrot Top was turning the big 5-0 and his girlfriend Amanda was throwing him a bash at the Chateau Club at the Paris Hotel. She invited me to go, and I was excited to be a part of his special birthday. The party was being held on the balcony of the club where it had the most awesome view of the Las Vegas Strip, and a good size crowd showed up.

While we were waiting for the Guest of Honor to arrive, we tapped into the back bar for cocktails to get the party started. I went with Dave and Kelle and, of course, Bob the Freeloader King was there, and a few celebrity faces were also there, such as Nick Cage's wife Alice, Flavor Flav, Dog the Bounty Hunter, and later on in the night, a few musicians from Rock Vault showed up after the show, namely Paul Shortino, Doug Aldrich and Andrew Freeman. Other than losing $700 at the blackjack table prior to the party, this was truly a fun night.

My gift to Scott (Carrot Top) was a bottle of the Milagro Unico II, the same as I had given to Vince, but it was much better received by Scott. Go figure.My Vegas life, at this particular moment in time, and completely unbeknownst to me, had reached the best it was going to get.

Shortly after the month of February, my life took a wrong turn, on the wrong path, with the wrong people.

Truth be told, despite the ultimate nightlife and the crazy socializing that was readily available to me, this was one of the loneliest times in my life. It didn't matter that I was successful at my job, making good money, and it didn't matter that I was a decent human being either. I had made some friends here and there, but most of those people ended up not being real friends and burning me down the road. (More to come on that later.)

Vegas wasn't a place where you hung out with your neighbors and had block parties, and it sure as hell wasn't the place where you're going to meet the girl next door, fall in love, and be all happily ever after and shit. It seemed like every single girl out there worked in the service industry, pretty much willing to serve you in any way to make a buck. They weren't the kind of girl looking to become a monogamous girlfriend, nor were they someone you would want to take home to meet your family. In all honesty, the best after work dates were the dates that I shared at home in the company of my bulldog.

I adopted my girl Lola after being in Vegas for a few months, and it remains one of the best decisions I've ever made. I always wanted a bulldog, and my new friends Kelle (Vince's former personal assistant) and her husband Dave found her for me. Dave was Vince's best buddy and was a drummer in a local band in Vegas. The lead singer's girlfriend, Britney, had moved to California and couldn't take her dogs with her, one of which was Lola. Lola and I bonded quickly, and she became my rock. She really did.

There were countless days where Lola and I would sit out on the upstairs balcony and look out across Vegas, Lola in her chair and me in mine with my glass of wine. Sometimes, we would sit out by the pool so she could sunbathe, something she loved to do. She was always so happy to see me, every single time I walked through that door, and it just didn't get any better than that. The only seemingly negative trait about her was that she hated other dogs and wanted to kill any dog that got near me, making it difficult to take her places where other animals might be, but that was okay. None of that mattered when we were home.

After I moved back to Dallas, where Lola and I spent another amazing year together, she was diagnosed with terminal cancer and I had to make that God-awful decision to put her down, but it was the right thing to do by her. I cried my ass off the day I found out it was terminal, and I cried well into the days after she was gone. I was fucking heartbroken. Heartbroken.

When I had to let her go, it almost killed me. She was such a kind, loving little soul, and that little girl got me through some of my most difficult times. She never judged me, she only loved me, every day of her life.

She let me know how happy she was in her life with me, and I was just as happy to have her be such a beautiful, blessed part of *my* life. Her urn now sits on my TV stand in the living room and not a day goes by where I don't think of her at least once. I still miss you, Lola girl ... and I think I always will. Until we meet again, run free.

*** 

The whole dating scene in Vegas sucked for me, though. I had been out with a few girls here and there, but nothing ever clicked with any of them. Some of the hottest women in the world live and work in Vegas, but the majority of those were party girls and I did my best to stay away from them. I even went so far as to hire a dating service that Kelle found and dropped $2,500.00, which ended up being nothing more than a waste of time and money.

When I met with the Owner at our first appointment, I described to her exactly the package I was looking for and she said, "I have tons of inventory; this will not be a problem."

So, trusting the expert and not knowing what to expect, I went on three blind dates with three different women. Clients were advised to not have any communication between them other than the female client texting the male client with the place and time to meet. After each date, both individuals are instructed to report back to the owner with their feedback. You know, share their thoughts, feelings, interests, next steps, etc. Although all three of the ladies I met with were nice to talk to, none of them were what I described as my ideal package. Not one of them. These were ladies that I could have met out in Vegas on any given night.

On my final call with the owner, I basically told her that her inventory fell well below my ideals and that I felt like the whole experience did nothing more than waste my time and $2,500.00. And that, my friends, was the last of my dating service experience and the rocky beginnings of my new life in Vegas. All in all, I realized that things could be much,

much worse, and I remained positive about my future. What else could I do? I was in Vegas. I was here, I was settled, and I was still more than ready to take on the world.

# OUTLAWS

## PART 6

# CREATION OF THE LAS VEGAS OUTLAWS

## CHAPTER 11

Well, I've told you of heartache, of success, of gains and losses, and some of the highs and lows that have defined my life. Now I'm going to tell you about the worst financial decision I ever made that, by the Grace of God, evolved into one of the best lessons I have ever learned.

I went from banging my head to Motley Crue's music to banging my head on the turf with their lead singer. Literally. I was the last one to the party to become business partners with Vince Neil and three others in the Las Vegas Outlaw Arena Football Team. Banging heads now meant with a helmet, pads, and a cup… not a concert t-shirt, a lighter, spandex, and liquid glue hairspray. (Ah, the good old days!)

Looking back on it now, I see that the cup was the most important piece of artillery I could have owned. Wish I had known that then, especially since I got repeatedly kicked in the nuts by most of the people involved in the endeavor and, well, by the entire experience as a whole with how it all ended.

Had I known then what I know now, things I found out later after the fact, maybe, just maybe, I wouldn't have let the whole *rock star idol* ideal cloud my judgment and prevent me from making a sound business decision. I should have made this decision based on the business savvy of the person, the professional credibility of that person, not based on the rock star persona that I was so in awe of, but I didn't. It was that lack of judgment that came back to bite me in the ass. Hard. Looking back on it now, shit, I would have used a much bigger cup, maybe even one that encompassed my entire body and one that was preferably bullshit repellent. And just maybe, if I had to do it all over again, I wouldn't have followed the same path, but I'll never know. The only thing that I can say for sure is that I will never allow myself to be put in a similar position ever again in my life. Ever.

This whole Outlaws thing went down back in September of 2014 when I was telling Bob about my ultimate goal of owning my own bar/restaurant. I told him how I was just two steps away from moving to Cabo when the gears changed because I chickened out. Instead of moving forward with making my dream come true, I took a nice, safe job in Las Vegas but was still keeping the dream on the back burner, keeping it alive for the future.

A few days after our talk, Bob called me, asking me if I wanted to buy into the Las Vegas Outlaws and become a co-owner with him, Vince Neil, Mark Daniels, and a guy named Sohrob. Now, I will admit, such a glitzy concept hit me like a rockin' tidal wave. Me? Co-Owner of the Las Vegas Outlaws? Really? Wow, like, I would become a legitimate business partner with Vince Neil? Are you fucking kidding me? I would be a professional sports team owner, just like Jerry Jones? (Okay, okay, I know, shut up. I realize it was on a hell of a lot smaller scale, but this was exciting, so screw you this was a moment.) I told Bob that I was definitely interested, and he said he would clear it through Vince and Mark, and if they both agreed to it, then he would set up the meeting to get it done. Just like that.

I believe it was on Saturday, September 20, 2014, that Bob set up a lunch meeting at Cabo Wabo on the Las Vegas strip to essentially seal the deal. This was the first time I had met Mark Daniels and my first impression of him was that he was a very level-headed, professional, and likable guy. Mark lived in Florida full-time and flew into Vegas for business, and he was the mastermind behind forming the team. He was supposedly a co-owner with Bob and Vince in another team venture, the Jacksonville Sharks, and he was now starting up the Las Vegas Outlaws project in an attempt to achieve some self-inflicted level of sports greatness.

Mark walked me through the presentation which included the layout of the AFL (Arena Football League) as a whole, the formation and growth expectations of the Outlaws, the connection to the city, fan turnout, corporate partnerships, TV, merchandise sales, and most importantly, the return on investment based on the anticipated sale of the team in three to five years. It all sounded fucking great to me and at the end of the meeting, Bob said that Vince had given the thumbs up so Mark made me an offer right then and there of a 5% minimum @ $125,000.00. He added that I could buy up to 7% if I wanted, but the 5% was on the table right now, we could talk about the rest later. So, I had to make the decision. Right then. Right there.

But I couldn't. Not yet. I firmly believe that if something is too good to be true, it probably is. Not probably. It is. Stick with that and you won't go wrong.

My first order of business in staying true to my own cause was to call my financial advisor, Greg Gardner, and get some real guidance from someone I trusted and someone who actually knew WTF he was doing. At least I had the clarity to do that much through the rock star haze that was swallowing me.

For the next few days, Greg read through the documents, checking how to make this a tax-free transaction for me. I had roughly $270k of 401k money sitting in an IRA, but that was everything I had to my name. Literally. Took me years to raise that much capital, don't kid yourself. Greg told me I could move forward as far as the legal BS went, but he also gave me a stern warning that this was a very high-risk investment. *Very* high.

That having been said, he also said that the highest risks could warrant the highest rewards and from what he could see, I could potentially walk away with anywhere from $600,000 to $1,000,000 if the team can sustain itself for three to five years, then be sold as anticipated in the business plans. Whatever that final sale price would be is what would determine my cut. I got it. It made enough sense to me at the time since I knew the League requires a minimum amount to form a team, which, by the way, Mark had told me the price tag was around $4,000,000.00. Within 3-5 years, they expected to sell a successful, well-run team for at least 3x that amount. Maybe even more.

Unfortunately, what I didn't see then, that I clearly see now, caused me to not be in the right mindset to ask the right questions when and where I should have. I was too focused on the idea of putting in those three to five years, doing whatever I had to do to get my just rewards, and getting the fuck out. If only it was that easy. It wasn't. It was way more complicated than that, and I found that out a little too late.

For instance, why was it life or death to get $125,000.00 from me when these guys had supposedly raised the capital to seal the deal on forming the team? Was that all they raised? Just enough to cover that formation of it all and nothing else?

Over the next two weeks, Mark and Bob were absolutely fucking relentless about getting the money. On top of that, I had Vince chirping in right along with them, always asking me, "Hey, where's the money, dude?"

It didn't matter how many times I told them that the transaction would take 10 business days. Told them over and over that the deal was approved, money would be sent in. Ten Business Days. I couldn't do anything to move it along any quicker.

I couldn't help but think that once those ten business days passed, things would never be the same for me again. After those ten days, I would be at the "Holy shit! I'm partners with Vince Neil!" phase. It was so surreal. I couldn't believe that I could actually say that I am a professional sports owner and mean it. Damn. I couldn't fathom how many women this would bring to my door, to say the least, and all while having a new adventure accelerate my career in Las Vegas. This was the type of opportunity that would open doors and introduce me to people that I never thought I would be introduced to, let alone become friends with, and it was all happening. In ten business days. Hell yeah, let's get this show on the road. But again, if it were only that easy. And it wasn't. I could have never imagined what would happen next.

On Sunday, September 21, 2014, at precisely 10:22 pm, the emails started with Mark contacting Greg and me, with Bob and Vince copied, explaining the terms with the Outlaws' stock purchase agreement under the company name of RSG (Rockstar Sports Group) and the Private Equity DOI, and he attached an IRA application. In that same email, Mark also sent over the buyer portion leaving it blank and leaving it up to me to put the deal in my personal name or set it up as a trust or corporation to achieve some tax/liability offset. Okay, cool. I felt I had my best interests being looked at on my behalf, I was solid.

Another email came shortly thereafter, at 10:29 pm, with a pdf version of the documents from the earlier email. Sure. Things are smoothly moving along, no problem. Everyone is backing everything up, documents are being sent, things are getting signed. Cool.

On Monday, September 22, 2014, at 9:27 am, I emailed everyone and told them that Greg was doing everything in his power to get it all handled within 10 business days or sooner if at all possible. Within an hour of my email being sent, Greg replied to the group asking that I be cut some slack on the timing as he could save me $75,000 - $100,000 in additional taxes or penalties if they did. Again. Easy-peasy. Nothing to see here, there's communication happening, it's all being properly handled. Or so I thought.

I was told to complete an IRA agreement and to not worry, that he would walk me through how to properly fill it out on the phone. Cool. He tells me RSG would need to sign some stuff and provide the supporting documentation, i.e., things like a copy of the signed Articles of Incorporation, the Private Placement Memorandum, blah blah blah, and needed to know if RSG was a C-Corp or an LLC. Again, seemingly easy protocol stuff. Mark replied with the relative documents and Greg replied he would provide an update status by the afternoon. Easy enough all around, right? So, it would seem. Yet again.

On Tuesday, Sept 23, at 9:29 am, Greg sent me an email noting that a C-Corp would be easy to work with, but the tricky part would be making sure all the i's are dotted and all the t's are crossed. He said to be on the lookout for a transfer later in the week once he receives an account number to receive the funds. He would then initiate the $130,000.00 transfer from my Schwab IRA to my newly opened IRA account. Again, easy peasy, right? If done properly, the transaction would not be taxable.

What I should have focused on was who was being included in these transactions as they were happening. I mean, where the hell had Sohrob been? Wasn't he an equity partner in this venture? Why wasn't he being copied on any of these emails? Stay tuned for *that* unfortunate discovery.

On Wednesday, September 25, 2014, at 9:53 am, I emailed Greg and told him that everyone, including Vince, was all on the same page and they all agreed to bring me in on the deal under RIG (Rockstar Investment Group) rather than RSG. I knew that Sohrob was currently set up under RSG, the entity that was created and solemnly designed specifically for the creation of the Outlaws. I was going to be set up there, as well, and carelessly assumed the switch of entity was a benefit somehow.

It wasn't, at least not to me. I later found out that it was beneficial to Mark, Vince, and Bob – but only to those three fucking greedy assholes! The three of them convinced me that RIG would be a better option for me because RIG was going to branch outside of the Outlaws and start working with all these other investments. They went on to say how they already had a deal in place and were partnering with the Seminoles, who also happened to be the owners of the Hardrock in FL, and that they would be starting up a Jeep rental business for tourists in Vegas, as well as a Lamborghini dealership, both based out of the Hard Rock in Vegas. So, of course, they told me this and I was like, holy shit, I'm going to hit the jackpot with this deal.

Man, they really greased me up. Such a fool I was. The only thing these three con men were doing was protecting themselves from Sohrob with their deviant plan to eventually push him out. They set up the corporate structure with Vince as the CEO, Mark as the President, Secretary & Director, Bob as the Executive Vice President, and my title would soon be VP. I relayed to Greg that Mark was redoing the stock and purchase agreement to show RIG and not RSG, and added that the AFL Commissioner, Scott Butera, had approved the deal.

I was excited as hell at this point because I could now join the group as an actual member of the executive team at the kickoff announcement that would be led by Carolyn Goodman, the Mayor of Las Vegas, and Robin Leach. Yes, that's right. Robin Leach, the voice of 'The Lifestyles of the Rich and Famous.'

Mark eventually sent over the Stock Sale & Purchase Agreement and I signed on the dotted line, now officially as a Buyer. Yet again, no Sohrob on the email trail, and he still wasn't included when Mark sent out a revised DOI document, signed only by Mark, supposedly validating the investment, but, whatever. I didn't give much more attention to it and ten days later, it was final. I was a professional sports team owner and an official business partner with Vince Neil. Holy Shit! One minute, I'm hanging out in Dallas and a month later, I'm a professional sports owner of an AFL Team in Las Vegas. Fucking unbelievable! Never saw that shit coming. But it did, and it was here, and it was... real.

The official kickoff to the city was on September 25, 2014, beginning with a press conference held downtown on Fremont Street. I was so fucking nervous, I almost couldn't stand myself. I even had my mom there for moral support and even that didn't help to calm me down.

To say I felt uncomfortable was an understatement. I was so uneasy about the whole thing because, well, it was something I just wasn't used to, especially not at this level. Not to mention, there was so much tension within the group that it made for an awkward environment and vibe to begin with at the pregame.

One of Vince's buddies, Michael Politz, set things off in the wrong direction right at the start of things. Such a putz that guy. He was beyond pissed that he was not part of the team, and he was going to make damned sure that everyone knew about it, too. Since his claim was bringing Sohrob to the table who invested $1,000,000.00 into the new venture, Politz automatically assumed he deserved the same 5% deal that I was given. He was such a weird fucker, too. The guys in the group made fun of him behind his back, calling him gay and all sorts of things. I'm not sure if he was actually gay, and it didn't matter to me one way or the other, but he *did* send me text messages of huge naked black men on many occasions.

Anyway, he was a weird dude and an extremely dramatic little bitch, except for the fact that he wasn't exactly little, more like overweight and out of shape. Asshole tried to derail me going into the deal and then tried to mess with my head by texting me the night before the press conference telling me that I was being used and getting screwed over. I didn't know him personally at that point, but what I did know is that I didn't really like him, nor did I trust him. Not for one second. I just blew him off, which only infuriated the little prick even more. I felt like I was back in high school with a bunch of fucking drama clowns circling me from every direction with their tiny little immature egos clashing everywhere.

Kelle told me that I could very easily, and very quickly, lose my $125,000.00 investment, but, what the hell. At the very least? It all came with a 100% guarantee that it would be one hell of a memorable ride. She told me to jump on it, to go for it, that it would be the ride of my life. And she was right. The only thing I needed to figure out was if I was being scammed and lied to, why did Politz still want in with the group of people scamming me?

I put that thought on the backburner of my thought process, which, as I look back, I shouldn't have, but I did. I squashed my inner squeak of concern and fully gave into the notion of being in business with a rock star, not fully understanding what that meant. All I knew is that it was too late to turn back now, so I buckled up and took the ride.

Before the press conference, we all met at the upstairs bar at the D Hotel on Fremont St. My mom was with me and I had filled her in on everything that was going on, as I've done my entire life. Here I was, getting ready to be introduced to the press and the City of Las Vegas as a professional team owner with Vince Neil and the others.

The weird thing was that I didn't feel that "connection" to what was going on. I couldn't help but feel as if I was being left in the dark, being left out, being kept on the outside of the real dealings. Now, I will give myself some credit because I'm not a dumb guy by any means. When I smell a rat and my stomach churns into knots, I know I am onto something, and most likely, that something isn't quite right. Hey, I knew right from the start that I was in over my head. I knew, deep down inside, that there was something about this team that wasn't legit, but I still wanted to see it through. Why? Because I couldn't *prove* anything. It was instinctual, and maybe, just maybe, my instinct was wrong. It's happened before in my life. Maybe it was just feeling nerves and anxiety. Maybe I was just overreacting to the unknown and it was making me paranoid. I honestly didn't know.

As we were sitting in the bar, in walked Sohrob and Politz. Again, I didn't know Sohrob and was told to stay away from him. When they walked up, Politz and I made eye contact and you could tell he was just fucking seething over me being a part of this when he wasn't. It was uncomfortable as hell, too. I was still new to Vegas, surrounded by people I didn't know, and I was now playing at a level I had never played on before. And that was only the beginning.

When it was time, we waited backstage and were given instructions on how the event would go, given the necessary precautions on the pyro that would be going off, blah blah blah. The mayor of Las Vegas, Carolyn Goodman, kicked off the press conference by making the Las Vegas Outlaws official. It was now real. It was now out to the public. Crue's song 'Kickstart My Heart' started pumping and the pyro began to ignite. I felt like I was on stage at a Crue show! The difference this time was that I wasn't a fan; I was one of the guys on the stage. I couldn't believe it. It was so surreal it was difficult to comprehend, even just a little bit.

As the Outlaws Cheerleaders, which Vince had named the 'Posse,' took the stage, Robin Leach introduced each of us, one by one, to the crowd. Of course, I was the last one to be introduced, but that lineup didn't matter to me. There's something to be said about saving the best for last, right? Here I am, looking into this massive cheering crowd, realizing that for the first time in my life, I wasn't one of the people in the crowd looking at the people on the stage. I *was* on the stage. They were all here looking at *me*.

There were cameras everywhere, capturing my every movement. There was pyro going off in every direction, and "Kickstart My Heart" was jamming in the background like it was a rock concert. I realized, at that moment, that this whole thing is a fucking dream come to life, and yet, I stood there, stuck in the shell of my own head, not enjoying the once-in-a-lifetime moment as I should have enjoyed it. As I heard my name being announced by Robin Leach, "… and we have Britt Amsler, from Longview, TX, blah blah blah…," I walked out onto the stage, looked out into the crowd, and froze. Just stood there. I didn't know how to handle this kind of recognition. I was always the one looking on, not being looked at, and I wasn't prepared for it. Not quite sure what else I could have done to prepare for it, though. How the hell do you prepare for something like that? You can practice and imagine all you want, but nothing can substitute for the real thing. It's just not possible.

My mom was standing to the right of the stage, waving at me and taking a gazillion pictures. She was so proud of me, and it was awesome to see. It was written all over her face and she just couldn't hide it. I felt bad in a way, though, because I had gotten snappy with her on the way to the event. I didn't mean to be upset with her, it was the situation that was fucking with my head. I wasn't upset with her by any means, but you know how it can be at times when you're stressed out. What didn't help matters was that we were running late to begin with, and I was under way too much stress from all the damned drama. I was uncomfortably in a position that I had never been before and admittedly not dealing with it as I should have.

To add to the situation even further, Politz had thrown some sort of a bitchy hissy fit tantrum to the point Vince agreed to let him be a part of the ceremony just to shut him up. Vince caved, and even though Politz wasn't an owner like the rest of us who had earned the right to be there, he got his way. Fucking little bitch cry baby. I wonder if he stomped his feet and threw a toy on the ground, too, during his little temper tantrum. Maybe even changed his tampon a few times.

Not to be outdone, though, when Carrot Top made *his* appearance, he stayed true to form and it was amusing as hell. He came in wearing an Outlaws helmet that looked like one of those mini helmets on his head because of all that bushy red hair. He was hilarious and did a fantastic job of breaking the ice with the crowd.

At our table, JB Berstein (the guy who the movie the Million Dollar Arm was based on, and who I think I was told was once the agent for Barry Sanders) was sitting to my right, Politz was to his right, Sohrob was sitting to my left, then followed by Mark, Bob, and Vince in succession around the table. Vince, Bob, and our coach Aaron Garcia all spoke to the crowd and in closing, we all got up and took what seemed like a million pictures with the local press. I had never been in this type of setting before and I felt like I didn't even know how to smile, how to stand, what angle was my best angle, what to do with my hands.

There were so many things I never had to think of before and now I had to think about them all at once. Damn. What should have been an incredible, life-altering experience for me turned out to be one of the most awkward, most uncomfortable, and most emotionally exhausting experiences of my life. It didn't give me that anticipated satisfaction, that targeted sense of security, that it should have. It just drained me of everything. The situation never once felt real. It never felt tangible, never felt it was *permanent*.

Come to find, I had a reason to feel what I was feeling, and it wasn't because I was being paranoid or misreading the signs. I would later have those feelings justified when I found out all of it was nothing more than a fraud. All of it. Down to every person pulling the wool over everyone's eyes.

After the press conference, we all went to Circus Circus for the private afterparty. I don't recall the exact name of the place inside, but something like R&R BBQ comes to mind. Nevertheless, there was a nice spread of food and plenty of drinks flowing. Naturally, Vince had his Tatuado Vodka and Tatuado Tequila on hand. Such a shameless fucking plug, because, you know, it was such a great selling product. Not.

Vince, Bob, Mark, and I were doing shots of the shitty tequila, and as much as I would have rather drank piss than that cheap, nasty shit, I went along to be a good sport and be a true part of the team. Vince had his name connected to a restaurant inside Circus Circus called *Tatuado Eat, Drink & Party.* Makes me fucking laugh. I don't think he owned one penny of it, more like he just received comps in return for the use of his name. Oooh, such a big-time baller, right?

Anyway, the bar used this plastic replica of a toilet to advertise their huge drink, you know, kind of like a fishbowl or a Scorpion Bowl at an old school Chinese restaurant. When the bartender brought it over to us and sat it down on the table, my mom, Vince, Bob, and I each grabbed a straw and sucked that bad boy down until it was gone, complete with customary slurping sounds at the very end. How ironic, though, that the drink actually tasted like water from a toilet, but, whatever. I've had worse.

By now, we were all pretty buzzed and feeling no pain, even my mom who is not a big drinker. The drinks kept flowing, the celebration continued and as was expected, Vince got totally hammered and his girlfriend, Rain, had to take his stupid ass home. I was used to witnessing Vince's erratic behavior patterns by this point, which fundamentally became his norm, sad as that was true. His Rolls Royce was parked right out front and once he got to his car, he wasn't anyone's problem anymore.

We all went back inside to continue the celebration and hit up a blackjack table for a bit. Funny, we ended up at a table that had Vince's face on the felt. It was like he was going to be there with us whether we wanted him to be there or not.

The night was long and filled with boozy fun, which expectedly didn't make for such a great start the next day. The only smart one out of the group-wise enough to call it early was my mom. That shitty toilet drink kicked her butt. (Now *that* should be the advertising!)

Even though I could now officially call myself a sports team owner, I never let it go to my head. I remained shy and reserved about it and, to be honest, I didn't know how to act any differently. I am who I am, but I do have to say again that it never felt like the situation was something of true substance and sustainability, something I could count on. Wish I could have understood at the time that all of these gut feelings were actually some foreboding of the shady shit I would soon discover. Wish I would have given credence to the premonitions of the awkward situations I would soon find myself in, situations that I never thought in a million years I would be in.

As the countdown to opening night began, on March 30, 2015, there was still a ton of shit that needed to get done. We literally needed everything. Everything. We needed sponsors, we needed a field, we needed uniforms, there had to be residences for the players and the families to live in, we needed an office to call our Headquarters. Hell, we needed a fucking team.

One huge thing we did manage to pull off was signing our coach, Aaron Garcia, on September 11, 2014. Man, we got lucky with that one. Aaron was one of the all-time great QB's in the AFL and he played 19 seasons before retiring from his last team. He was a true gentleman, a real sportsman, a dedicated family man, and a genuinely humble individual who knew the game inside and out. He was a true asset to the group and I honestly can't say enough good things about the guy. As much as that hiring was a step in the right direction, it wasn't nearly enough to get us rolling. What we needed most was a true leader to bring it all together, and we didn't have someone like that in place. And that wasn't the only big issue.

On top of not having anyone to lead, there wasn't any type of system or protocol in place for us to follow on our own. No one knew what to do. No one knew how to get it all jump-started and truly up and running. No one knew how to get the whole concept actually functioning. Everyone thought it was so cool to be an owner, yet the biggest problem we faced was that none of us knew how to actually be one.

Getting us all on the same page was proving to be impossible. We were worse than herding a group of feral cats. Just one example: When I received my first copy of the sponsorship presentation, I noticed right away that it said on the cover "as presented by the ownership group. " The presentation was decent enough, but I had a real issue when I came to the section highlighting the ownership group. As I flipped through the pages, I saw pictures and bios of Vince, Bob, and Mark, but no mention of me or Sohrob at all. I mean, I didn't exist. There wasn't even a blank spot "to be announced" or "coming soon" or some shit like that. There was absolutely no mention of owner, Britt Amsler. I was so fucking disgusted, so pissed off. This was stupid, and beyond unprofessional. You leave out an owner from the information on the ownership section and not one person noticed? Really? How many of these have gone out like that?

Screw that. There was no excuse for this amateur BS at this point. When I called Bob with a bit of an attitude, he told me to call JB since he was the one who *did* the presentation. Now, JB was a very nice man, and after a few friendly emails were exchanged, I was added to the team presentation. But that wasn't the point for me. It was the fact that I was left out to begin with that caused an issue.

Whatever. I felt like I achieved something, but that glory was short-lived. The only thing I got in return was an even greater sense of falsely believing I was an integral part of the organization. Didn't matter at that point, I guess. I was too far in to quit and not far enough in to be able to decide anything more. I needed to focus on the fact that there was some hefty work to be done, and a lot of it. Our success depended on it.

The next big-ticket item was finding office space and getting those offices set up. Should have been easy enough, sure, except for one obstacle. One big obstacle. Apparently, we needed a sponsor to pay for those offices, and well, of course, that wasn't in place yet. Of course not.

I don't know how, but by some undeserved stroke of Divine luck, the owner of a Dollar Loans Center in Las Vegas stepped up to the challenge. Charles Brennan was a former rock concert promoter and had some type of involvement with LA KISS. I'm not sure exactly who reached out to whom, but a meeting was set up for me and Bob to go meet with him. We went to his office one afternoon and his office was cool as hell. He was a huge rocker like me and his office was decorated in ultimate true rocker fashion. I was so damned jealous. I wanted that office. I can't remember who the bike belonged to, but he had a rock star's bike on front-and-center display and that bike was one badass fucking bike. Truth be told, the damned thing was truly a work of art, deserving of the display.

Bob and I met with him, and we walked across the parking lot to one of the buildings he owned that had a vacancy on the bottom floor. Now, at this time, I was not authorized to sign any documents (Go figure, huh?), but we ended up taking that vacant office which became the Outlaws' first home. Bob told me that we got the first year for free and over the next four years, we would pay rent on it. Again, it seemed simple enough, so I left it there and never asked about the leasing arrangements for the office again.

Now, one might think that with an official office being formally set up, the team would meet there on a regular basis, right? You know, to handle those pesky little things involving a business, like planning, strategizing, hiring staff, etc. That's what you do when operating and building a business, right? Well, the standard answer here would be correct for any normal business. But with this group? Shit. Not with clowns like Bob and Vince. Hell no. We always had to meet at some fucking bar and try to discuss business while these two jackasses would drink themselves stupid.

On Sunday Fundays we would meet over at Red Rock Casino to discuss draft picks for the team, and now and then a player would stop by and join us for the day. The guys would always treat the players like royalty while they were there, but really, it was all about slinging all kinds of shit to get the dude to make a horrible decision and sign with us.

Coach Aaron came by a few times and we would try to plan while non-stop drinks were flowing. Aaron wasn't a big drinker and always held himself with dignity. I think he almost felt out of place because of it. I can't speak for the guy, but looking back, I wonder about it. My point is that everything about the team was built in a bar, maintained in a bar, and handled by people who reach a point of oblivion every time they meet. How anyone thought that something good, something solid, could come from that scenario, I have no idea. I just kept going with it, hoping and praying for the best possible outcome. Naively hoping that through a natural course of business, things would fall into place. They had to.

One thing had to lead to another, or there wouldn't be a team. There wouldn't be anything.

The next attack plan was the field. We needed to order one since there isn't anything like The Field Store anywhere to just go pick one out and have it delivered. I was told the field we needed cost around $100,000.00, and of course, we had a dire need of sponsors to pony up for this, too.

Now, that really started to confuse me. I had been told there was $4,000,000.00 granted to the team by the League, so I assumed at this time we were whole. I also assumed that, out of a cool $4 million, we could easily, and readily, afford $100 grand for the field. Why was there so much pressure to find deep pocket sponsors for the dashboards along the walls and local beer distributors? Why now? What's going on with the League money? Stress was at an all-time high, everyone was on edge, but I needed to do my part to keep the team moving forward. I had discussions with my company about partnering up with our team to connect fans with the team and get them to games.

The idea that I came up with was surprisingly approved, and a "sweepstakes necker" was created that would hang on a bottle of Sailor Jerry Rum, the biggest brand in my portfolio in the Nevada market. I don't remember the details of the program or the sweepstakes, but it was an investment my company was willing to make. As time quickly passed on and we inched closer and closer to March 30th, so did the pressure of needing funding that we weren't getting.

What set out as an originally very cool investment took an unexpected turn and quickly became a derailing runaway train. On top of it all, the League was becoming more and more suspicious of the team's activity, questions were frequently being asked, and lies were being told on behalf of the team to cover it all up. I knew right then and there that I was in trouble, and I somehow knew it was only going to get deeper. I knew right then and there that I could just kiss my fucking money goodbye, money that I worked so hard to save. And these asshats couldn't have cared less about anything business-related that was going on around them.

I continued to bring solid and creative ideas to the table but was always denied approval and I couldn't move forward with any of them. Every fucking time, too. Surprise, surprise. More stupid decisions abound. I may not be of the Sir Richard Branson mindset, but I can hold my own when it comes to business. We needed to get serious, and fast. We needed to be in our office conducting business, setting goals, developing merchandise, building budgets, finding sponsors, etc., not drinking in bars, chasing after hookers, and allowing the unreasonable voice of alcohol to pave the way.

There was a multitude of things that Bob, Mark, and Vince kept from me, too. Sohrob was our partner, but he was always kept at a distance for no other reason than Bob just flat out hated him. Like, despised him. I now felt in that category. Bob was always whispering in Vince's ear, always stirring the pot, and always trying to build a case against Sohrob, constantly saying he was out to fuck us. As a matter of fact, I was told to stay away from Sohrob and to have absolutely no communication with him at all if I wanted to be part of the team. In other words, in their twisted, deviant little circle of trust.

It was a tough situation because the more I was around Sohrob, the more I could see that he wasn't a bad guy. In fact, I grew to like him because he was actually a decent person. The only reason Bob was in Vince's ear about Sohrob all the time was that Sohrob was wise to Bob's bullshit and

Bob knew it. It scared him. Bob was nothing more than a cheap con artist, a complete fraud, a habitual liar, drunk and Sohrob saw through all of it.

Sohrob had skin in the game, but he wasn't running the show, unfortunately. He should have been, though, and Bob knew that, too. Bob further knew he would be out if that ever happened, so he kept the shit pot constantly stirring. He did his utmost best to keep Vince under his arm, always in clear view, and always just an earshot away. Vince was always drunk and just went along with whatever Bob said, so that made it easy for Bob to continually play Vince like the drunk he was.

As the shit pot was starting to overflow, JB and I decided to just hold tight on reaching out to local businesses and my company for sponsorships and protect ourselves and our reputations as much as possible to make sure we didn't completely ruin our names and jeopardize relationships because of this shitshow. It was one thing to go down with a ship with the potential for a comeback. It was another thing to never be able to recover and have your entire future ruined, too.

On January 27, 2015, Sohrob sent out an email to Commissioner Scott Butera and copied Vince, Bob, Chris, Mark Krum, Jay Coogan, Eric Hewko, David Kaminski, and me, laying out the terms which I've covered up because, well, it's a legal document, but take a look at it… you'll see where I'm going with it.

Dear Commissioner Butera,

Please see the deal terms below. **Each party will reply to this email with "I AGREE"**, and we will draw up a formal terms sheet for everyone to sign prior to formal deal documents, which we anticipate closing on early next week. We will also draw up a loan agreement that will be signed by the parties allowing me to fund the team in the near term until full deal documents are signed.

Thank you for your support through this.

Best Regards,

Sohrob

Outlaw Investment Group ("OIG")

- $500k additional cash investment for 50% ownership in Rockstar Sports Group LLC ("the Team")
- 150k of the $500k will be provided as a bridge loan on signing of term sheet, loan will be fully collateralized by all assets of the Team, including 50% of the franchise rights. Loan converts to equity on signing of final deal docs.
- Will receive 2 board seats, one to be filled by Sohrob Farudi (as co-chairmain) and the other to be selected by OIG needing approval of both Neil and Salamone (not to be unreasonably withheld)
- Sohrob Farudi will be CEO and Managing Partner of the Team
- OIG and it's members will sign releases and waivers with the Team, Rockstar Investment Group Inc ("RIGI"), Daniels, etc.

Chris Salamone ("Salamone")

- Will receive 20% ownership in the Team
- Will receive a Board Seat
- Will serve as President of the Team
- Will release Mark Daniels ("Daniels") from $435k of personal debt
- Will provide copies of the signed loan agreements between Salamone and Daniels
- Will sign releases and waivers with regards to the Team, RIGI, and the Falcon, etc.

Mark Daniels

- Will receive a 5% profit interest (non-transferable, no ownership, no voting rights) in the Team, which shall expire after 5 years, up to $150k
- Will receive $50k cash from the Team, $25k paid on execution of final documents and $5k/mo until the balance is paid in full. This $50k will be deducted from the 5% profit interest
- Will resolve issue of $26k fuel expense with Salamone (by assigning 25k payment to Salamone)
- Will receive release from Salamone of $435k in personal debt obligations
- Will receive release from Neil of Falcon debt

- Will sign releases and waivers with regards to the Team, OIG, and it's members, RIGI and it's members, Salamone, Neil, and the Falcon, etc.

Vince Neil ("Neil")

- Will receive 20% ownership in the Team
- Neil will receive a Board Seat
- Neil will be Co-Chairman of the Board
- Neil will receive resolution on the Falcon (as noted below)
- Will sign releases and waivers with regards to the Team, OIG, and the Falcon, etc

Bob Hewko ("Hewko")

- Will receive 5-10% ownership in the Team (depending on agreement with Amsler)
- Hewko will be GM of Football Operations
- Will sign releases and waivers with regards to the Team, OIG, etc.

Britt Amsler ("Amsler")

- Will receive 0-5% ownership in the Team OR a note from the Team for $125k + 6% interest payable monthly (depending on agreement with Hewko)
- If agree on the note, Amsler will receive 2 front row season tickets for 5 years to Team home games.
- Will sign releases and wavers with regards to the Team, OIG, RIGI, etc.

Other Terms

- AFL Commish (or other neutral party to be agreed upon by OIG, Neil, Salamone) will break any board deadlock
- Distributions of the Team will first pay back cash invested, then be split pro rata among the parties
- Neil and Salamone will jointly agree upon a resolution with regard to the Falcon jet ("Falcon") in which Neil either a) is repaid his $150k by Daniels or b) Salamone allows Neil to purchase the Falcon at a reasonable price agreed upon by the parties ($200k-$220k) or c) the Falcon is put up for sale and the parties split the proceeds, or d) Daniels agrees to assign his 5% profit interest in the Team to Neil, with Salamone agreeing to "backstop" Neil's $150k investment with proceeds (after Salamone recoups his original investment) from the sale of the Falcon if Neil does not receive 150k through the profit interest
- Neil, Salamone, and Daniels will not sign releases with regards to the Falcon until a resolution is reached by the parties.

Okay. Before I continue…. It's important that I point something out in case you missed it. Did anyone else catch the person whose name hasn't been mentioned once yet, whose name has now magically fucking appeared on a legal document with ownership terms he is to agree to? Who the hell is Chris Salamone? Why haven't I heard of this guy before? Here they go again with the shady ass shit with this group. I had no idea who this person was, and I'm in a legally binding agreement with him? WTF!

As I sat back, a hint of a recollection came to mind. I think Chris was *that guy*, the big dark secret, back in December when Vince was playing a show at the Red Rock Casino. The show was somehow connected with Dollar Loans, I think. I don't remember the exact date, but it was near the holidays and what was weird about the whole thing was that on the day of the show, I still didn't have my tickets. Bob said to just show up and then I couldn't get ahold of him or anyone else for that matter. I remember going over to T- Bones for dinner and I'll be damned. Lo and behold, there sat Bob, Vince, and who I would now meet for the first time, *this guy Chris* and his girlfriend. Totally surprised the shady fuckers when I walked in, too.

It was so incredibly wonderful to see their faces drop when they saw me. Apparently, they were there trying to bring in another player, and, well, naturally, neglected to tell Sohrob and me about it. I was so livid and so done with feeling betrayed and played by these two scheming little cunts. Seriously. Nothing these two did surprised me anymore, and I don't care for those odds when it comes to my life.

To add insult to injury, during this entire time, Dead Beat Bob was staying with me because his sorry ass couldn't get any more hotel comps, couldn't afford a fucking hotel, and didn't have anywhere else to stay.

And I also fed the fat bastard every day for a week, paid all the bar tabs (nothing new), *and* I let the motherfucker drive my car! Never once got a 'thank you' or a penny in return from him. Nothing. No expression of gratitude at any time.

I remember one morning I went into the laundry room, which was upstairs and right across from the guest room Bob was staying in, and I saw a green card laying on the floor with a photo of a naked woman on it. I picked it up to see what it was, and it was a phone sex card. Oh, man! Bob is jerking off to call girls in my house. Eww! Now I'm gonna have to get the damned carpets and walls steam cleaned after he leaves. His tired ass claim to fame was that he was this starting QB for the Florida Gators so far back I don't even remember, and he graduated to mooching off people and becoming the Jerk Off King to call girls in someone else's house. Nothing this deviant douchebag did could surprise me. Nothing. It was a way of life for him and he was good at it.

All those on the email apparently replied to the email with an "I agree!", which immediately opened the floodgates for my resentment and bitterness to fester even more. I couldn't believe how blatantly I was getting screwed, and yet I had a lot of skin in the game and was really stuck. I had a lot to lose. Maybe too much. I didn't have anything, or anyone, to hide behind. It went beyond the "Hmm, I wonder if that means… " type of scenario and way of thinking now. It was more like, "Holy shit, add *this* to the fucking list of me getting screwed!"

I had no idea who this Chris guy was, let alone venture to guess how *he* became involved, what he brought to the table, or what he was offered behind the scenes that I would be held liable for fulfilling. Anything was possible, and it was becoming frightening. The icing on the cake was when Mark achieved getting himself banned by the Commissioner. He lost his seat on the Board and could no longer have any say whatsoever in the team's operations. And when I say banned, I mean, *totally* banned. No passing go, no collecting $200, no get out of jail free card.

Being banned meant that Mark could never get his ownership card back. Ever. I was actually getting closer to Mark when all this shit started to go down and when it was over, I was really left standing alone with absolutely no one to trust. I felt like prey being constantly circled by hungry vultures, and not by your ordinary vultures that prey off the weak and dead. These vultures actually preyed on each other while still alive, too.

As it turned out, Chris was brought in to "relieve Mark of a $435,000 debt" that was tied to some plane he called The Falcon being auctioned off in Florida. Something about it being seized in a drug deal gone wrong or some shit, who the fuck really knows. Or cares. There were so many lies flying around this group it was virtually impossible to determine truth from fiction. I don't know what it was about that particular plane, but it was all Vince talked about, all day, every day. The plane this, the plane that. And he called it *his* plane, too, making sure everyone had the impression that he was the one who purchased it. Him. Vince. He bought it. It was *his* plane (drops toy on ground, stomps feet, holds breath). Fucking drama queen. Just made me want to punch him in the face. He was more worried about that stupid fucking plane than he was about the success of the team. Oh, wait. That's right. Duh. He didn't have any money in the team. He literally had nothing to lose! (*Insert self-inflicted throat punch here.*)

When Bob tried to strongarm me into accepting the deal drawn up by Sohrob, and I steadfastly refused, the shit really started to go down. Bob's brother was some sort of a lawyer back in Florida, so Bob put me on the phone with him to try and sort things out. The guy basically told me to take the deal and move on, but I didn't want to and I let him know he wasn't going to change my mind. I was like, "Hell no, I'm not bailing out, I'm staying in for the ride, so stop asking me to change my mind."

I had no clue who to trust. I already had come to terms with the fact that I was never going to get my money back, so I just figured *screw it* and saddled up for the crash and burn. If I'm going to lose my money no matter what, then I may as well have some fucking fun while I watch it all slip away. Bob was so pissed that I wouldn't settle, it was almost funny. He really wanted my 5% share to bring him up to 10% and he didn't give a damn how he did it. Fucking evil little cocksucker. Living in *my* house, trying to steal my stake in the venture when he wasn't brought in originally. Remember, he was there by temper tantrum through Vince.

The next morning, Bob was sitting at my breakfast table and I was working in my office.

He yells, "Hey, bro? Just take the deal and walk. It's the best thing you can do."

I responded, "Fuck you," shut the door, and called Sohrob.

Wow, did the truth come out then! Turns out, Bob had absolutely no skin in the game. None. Explained why he wanted me out so badly.

I hung up the phone, walked out into my kitchen, looked at Bob, and said, "What the fuck, Bob! You have no money in this team? None, dude? You're such a fucking joke!"

I was so pissed I called Vince, too. Despite the bullshit, he was still the President. Much to my surprise, Vince sided with me, causing Bob to lose his mind and causing us to finally get into it. I had had enough and instead of pummeling the bastard right then and there, which he more than deserved, I told him to get his shit and get the fuck out of my house. The sad part was that by the end of the day, Bob had already gotten back in Vince's ear and, of course, Little Vinnie Vin Vin retracted his comments and reversed his opinion, absolving Bob of any wrongdoing. Spineless piece of shit.

Of course, they had to cover up for each other since Vince didn't have any money in the team either. Not one red cent. Just like with the restaurant inside Circus Circus, they were only using his name. His name. Not his money, not any equity he may have had, not his ideas, not his vision. His name. All I can say is that these two fucking morons really deserved each other.

It was all starting to make perfect sense now. Mark, Chris, Sohrob, and I were the only people who had money invested. Hell, out of the $4 million I was told we had from the League, we didn't even have half of that. Not even close. The multiple layers of bullshit were all coming to the surface now, proving that I and my money were nothing more than victims of these wannabe douchebags. Wow.

There was no ultimate goal. There was no true professionalism or business being conducted here. There was no true desire or plan to have a winning team. Everything that was done was done in the name of self-professed glory of the present moment, and nothing more. All to be done on someone else's dime and energy. Sohrob was on to them, too, and he had them by the balls. The Commissioner was on to them, too, and it was just a matter of time before the whole thing imploded. The saddest part of all was that there was nothing I could do to salvage what I had invested. It was too late. I had no choice but to sit back and watch it all burn before me, standing close enough to the flames to smell hair burning.

Sohrob sent out another email on February 17th entitled "NEW Rockstar Sports Group LLC Operating Agreement" to Bob, Chris, Mark, Vince, and copied Jay Coogan from Piper Global Law Firm. "NEW," it said. This was a NEW agreement. Another one. This far in. Now a NEW agreement. You fucking kidding me with this? Within the email, it read, "Please review this and get back to Jay with any comments by tomorrow. There will be plenty of other documents that we need to execute to get this deal finalized, but this is the main document that will govern the team so we can get everything in place we need to play this season. Please review ASAP! Thanks! Sohrob." This "main document" was 37 fucking pages long and my immediate thought was WTF is this now? Fuck! So, I have to get an attorney to review all this shit now?

Then, two weeks before kickoff, there came a follow-up email saying all the binding terms needed to be signed by Wednesday, or we "wouldn't be playing this season." It was the next email that laid the tracks for the utter and final destruction of the team, and well, basically the whole venture.

Sohrob's email indicated that some language had been left out, accidentally of course, and a revised document was attached that added that left out language: "*AFL Commissioner will break any board deadlock.*"

It didn't end there. Next came the reply from Chris Salamone's attorney, requesting changes, one of which referred to that stupid fucking plane that got Vince's little whiskey dick hard. You know, The Falcon. The one that was his? The one where he publicly said that he would fly to all the games and then reward the MVP of each and every game with a ride back on it? Such a crock of shit. That never happened. Not once. That fucking plane never even left Florida because it was such a piece of shit it couldn't pass inspection. Vince and Mark said it came from an auction as it was confiscated as a drug plane.

Ah, but the doomsday emails didn't end there, nor did the rapid deconstruction of everything we knew as the Outlaws.

A month later, we got a follow-up email from Sohrob telling the group that if the recently distributed documents didn't get executed, checks were going to bounce. Starting tomorrow. An entire month goes by without any action being taken, and now it's down to … tomorrow. He then proceeds to tell us all that there was about $1,000 in the account and there were about $12,000 worth of checks being deposited. Tomorrow. A bit of an issue since some of those checks were to be used for deposits for player housing, something that couldn't be put off any longer.

In that email were also changes to the Term Sheet, effectively immediately, which included giving Vince, Bob, and me equal equity split. Sohrob also added some language for a performance clause for Vince, language addressing Daniels' debt, and included language for buyout options. Since no one had responded to the email yet in over a day, Sohrob sent out another one to the entire group providing revised language to the buyout options to include options for Vince and Bob to buy out all the equity of the company. Seemed legit enough, until Mark Daniels sent out his reply.

Mark reminded the group that he was excluded from any negotiations that had taken place and as such, his rights weren't considered. What did that mean? It meant that he rejected *everything* proposed in Sohrob's emails and reminded everyone that if it wasn't for him, there wouldn't be any assets for them to be fighting over. He also added that he was involving his attorney to protect his rights, and this wasn't an issue that was just going to go away on its own. Pissing match ON.

Jay Coogan replied by sending a revision that would give Mark this teeny tiny non-voting percentage offering, thinking that would appease Mark. It didn't. Sohrob took the opportunity to piggyback on Jay's email, stressing that the deal get done *today*. Checks written for the player housing were bouncing, there was no cash to purchase the field, and there was still the huge issue of still needing cash from sponsors for the field dashboards.

If cash wasn't put into the account tomorrow, we no longer had a team to manage and everything from that point would be done at the sole discretion of the League. Basically, as of that email, we didn't have anything. Didn't matter what everyone thought we had. We didn't. Sohrob pleaded, yet again, to get signatures to him by midnight. Well, I'm sure I don't even have to say the pleas fell on deaf ears and blinded eyes. None of those signatures happened.

You know, you just have to love customer service at Bank of America and their friendly, timely, and unforgiving account alerts. That very next afternoon, March 19, 2015, at precisely 12:36 pm, the alerts started coming in.

"We are letting you know your account is overdrawn and has insufficient funds." The Outlaws account was already overdrawn by just under $6,600, bank fees were already being charged to the account and accruing, and it had only been half a day! Sohrob pleaded to the group, pathetically begging a supposed bunch of businesspeople to conduct business. He needed to collect all signatures within the next two hours. If it was all handled within the next two hours, he could make the bank cutoff and try to halt the overdrawn amount from rising.

Did that work? Of course not. Why would he be taken seriously with this bunch? It wasn't until four days later that Sohrob tried again in a final attempt, this time adding that he would personally make an interim, short-term, interest-free loan for $150,000 from his equity in the Outlaws Investment Group to help fund all of the things that needed to be funded and temporarily solve the funding crisis. He suggested that we would then hold an official board meeting to lay the plans for funding the team moving forward.

Oddly enough, it was Vince, the one who kept silent through all of this since the inception of the team, to be the first one to reply to Sohrob's offer, and that's when the circus really got started. Staying true to the fucking tool that he was, Vince's reply was, "What scam are you trying to run now?" Ha! Nothing about solving the issue, keeping the team afloat. No. Apparently, Vince was under the impression that Sohrob committed to putting in $250k, not just $150k, and he thought there would be about $550k available to the team once added to the League's donation.

It took all of about 10 minutes for Sohrob to reply to Vince, officially listing the equity he has paid, officially listing payments made on behalf of the team and for what items, and said he would be more than happy to meet to discuss it all the next day. Since I was always left in the dark on everything, I'm still not sure what happened next or what may have gone down between Sohrob and Vince, or what happened with the bank account. All I know is that we kicked off on Monday night, March 30, at 7:30 pm, at the Thomas and Mack Center in Las Vegas for Game 1. The Outlaws finally became real, and so did all of the problems that came along with that reality.

# OPENING NIGHT

## CHAPTER 12

On Sunday, March 29, 2015, one day away from the Outlaws' season opener, Vinnie Paul (an individual who should need *no* introduction) threw one of his infamous Sunday Funday parties at his house in Las Vegas. He had a cool compound-like place just around the corner from the Palms Casino, making it conveniently located near the Las Vegas Strip. It had the greatest view, too. You could see Mandalay Bay from the pool in his backyard.

If you've ever been lucky enough to have attended a Sunday Funday party at Vinnie Paul's house in either Dallas or Vegas, you know how beyond fortunate you were to be a part of such an amazing, over-the-top kind of day. Vinnie was an unbeatable host, a true friend to many, and a man with a kind, gigantic heart. That's who he really was, too. He stayed the same person he was from way before he was *the* famous rock star, and he never deviated from it. He consistently remained the humblest human being I've ever met in my entire life, and I'll be surprised if I ever meet his equal.

When I look back on it, it's truly bizarre how such a shining example of a person like Vinnie Paul came into my life at the time he did. It was the *Tale of the Two Vinces*, as we used to say. On the one hand, you had Vinnie Paul, the finest example of a decent, unpretentious, genial human being. And then, on the other, much lower, dishonorable douchey hand, you had what was known as Vince Neil, the polar opposite.

At his parties, Vinnie always cooked up a feast fit to feed an army, and he loved doing it. He would roll home in the early hours of the morning from a night out before, only to wake up soon thereafter with the sole purpose of going to Costco for groceries and supplies for the party that day. He always put his friends first. Any guest that his friends brought was also considered a friend, and always welcomed. That was real. Not some kind of hype or image bullshit. There wasn't a headcount being kept. There wasn't someone there monitoring how much food someone ate. There wasn't someone there telling you he's trying to monitor the booze because it's not for everyone to drink. You know, so he can bring home what's left for himself. Vinnie Paul was the real deal, as real as it gets.

As for Vince? Shit. Not only did that asshole not have any friends, but there also wasn't a person out there looking to fill the position either.

My stepdad Bobby had flown into Vegas to spend a week with me and go to the home opener. My mom was on an Australian vacation with her friend Marie at the time, but that was fine by me. She's supported me through so much, she deserved a vacation. My brother Aaron was flying in that Monday, the day of the game, so I had a family support system with me and was grateful for it.

When I told Bobby that we were going to Vinnie Paul's house for that week's Sunday Funday party, man, was he excited! In fact, he still talks about that party to this day! True to Vinnie's character, he greeted Bobby with a huge warm welcome and Bobby immediately felt like he belonged.

My good buddy JMAC was also in town for the party and to support me at the opener. He was best friends with Vinnie and was there at the party as acting chef and managing the grill. If you remember, JMAC was the friend that connected me and Bob Hewko, but after the disaster of the Outlaws, JMAC punted Bob as far as China for being a fraud and a con artist. It didn't sit well with JMAC that this guy took advantage of me as he did. Now that's a great friend, and it was good to have JMAC there with me. We always had a good time together, especially at Vinnie's parties.

You see, these parties always came with an element of surprise because you never knew who was going to show up. Guests ranged from Carrot Top to off the chart musicians from Five Finger Death Punch and Volbeat. We partied that entire afternoon away, getting geared up for the big kick-off the next night. I was super pumped, and everyone seemed to be excited not just for me as a show of support, but excitement towards the event about to take place. I told Vinnie I reserved an entire row of tickets for him and JMAC and told him to be at the arena early for a special VIP party for, naturally, our VIP special guests.

Another steadfast thing about Vinnie was that he always supported his friends and his counterparts within the music industry. Always. If there was some show or some kind of event, whether it be in Dallas or in Vegas, and he was in town, you could bet your last dollar he would be there. Every time. And he was more than happy to do it. There wasn't anything selfish or self-serving about it. I'll say it again and will keep saying it whenever I see fit. Vinnie Paul was one of the humblest, most genuine people I've ever met, and probably will ever meet, in my lifetime. I'm a better person for having known him.

The Big Day finally arrived, and on Monday, March 30, 2015, I was able to wake up that particular morning as an official owner of a professional arena football team. I was an owner of the Las Vegas Outlaws. Me. An owner! The feeling was overwhelming in so many ways, on so many levels, that I can't even properly express it. Sure, it was a feeling that I would love to experience again in my life in a lot of ways, but, in a lot of other ways, I'll take a pass on going through that again. Without a doubt, the highs of that feeling were something to cherish, something to remember; however, the lows haunt me to this day and perhaps will for the rest of my life.

I was psyched my brother was in town. He was staying with a coworker who also lived in Vegas, so that's who he was bringing as his guest to the game. They had some business to take care of that afternoon, so I told them to meet me at the arena around 5 pm. At least I think that's what I told them. I was incredibly scatterbrained that entire day, with various thoughts about the kickoff constantly fucking distracting me.

Right after lunch, Vince, Bob, Mark, Johnny, me, and Bobby met at the arena for a walk-through. The turf was beautifully done, I must admit, and it was a sight to behold. The dashboards evenly graced the walls along the field and the goalposts were going up as we arrived. It was starting to look like a professional sports arena. Everything was coming together. I don't know how it was, but it was happening.

We were actually going to kick the ball off, on time, that night. Despite all the bullshit of the last few months, somehow, it squeaked by just enough for this moment to happen. We walked out onto the field and tossed the ball around, played pass, and shared some laughs. Sad in a way, because that was probably the only moment the ownership group interacted as friends just having fun and enjoying the moment. Before heading home to shit, shower, and shave, Bobby and I decided to walk over to the locker rooms to check them out. Taped to the wall outside the main door was a list of scheduled events for the evening. Here it is:

## Team Schedule: March 30th, 2015
## Las Vegas Outlaws vs. San Jose Sabercats

| Real Time | Game Clock | Element |
|---|---|---|
| | | Starting Line-Ups DUE to Public Address Announcer |
| 6:18:00 | 79:00 | VISITING Warm-ups |
| 6:28:00 | 59:00 | BOTH team on field for warm-ups |
| 6:48:00 | 49:00 | HOME Warm-ups |
| 7:04:30 | 32:30 | 5-Minute Warning to SABERCATS |
| 7:08:00 | 29:00 | HOME team to leave the field |
| 7:12:00 | 25:00 | SABERCATS Team Introductions<br>1) Team introduced as a whole, no individual names<br>2) and then the Head Coach<br>5-Minute Warning to OUTLAWS |
| 7:17:00 | 20:00 | OUTLAWS in tunnel |
| 7:17:40 | 19:20 | OUTLAWS Team Introductions<br>1) 8 Introduced<br>2) Head Coach<br>3) All other players/assistants/rings/etc/<br>4) Vince Neil |
| 7:19:30 | 17:30 | Honor Guard |
| 7:20:30 | 16:30 | National Anthem – Vince Neil |
| 7:23:00 | 13:30 | Ball Delivery – Scott Butera |
| 7:34:00 | 3:00 | Coin Toss – Carrot Top |
| 7:37:00 | 0:00 | Kickoff |

- Half-time is 12 minutes
- There is a special half-time ceremony; players are not allowed on the field of play until the 3:00 mark. A team representative will be stationed at the locker room for instructions

Unfortunately for us, the locker room was set up for a basketball team, not a football team, but we made it work. We had to. It was either that or our players didn't have a locker room. One of the biggest drawbacks was that the space was really cramped. For Outlaws games, it was set up with a red fold-out chair placed under each player's locker, and the locker had the player's name taped to it. There was an Outlaws helmet on top of each locker, and an Outlaws jersey hanging underneath on a hook.

Might not have been NFL standards, but it was my moment in time, and you better believe I was taking it. This one belonged to me, and no one was going to piss in my Cheerios. Not today.

That morning, my phone had been ringing off the hook, text messages coming in by the dozens, and in the midst of it all, I had to make sure there were enough tickets to cover all the guests. It was the definition of mayhem, but I kept it together. I had to. Especially since I knew no one else was going to. Quite frankly, I didn't trust anyone involved in this shady circus act. This act had circus clowns with egos that stretched well beyond the fact that they were nothing more than washed up, worn out, has-beens that used anyone they could to get something for themselves. These weren't people you could rely upon, and I wasn't going to make that mistake again.

I have always believed that a person needs to dress for success. If I was going to accurately represent this team as an owner, I wanted to do it in a professional, classy yet sassy kind of way. Since everyone loves a sharp-dressed man, I sprung for a couple of custom-made 3-piece suits to make sure that I looked the part. As a collective group that day, I thought we all looked pretty stylish. I was wearing the new grey suit, styled with black shoes and a white Outlaws shirt. Vince wore a dark, greyish pair of pants, black shirt, black jacket, black shoes, and naturally topped off the look with a pair of shades to hide his bloodshot eyes, which was probably for the best. At least it kept the focus on the fact that he did look nice and looked the part. Sohrob also wore dark pants and had on this grey jacket and white lace-up shoes, Bob was in all black, and I'm not sure about Mark but who cares.

We posed for so many pictures it was on the brink of being tiring, but hey, at least we looked good in those pictures. Throughout the entire process, I felt like I was in the Twilight Zone, the new and improved edition. I was nervous as all hell, too. Once I saw the TV cameras that were already setting up, my nerves really started to run away with me.

I had no idea how I was going to do this, or even *what* to do in this situation. This was uncharted territory, for sure. When we were inside the Center, a security guard asked for our credentials, and I said, "I am Britt Amsler, one of the owners of the Outlaws," and he waved us in.

That was a proud personal moment for me, I won't lie. As we were escorted in, I could see Vince's Rolls Royce off in the distance and as my eyes passed the car, I saw the game-ready field for the first time. Holy. Shit. I stood there for a few seconds, soaked it in, and then snapped back to reality. Back to business. I was an owner. I could get all weepy-eyed later.

I walked over to the VIP check-in where staff were controlling the tickets and credentials and was more than relieved to know all of my requested tickets were actually there. Another potential issue no longer an issue. Check. One more obstacle down. You know, it's fucked up owning part of the damned team and you still had to worry if your guests were going to be let into the arena. So much energy wasted on shit like this.

While Vince and Bob were being interviewed by the press on the field our VIP guests began to arrive. It was time to get the party started!

The VIP party was being held at the back of the arena. Normally, when you have a VIP party at an event such as this, you would require some help with the organization of it all, right? Say, maybe hire an event coordinator to assist with the planning and then be on-site the day of the event to make sure that everything goes by design? Yes? Wrong! With Vince and Bob, everything was always done on the fly and under the influence of alcohol, so to find out that things they handled were fucked up no longer came as a surprise or a shock. The only thing those two organized in their life was their next drink and next sleazy lay.

A small side note here to support the first point. Since alcohol was of such extreme importance to them, I was asked to supply the booze for the party. Sounds logical and not so far-fetched, right? Sure, under normal circumstances. But there's a catch with this one. See, liquor wasn't permitted at this event.

That's right. It wasn't allowed on the premises, and not like it wasn't served there. You weren't allowed to BYOB, not as an event goer, not as part of a party or event. Yet I was still asked to supply the party with booze. Why? Well, because we had a big bad rock star on our roster, and Mr. Rock Star was gonna show everyone out there that we didn't have to abide by the rules. So, there! Hmph!

Even though I knew better, I did it anyway and brought my premium to super-premium portfolio of Vodka, Scotch, Rum, Gin, and Bourbon to the party. If you know anything about liquor, you know that such a portfolio can end up being a very pricy donation when considering the quantity needed for this party. I can't confirm the amount spent, but I believe the arena supplied the beer and wine at a hefty marked-up price, which is why they didn't want outside liquor being brought in. See that, class? Did you learn something here? Why, yes, we did. We learned how to work around what we were told, not respect it.

It's no wonder it was the Cheap Cocktail Clown Posse who asked me to bring liquor, even though they knew it wasn't going to jibe with the regulations set by the arena. They didn't care. It wasn't *them* doing it. The reign of free booze didn't last too long, though. Right as the party got started, Kelle came over to us and said that the liquor had to go *immediately*, or the arena was going to confiscate all of it. She somehow managed to convince security to let her get it packed up and taken outside so she could save it.

All the booze I brought was immediately boxed up and put in the back of Vince's Rolls. Not my car. Vince's car. Never to be seen again, too, like it never existed. I asked Vince about it, too, and he was like, "Booze? What are you talking about?"

I reminded the dumbass it was the booze placed in the trunk of his car at the arena after they told us it was not allowed, and he still played fucking stupid. Still claimed he "had no clue, bro" about $2,000.00 in booze that just magically disappeared into the trunk of *his* car. So, nobody has a fucking clue where it went then? Really? Nobody? Fucking alcoholic entitled douchebag.

Even Kelle laughed out loud and said, "You think Vince is going to give up that free booze? No fucking way." She was right, too.

I never got back any of the booze or any of the money I laid out. Just one more "fuck you" to add to the running list. But that was a real thing with him. That was the real Vince, the real person, not the singer frontman Vince. The real Vince was the guy who could look you directly in the eye swearing loyalty and morality and then fuck you over as soon as your head turned. He just didn't fucking care. He had absolutely no moral compass of any kind whatsoever. Everything this piece of shit had access to, everything that he already possessed, and he had to fuck me over for a few bottles of alcohol, and then lie about it? Such an ass. Like he won something? Like he deserved something? Like he was smarter than me? But to lie about it afterward made it even more sickening if only for the fact that he believed everyone else was too stupid to see it. Such a smug little prick. Anyway, back to the party.

When Vinnie, his crew, JMAC, my brother, and all of my other guests started to roll in I started to focus on the party. I made sure I greeted everyone as they walked in and then took them to the bar to grab a beer or wine. Vince was predictably standing at the bar and when I walked over to him with Vinnie, honestly, I was embarrassed by the way Vince greeted him. Vince was already getting hammered, and I'm not sure why I expected him to act any differently, but still. Vinnie stayed true to form, remained calm and unphased, and kept his class act composure as he always did. He just brushed it off. He was simply happy to be there with his friends. I also tried introducing my brother to Vince and that greeting wasn't any better. Have you ever simultaneously experienced the sensation of a cold chill running down your spine while a hot flash of embarrassment washes over your entire body because you thought someone would act better? Act like a mature adult, especially when they are meeting your close friends and family? That's how I felt. Totally embarrassed, and more for him than for anybody else. This was who he really was, inside and out, tried and true. This was Vince, and it shouldn't matter that he was a "famous person."

People like Vinnie Paul and Carrot Top were "famous people," and they weren't douchebags. Carrot Top is another genuine person that you can count on. He's a class act, very friendly, inherently very funny, and always engaging when you talk with him. He was tight friends with both Vince and Vinnie, so I can imagine he was put into similar situations that I had been put in. He was at the opener there to do the coin toss for us before heading out to do his own at the Luxor.

He didn't disappoint either. He brought his own coin with him that was the size of a drum snare and he had it all bedazzled and shit. It was pretty cool and funny as hell, but the ref wouldn't let him flip that one no matter how hard he comedically tried to persuade him. Nope. He had to flip a real coin, and he did just that.

But hey! Great idea, it looked cool, and it got people engaged. It also showed that he cared to be there, that he thought about how to be a part of the moment and not just some half-assed, lame part. A class act always wins, and that's why Vince the Selfish was always losing. That's why Vince the Sloshed was always bottom of the barrel in everything he did. This opener was no different than any other day to him. It was just another reason to drink and be an egotistical asshole and he certainly didn't let anyone down on those expectations.

Soon after the party was getting started, Johnny brought in a blue ice chest from Vince's car. In it were two bottles of Grey Goose, several bottles of Santa Margherita Pinot Grigio and Veuve Clicquot Champagne, some ice, and some blue Solo cups. A couple of things instantly came to my mind, the first of which was how shitty Vince was going to become before the night was over. The other was thinking it was cool that he would bring in the booze for our inner circle to enjoy, or so I thought. Johnny ended up rolling that blue ice chest behind the stands and against the wall, making sure it was hidden from the eyes of those who shouldn't see it. Guess it didn't matter that all of the alcohol that I brought in was in jeopardy of being *confiscated*. Guess that when you are a rock star with a boundless ego and an insatiable need for alcohol to function, you do shit like this.

Then I thought, fuck it, I'm getting a drink. I walked over, poured myself a blue Solo cup's worth of pinot grigio, and walked back to the bottom of the ramp.

Next thing you know, Vince comes stammering over to me and said, "Hey, bro! Easy on the booze. I don't want to fucking run out. That's not for everyone to drink."

I was stunned. Really? I just had at least $2,000 worth of booze confiscated and being held hostage essentially by him, and he was going to tell me to go easy on the few bottles of booze he brought in? Man, what a dick. A cheap, little, pathetic, narcissistic dick. Would be one thing if he were joking, but he was dead serious.

The issue I seemed to have was that his restrictions were seemingly only directed to me. Not Bob, his butt-kissing booze buddy. Nope. Not even a few other people that were always around. Nope. Me. It was always me. It was like he was always in competition with me for some reason. If it had anything at all to do with *me*, there was always an issue for him. Always.

There was no way that little prick was going to drink a dent in that many bottles even with the way he drank. Not everyone there was looking to get shitfaced like him and drink everything they could get their hands on. I wanted to socially drink, have one or two drinks, and stay coherent. As an owner, I needed to greet, intermingle, and face people with a sober mindset when I shook their hands and spoke with them. We weren't at some rock concert where it was considered "cool" to be all fucked up and bond with other fucked up people. We were there conducting business and we were still in dire need of sponsors and loyal fans to make this venture work. To turn all that away, and possibly not be able to get it back, just because some of the owners had too much to drink was professional suicide.

Ah, but trust in that Dumb and Dumber were not worrying about that, though. All that mattered was cracking open those fucking bottles. Didn't matter to them that this was a business. Didn't matter to them that this was a crucial step in the success of the team.

It did matter to me, though, and I was going to do my best to set a good example. Well, the best one that I could for this dysfunctional group under the circumstances we were facing.

At one point, Vince and I were standing at the bottom of the tunnel, behind the back of the end zone, talking about our taxes of all things. Hey, it was tax season. He told me how much higher the taxes were for him when he was living in California versus living in Nevada and then proceeded to tell me that he owed the IRS something like $2 million or some shit. Fuck that! I could never even imagine being in that situation.

Then he told me he's nervous, and it wasn't over owing the IRS so much money; he was nervous about singing the National Anthem.

I laughed and reminded him, "Bro, you sing in front of 20,000 people at every show you do with Crue."

He just looked at me and said, "Tonight is different, bro. Way different." He then told me he rehearsed once in the shower early today. Once.

What else could I say but, "You got this" and off we went.

Wow. Needless to say, he didn't "have that." Holy shit did he *not* have that in any way, shape, or form. If the question was whether or not he butchered it, then, ya, he fucking nailed it!

***

Just before 6:30 pm, both teams took to the field to warm up and as I stood there with Vince watching them, it dawned on me that I had never once in my life seen an arena football game. Like, not even a news snippet. Hell, I wasn't sure I even knew the rules of the game. I had been to several practices and interacted with the team leading up to tonight, but truth be told, I had never taken the time to read the rule book. Haha!

Okay, okay, chalk that one up as a failure for Team Owner Britt. My bad. Whatever. I had more important things to focus on at the time. There wasn't any sense in learning the rules of the game if there wasn't a team to play it, right? It was still professional football, and I was still excited to be a part of it.

As we were standing there, Dave walked up and told us that the line outside of fans waiting to get in was wrapped around the building. That was such awesome news you have no idea. It was imperative that we captured and maintained the City of Las Vegas' support to survive, so this was beyond encouraging to hear.

I don't know the exact number of tickets sold for that opening game, but I do know that for each home game we played, we needed around 7,000 tickets sold. And that was a bare minimum number just to keep the team afloat. Those numbers didn't generate the kind of revenue needed to expand and grow the team, let alone create a cushion for any unexpected or last-minute issues or emergencies. For right now, our immediate goal was just to stay afloat. To have such a decent turnout for our opener, especially since we didn't really advertise or market the event, was a true gift.

Don't be surprised, either, that there wasn't any marketing done. You need proper people in place to *do* that kind of stuff, and, well, you know how this shit show was run. The only advertising that managed to get done was getting a few billboards with Vince's face sprinkled around Vegas and on the freeway. Because, we all know how well Vince's face can sell a product, let alone sell out an entire arena for an event that no one knows about. Obviously, that didn't happen.

Opening night ended up selling around 6,569 tickets, not even close to a sellout and less than the average we needed per game. Sadly, opening night would turn out to be our bestselling night of the season. From there we only averaged about 4,731 sold tickets per game, and the estimated attendance for the entire season was estimated around 42,584 fans. At least that's what Google tells me.

*** 

As kickoff neared closer and closer, the jitters got worse, and it was like a ball of nerves right in the pit of my stomach. As I stood there with my stepdad Bobby and my brother Aaron, the moment evolved into one of the most memorable experiences of my life. It was like a dream, it really was. As I was standing there, basking in the natural high of the moment, Vinnie Paul, Christian Brady (#Hellyeah), JMAC, and the crew walked over to me and wished me good luck before heading to their seats. We had a group picture taken of all of us standing in the endzone. This picture remains one of my all-time favorite photos and it sits on my desk at home to this day. Forever memorialized. We brought an entirely new, untainted meaning to representing a Motley *Crew*. Don't believe me? Here's the pic:

*From left to right: JMAC, Me, Vinnie Paul, Vinnie's GF Chelsey, Christian Brady, Bri- Dog's GF, Bri-Dog, Jamie's GF, Jamie Sexton, Timm Bland, and my good friend Chance McDaniel.*

As my crew of friends headed to their seats, the Outlaws' cheerleaders, known as 'The Posse,' stormed the field and the fans finally started to get a little louder, get into the moment. The Posse performed to the song "Pour Some Sugar on Me" by Def Leppard and as soon as the song was over, each one of them ran to the tunnel and hopped on the back of a motorcycle that was waiting for them. With the music blaring and dry ice filling up the endzone, the bikes drove out onto the field, one by one, busting through the dry ice cloud with the Posse chicks pumping their pom-poms into the air.

Once all the bikes were out on the field and lined up, "Kickstart My Heart'" started blaring and a bunch of dudes ran out onto the field waving Outlaws flags. It was almost time to get this show started. Robin Leach was standing at the back of the tunnel with Vince, wearing a fucking white suit that made him look like he just stepped off the set of a 70's sitcom. It was unreal. It made me flashback to Dime wearing that purple suit at the Stripper Christmas Party. I imagined the two of them standing next to each other, like some tacky throwback velvet painting you would find in an outdated casino, and it made me laugh out loud.

Hard to believe, but what was even more noticeable than the suit was that Vince was drinking from one of those fucking blue Solo cups. Cheap little mother fucker! He just stood there with Robin, waiting for his cue, getting nice and fucked up. Once all the players were all introduced and standing on the field as a team, the announcer yelled "Head coach, Aaron Garcia!," and then right after, "The owner, the legend himself… Mr. Vince Neil!"

Vince put his cup down and proceeded to storm the field with his arms spread wide open, with his burnt bleached blonde hair waving behind his head and all. Probably the most exercise he'd gotten in years. When he reached the field, he went down the team line and hugged and high-fived the players. Once "Kickstart My Heart" ended, the Honor Guard took the field with Commissioner Scott Butera in tow. It was time to get serious.

At that point, both teams were standing on the field, helmets in hand, and Vince was escorted to the center of the field by two members of the Posse. When he got to where he was supposed to stand, he starts mimicking like he's reaching for a microphone that's not there and yells out, "Who has a microphone?"

Some dude walked up, nonchalantly handed Vince a microphone, and also handed him a game ball. Vince took the microphone, said, "Here we go," and then proceeded to butcher the shit out of our National Anthem in a way that no other person could hopefully ever achieve. Holy shit was it bad. It was so bad it couldn't be … more bad. Immediately at "Oh say can you see" I was like, damn that's horrible. It was so bad I had to drop my head as he continued. I'm serious. I couldn't even look at him.

It made chills run down my spine and it felt like my skin was melting off my body. It was like a nuclear cloud that just kept growing and getting worse by the minute. He continued to sing on, seemingly not even *trying* to make it sound good and … and … well, he had absolutely no shame to him with anything else, so, no shocker here.

When I tell you I was embarrassed, I was embarrassed to the point where I felt like my shoes were frozen to the turf, like I was frozen in time. *That* kind of embarrassed. As I raised my eyes and looked around, I saw everyone, and I mean fucking *everyone*, with this shocked look of OMFG written all over their faces. Every person there was stunned. It was so bad that I thought about tackling him, like in a movie, and then have someone yell, "Cut!" and turn the fiasco into a staged joke for opening day kind of thing.

The saddest thing of all is that Vince thought he did a great job. I'm not kidding. He really thought that. He had no perception that it was as bad as it was, but, you know, when you're shitfaced, everything is good, right? So, I guess that means everything must sound good, too.

The Posse was standing behind him on the field, forcing smiles and trying not to react in the way they really wanted to react. Poor girls. Imagine having to stand there and having to pretend that what was happening was so good, so cool, so well done. Yay, go team!

After what seemed an eternity and he finished singing, he was like "Yeah," raised the ball up in the air, and then yelled, "Let's go!"

I was like, holy shit that was reality. That really happened. I just had my very own personal *This is Spinal Tap* moment. Right there in front of a festival crowd. I just witnessed, first-hand, what had to have been the worst performance of our country's national anthem ever performed, and it was performed by my partner, the one and only, Mr. Vince Fucking Neil.

Rosanne Barr's version may have been distasteful, but Vince's version was disgraceful. Roseanne may have gone to 10, but Vince went to 11. A negative 11. Not surprisingly and rightfully so, the media crucified him the next day. Absolutely merciless, too. At the end of the day, the sad thing was that none of them were wrong. See for yourself some of the headlines:

- The San Diego Union-Tribune - "Vince Neil 'sings' the national Anthem and kills it, really

- Deadspin – Watch Vince Neil Coke-Fart All Over the National Anthem

- The Daily Dot – Vince Neil of Motley Crue butchered the national anthem at the Las Vegas Outlaws' First-Ever Game

- CBS News – Watch Motley Crue's Vince Neil's head-scratching performance of the National Anthem

- Dan Joseph - Vince Neil Absolutely Butchers the National Anthem

- CNN – Vince Neil Slays The National Anthem

Once the horror was over, Scott Butera took center field and gave Vince a ball as the new franchise owner of the Las Vegas Outlaws. Vince took the ball, raised it in the air with the biggest shit-eating grin on his face, totally unphased by his appalling performance.

Scott handed the microphone to Vince who yelled, "Thank you guys so much! It's game time, so let's go!" He then walked off the field.

I was like, what a fucking tool. More like a wanker. He sure wasn't any Duke Fame selling out the "big" arena. (*Personal shout out to Paul Shortino, a friend of both writers who was the actual Duke Fame! Paul's wife, Carmen, told Christine one night when they were drinking wine that the outfit Paul is wearing in the movie was what he was really wearing that day … he went to the audition in it! No wonder he got the role! Classic!!!)*

CBS Sports covered the game and soon after the coverage began, my phone started blowing up with texts, screenshots, photos, Facebook tags, all showing me on TV, sitting there in the front row. Me. One of the owners. On a side note, that grey suit really did look fucking nice. It was a remarkable feeling knowing that my friends back home were watching and that they were all there with me in spirit, supporting me, cheering me on, wishing me success.

The ball kicked off and all the hard work, the extreme bullshit, and the continual highs and lows that went along with it, the end goal still became real. It was real. No matter how distant I felt from it all in the past, it was here, and it was real. We were all there, and the team was on the field. The game moved fast, and I was captivated by it. From bouncing off the walls of the field to the head-to-head contact to the full speed of the game, it was an impressive game. This was a very cool exposure to my first arena football game.

I sat next to Dana Strum and his wife, my brother was next to me, and Bobby was sitting behind us. Dana was the bassist for the band Slaughter, he was also the bassist for Vince's solo band, and he was also Vince's financial controller, or so he told me. He shared a few outrageous stories with me during the game, but I'm going to keep those to myself out of respect for Dana. He was a pretty cool dude and for sure deserves that respect.

We sat on the front row at one end and Vince, Rain, Bob, and crew sat on the other end. You Sports Illustrated – Vince Neil sings strangely cavalier National Anthem won't believe this, but Vince was shitfaced and at one moment during the game, he got really excited and almost fell over his seat, which would have promptly landed his soused ass on the field. It was one of those roll-your-eyes-yet-have-to-laugh moments. There wasn't anything you could do about it, so you just had to let him be him, hope for the best, and laugh when it was funny. Life is too damned short. The least you can do is laugh when shit is funny.

***

The Halftime Show was pretty cool with Zowie Bowie performing with Lydia Ansel and the girls from a new local show, SEXXY, were there doing their thing (** *Personal shout out to Zowie Bowie, Lydia Ansel, and Jennifer Romas from Christine!***). Everyone all put on a great show and the fans genuinely seemed to enjoy it. During halftime, Vince went to the press box for an interview with the CBS Sports crew.

Though I didn't hear the interview, my sister-in-law called me like a 911 dispatcher and said, "Britt, someone better get up there and take the microphone away from him – he's barely making sense, he's so drunk!"

I just had to shake my head, laugh, and tell her that's how he always sounds. Next thing you know, the Outlaws had fallen behind and were down 28-0 in the second quarter. The San Jose SaberCats were the 2015 AFL Champions, so needless to say, they were good. Our quarterback, JJ Raterink, scored our first touchdown and by halftime, we trailed 35-13. We came out hot in the second half and actually outscored the SaberCats 28-24 but ended up losing the game 59-41.

Even though we didn't get a W on our record for the first game, we sure as hell got a damned W for just kicking off the ball. The fans really got into the game, and it was endearing to witness, it really was. We needed those fans to survive the season, and it was pretty fucking awesome to see fans wearing our team's Outlaw gear.

When the game was over, we all went onto the field and were joined by some of the more zealous fans. The AFL permitted this type of interaction, and it was cool to see the fans, especially the kids, interact with the players and take pictures with them, enjoy the moment together. Well, ya, okay, for me it was nice to take pictures with all of them, too.

At first, it was weird to have people come up and ask if they could take a picture with me. I didn't know how to act, but I just smiled, shook a lot of hands, and went with the flow. This type of interaction would become the norm after every home game. Did I get better at it? Ya, I think so, even for nothing more than something becoming a routine and more familiar to you as you go along.

As we all made our way off the field to exit the arena, it finally happened. Right there in the tunnel. The alcoholic bomb was about to explode. There he is in all his douchey glory, three sheets to the wind Vince, throwing his customary temper tantrum, front stage and center, right there in front of everyone and anyone who happened to be standing there in time for the show. He was pissed off because Rain was doing the responsible thing and trying to convince him not to drive, and she was forcibly trying to take the keys away from the dumbass. He was just being his usual, drunk, self-centered asshole, not-caring-at-all-about-anything-going-on-around-him self. This was our opening fucking night, and here's a crowd of people witnessing an "owner" being an enraged, deranged, inebriated, out-of-control loser.

Bobby and I were standing right there, joined by referees, arena and Outlaws staff, CBS staff and crew, and all kinds of other press members and fans Vince had that time-honored demented look in his eye, the one I have seen too many times, and he was cussing, stomping, and just downright making a scene and a complete ass of himself. When the little boy tired of throwing his pissy fit antics and realized he wasn't going to get his way, I remember him sitting on the curb, pouting and scowling.

It took a village effort of Rain and several of us to convince him to let Rain drive him home and to chill the fuck out while there were so many onlookers. The last thing we needed was for his negative behavior to hit the press before anything positive hit about the opening night. It would totally derail anything positive or optimistic about the team and we didn't need that. Not a good starting point for our fan base, especially since we lost the game to a less than sellout crowd

We somehow got the little fucker in the passenger seat of his car and as Rain started to back up, you could see the ungrateful piece of shit just raging at her in the car. I felt sorry for Rain because I've been there. There was nothing anyone could do about Vince just being a drunken idiot and a spoiled rotten douchebag. Nothing. Nothing in this world would ever change that aspect of him, not even a special night like tonight. This night meant nothing more to him than just another alcohol-laced evening.

As troubling as it was for me to have to witness this and stay focused, I managed to look beyond it just enough to see some positive, once-in-a-lifetime moments of the evening. Vince's erratic behavior truly left a huge grey cloud of uncertainty over our future together. As far as I knew at that time, the team was real, we had one game under our belt, and everything was moving forward according to plan. How unfortunate it didn't work out that way.

# THE SEASON

## CHAPTER 13

**A**s the season moved on, the tensions rose, relationships dismantled, trust barriers broke, friendships ended, and chaos became the norm as everything spiraled out of control, and I mean fast.

On April 4, 2015, we won our second game at home against the Arizona Rattlers 70-53 in front of 3,227 fans. Way below our expectations and embarrassing to me to see so many empty red seats. The win was super exciting for everyone and being 1-1 gave us some momentum going to LA to play our rivals the LA KISS the following week on April 11 at the Honda Center in LA. I did not make the road trip by choice, as a matter of fact, I did not make any of the road games. Vince was playing a solo gig on April 11th in Tyler, Texas which was 30 minutes from where I grew up in Longview, Texas. So, I made the trip home to see Vince play at the Oil Palace. A lot of friends in the area were planning to be in attendance, also.

Vince knew I was going to be there as we had discussed it a few weeks prior, and I told him that I was going to bring my grandpa. I was super pumped.

The day of the show, Vince texted me, "Hey bro, I'll be in Tyler around 9 pm tonight."

My reply was, "Sounds good, bro. See you there."

Vince replied, "Cool."

Kelle called me that afternoon and said that Vince was sitting by the Ritz Carlton pool in Dallas and that he and Rain were taking a limo down and would arrive prior to showtime. I told him I looked forward to it and would see him there.

I had asked for side stage access with a chair for my grandpa and a couple of days before the show, Kelle gave me Dana Strum's contact information as he was in the know because Kelle filled him in. Kelle said Dana would make sure that my grandpa and I are set and to contact him if we needed anything, and they would make sure that our tickets would be at will call for pickup at the venue. Dana played bass in Slaughter and was Vince's bass guitar player in his solo band. From what I was told, Dana ran the show and managed the band's tour schedule, the finances, etc. I had met Dana at our home opener, actually sat next to him at the game, and we shared quite a bit of back-and-forth conversation. He seemed like a pretty cool, genuine guy.

That afternoon, a few hours before showtime, my grandpa and I met up with my cousins and over 30 friends at a local bar just down from the Oil Palace for dinner and drinks. My grandpa was in his 80s and he was so excited to go to this show and meet Vince. He had heard a lot about Vince over the years and this was going to be his very first rock concert he ever attended. I was so pumped to be taking him; what a rare opportunity to be given in life.

While we were all at the restaurant, we took a group picture with my grandpa front and center surrounded by everyone. I texted Kelle and asked her whether it was cool or not to send that pic to Vince because of all the damned tension that was around. When she didn't reply right away, I sent it to him anyway.

When she did reply, she recommended sending it after the show in case he assumed that I wanted him to meet all those people. "If you do that, you risk him totally ignoring *you* and the fact that you are even there."

So I then texted Vince, "Hey Bro. My 86 yr old grandpa, family, and peeps are pumped!"

Vince replied to me immediately. "Very cool!!" So I guess there was no harm done there. This time.

Everyone was excited about the show, and it was cool to have the connection I did with Vince, but it wasn't without its struggles. When I got to the show, I went to grab my tickets, opened the envelope and immediately realized that some things were missing, in a big fucking way. There weren't any wristbands, there were no side stage access passes, etc., there were just tickets to the show, of which they were even one short on those. I had been texting back and forth with Kelle and I told her they were a ticket short, but the lady at will call made it right somehow. We didn't get any passes, but the tickets were for the second row and we were grateful for that on its own.

When Kelle did reply, she was like "Hmmmmm….Interesting. Something must be going on behind the scenes. Dana rarely makes mistakes. He is clearly preoccupied. But the second row is great. You guys got the family seats (even taking over other bands' tickets). No passes is about VN. Wait for him to get there. Text Dana about 930 to see if Grandpa can get a quick photo with VN."

Everything worked out in the end. Kelle and I continued to communicate via text messages, trying to arrange for a meeting after the show so we could all get a picture by the bus and keep tabs on the Outlaws vs LA KISS game that was happening.

At this point, my grandpa was having the time of his life. He could barely see or stand due to his age and blindness in one eye, and he almost fell when we were walking in the arena, but he was enjoying himself. He was drinking beer and grinning ear to ear. I know he had no fucking clue what he was listening to, but I know he was happy just to be there with me, be there in that moment. This was a very special moment for both of us. As I stopped and looked over at him, I blocked out the music and said to myself, *That's my grandpa, and I sure do love him.*

To be honest, I was trying to hide the BS from everyone, that I was hiding some embarrassment and feeling quite upset. I feared what was taking place behind the scenes because my grandpa was staying up way late past his bedtime. Fingers crossed. I got the text telling me to "get situated," which meant I had to go speak to an usher near the backstage and charm the pants off of him to allow my elder grandpa and me to get backstage, to get a picture, and without the passes, we needed to get there. Awesome. To get that photo would be priceless, but my grandpa moved slowly, okay? And Vince was always so damned impatient. Honest to God, it was nerve-wracking.

After a few more texts, with Vince involved in some of them, and after no replies, we left it alone. Prior to the show starting, I had texted Vince and said, "Bro, we are kicking the shit out of KISS!" I didn't get a response,

but during the show, I made my way up to the stage for a few songs while my cousins sat with my grandpa.

While up there, I heard Vince asking, "Where's Britt? The Las Vegas Outlaws just kicked KISS' ass!" He then saw me, made his way over to me, reached down, grabbed my hand, and it endorsed our mutual victory that day.

After the show, I texted Vince to give one final shot at getting a pic with my grandpa. When all I heard were crickets, I couldn't hide behind the fake smile on my face. I was devastated to look so stupid in front of my grandpa, but he said he didn't care. He told me that he had the time of his life and that he was proud to be with me. Those are the memories that fill your heart, and they did mine.

But I couldn't just let go of what went down, and how it went down. It was clear to me that something happened. Something *had to* have happened to derail that night.

Once back in Vegas, I found out that Bob saw my post on Facebook, the one with the pre-concert picture of me, my family, and friends in it. My post stated: "Vince Neil concert pre-party with my 86yr old grandpa, family, and friends from East Texas! Nothing like being back home! We are ready to Rock-n-Roll."

So, cock block Bobby Boy took a screenshot of that, immediately sent it to Vince, and made it appear that I was expecting VN to meet all of those people in that photo. All of them. Like, give that entire group individual attention. Basically, Bob derailed the whole thing on purpose. And that, my friends, is the kind of shit I dealt with on a daily basis with these fucking clowns.

We may have beat the LA KISS 61-48 in front of 8,565 fans in LA, but we lost to the Jacksonville Sharks two weeks later on the road, right after a bye week 60-28 and in front of 9,682 fans.

May 4th was our next home game and it was a big one as the LA KISS were coming to Las Vegas. It was going to be a Monday game, and everyone was pumped. We had high hopes of packing the Thomas & Mack Arena with fans. It was the ultimate match-up as Motley Crue meets KISS in a deathmatch in Vegas, and it was rumored that Gene Simmons, Paul Stanley, and Doc McGhee were going to be present. Fuck ya, that's good press!

My mom and Bobby flew out for the game and I was so excited to see them. At this time, I was seeing a Playboy model off and on and I was worried about what mom would think about her because even I had certain feelings about it. I always thought it would be cool dating a Playboy model, but that depends. Think about how you would feel if all your friends, and I mean *all of them*, can Google your chick and see all her goods. Weird, right? I understand the rare chances in life that allow you to date a model that once appeared on the cover of Playboy Magazine, but it weirded me out a bit.

Funny, because mom liked her, but in all fairness, I don't think that I told her she was a Playboy bunny. I think I just told her she was a girl I was talking to at the time.

When we arrived at the arena, I had to once again sweat the fact that I may, or may not, have the tickets I needed for my guests. Crazy, right? Every fucking time. By now, I had already been told that Vince didn't want me in his section because *his* section was reserved for special VIP/celebrity guests only. I didn't give a shit, and I took the entire front row of the section instead. Hell, that location was better anyways because it sat right at midfield. Fuck him and his section.

As I walked down the ramp into the Thomas & Mack Arena, there stood my good friend Johnny O'Donnell, who we called JOD. Johnny is and remains a good friend today, and he is known as the "Mayor of Vegas" because everyone knows him. JOD was once voted the #1 bartender in all of Las Vegas, so that is definitely a boost for a person's popularity.

He was there with Steve Levy from ESPN who the last time I saw was at the Red Rock Casino involving an altercation that Bob created at the blackjack table. Ah, Vegas. Steve was a cool cat and we all three took a picture together with some high fives. Not going to lie, this being an owner thing was pretty cool some of the time.

Kelle and Dave came, and we all hung out before the game in our spot, which was the tunnel area behind the endzone. Carrot Top was also there, and he and mom took a picture together. JB Bernstein was present, and I introduced mom to him, and she thought he was cool as the movie the Million Dollar Arm was about him.

Bob had invited his old college coach and former Denver Broncos head coach Mike Shanahan, with who I met and took a picture. He was a cool man and it was an honor to have met him. Roy Jones, Jr., was also in the house, and I had the pleasure of meeting and taking a picture with him after the game. Mom reacquainted with Vince and they took a picture and exchanged their "hellos" to each other. Vince was always nice to my mom, always, and I think he genuinely liked her, as well. Things were moving along nicely.

Before the game, the press was on the field with Vince, Paul Stanley, and Gene Simmons. There were some cameras and a microphone with a member of the press asking questions and building up the rivalry between the Outlaws and KISS. Gene had this trophy in his hand which was of a gold football helmet that had KISS on one side and the Outlaws on the other. The owner of the Dollar Loan Center, a sponsor of both teams, had created this trophy. The winner would take it home with bragging rights.

I walked over to Gene, extended my right hand for a handshake, and introduced myself as Britt Amsler, one of the owners of the Outlaws. Gene said he didn't shake hands due to germs but gave me and knuckle-to-knuckle shake instead. Fine by me.

He said, "We are going to kick your ass tonight."

I said "I doubt that. We are going to kick your ass and take that trophy home with us."

We laughed and took several pictures together of both of us holding the trophy. He was a cool dude and he even took a couple of pictures with my mom. That was a very cool moment. Growing up my whole life as a KISS fan and my mom telling me in Jr. High that I could not go see KISS in concert to talking a little smack a few decades later with Gene as a rival while taking pictures with him and my mom. Pretty cool if you ask me.

It was game time and to our seats, we went. All my guests were present as the game started. During the game, I looked across the arena and saw Gene, Paul, and Doc all sitting together. They carried themselves with such character and respect and then I looked to my left in the section over from me and there was Vince in train wreck mode. Several times during the game, I saw Gene, Paul, and Doc many times interacting with our fans while our leader was there getting shitfaced in the stands, drinking from a fucking blue plastic Solo cup. Interacting with the fans was totally out of the question for Vince.

I often wondered what was going through Gene, Paul, and Doc's mind looking over across the field at Vince seeing him in the sloppy state he was in all the time. Here you have total opposites with those guys exuding class and respect, and our leader acting like a train ready to derail at any given moment. I was totally embarrassed and maybe, just maybe, that's one of the reasons why we only had 2,542 fans at the game. Maybe.

Our attendance was just fucking awful, and we were sinking. While out on the road, other teams were normally pulling in 8,000 to 9000 fans per game, but here in Vegas, we could only get 2,542 to come out and see us play the LA KISS. I knew we were doomed. I knew it was a shit show that wasn't going to get any better any time soon.

Over the next five weeks, we lost every game and were at 3-7 overall. The drama was at an all-time high, and we were financially broke as an organization. We needed someone to either buy us out or we needed to find a partner with deep pockets to help us stay afloat. At this point, I didn't know who to trust anymore because Mark Daniels was banned from the league by the commissioner, which to me was a bunch of bullshit. Sohrob and I became closer and as I got to know him more, I realized that he was a level-headed, cool, and smart man. It had all come full circle that Bob was the nucleus of all the bullshit within the organization. The man that constantly drank himself silly, moved from hotel to hotel like a gypsy, had no car, no home, and no real skin in the game. All he had was a few suitcases and a line of shit that would pave a road to California and back. Twice.

Players were now calling me, telling me that Bob would call or text them drunk in the middle of the night and leave them nasty messages threatening to not pay them and shit like that. He was a piece of work but let me tell you, the man's only claim to fame was that he was the starting QB for the Florida Gators back in the '80s. You would have thought he was Tom Brady by the way his ego carried him around Vegas, yet to the players, he was a fucking joke and they all laughed at him behind his back.

On May 23rd, we played the Spokane Shock at home. Bob called the week prior and asked if I knew of anybody local who could sing the National Anthem. Vince had this thing that all entertainment, including the National Anthem, had to be sung by local Vegas entertainers. As the season started, a high school friend and guitarist for Madonna hit me up and offered to play the National Anthem at one of our games. He even sent me two videos of him performing it, so I met with Vince and Bob to discuss it. Before I could show them Monty's videos, they both chuckled when I said he was Madonna's guitarist, and they blew it off. I had to keep my inner voices on the inside and not openly call them out on the goon dick assholes they really were as people.

So, since my suggestion wasn't good enough for them, Bob still needed someone to sing the National Anthem since Vince was out on the road with Motley. I asked my friend Paul Shortino if he was interested, and he told me that he would love to do it. I walked out onto the field with Paul,

I stepped to the sideline, he stood at midfield, and he absolutely nailed it. I mean, nailed it. He had the fans roaring when he was done, and for the rest of that season, no one else even came close to performing it as well as Paul did. I had to shoot Bob a glance that just said, "Fuck you, cock sucker," without having to utter a damned word.

Once off the field, we were all sitting in the stands together in the front row having fun and enjoying the game when, all of a sudden, we saw this little kid walking towards us with a game ball and a Sharpie in his hands. Apparently, he had just caught the ball in the stands and when he got to me, he stuck the ball and the Sharpie out and said, "Can I have your autograph?"

I wasn't expecting that, so I asked the little guy if he was sure it was me he wanted the autograph from.

He said, "Yes, Sir. I know who you are."

I asked him if he wanted autographs from the other two guys that were there because they were rock stars, and when he told me that he only wanted mine it was a moment that I will never forget. Ever. I mean, here I am, sitting next to two rock stars and this kid wants *my* autograph. I signed his ball, gave it back to him, and watched him run off, all happy and shit.

From that moment on, a few autographs were given and a few photos with fans were taken. After every game, we would let the fans take over the field and interact with all the players, coaches, Posse Cheerleaders, and of course, the owners.

One particular night after a game, I was standing by Vince, Mark, and Bob and three chicks walked up and asked if they could take a picture with me. The four of us grouped arm and arm and I said, "Thank you for coming."

The one girl said, "As long as you are here, we'll keep coming."

Hellyeah! Boom Bam! The best part was that they walked away without asking the other guys for a photo. You should have seen the look on the faces of Bob and Vince. It was priceless, truly priceless, and I laughed my ass off on the inside. It got even better when it went to another level where girls threw themselves at me on a couple of occasions. I was like the rock star, and you know what happens next.

***

So, back to that Playboy chick who I won't call out by name but will say that her ex was the drummer from One Republic. Anyhow, I met her in Reno at a liquor trade show. Her booth was next to mine and she was representing some tequila I had never heard of before. She was a tall, pretty brunette and I remember she had on tight-ass red pants. Unfortunately, she also wore a ton of makeup, which I had to overlook as I am not a fan of makeup, but I was determined to get to know her, nonetheless.

I started flirting with her during the trade show, and the next thing you know, I am buying a Harley Davidson sweatshirt at the casino because it was nighttime and chilly as shit outside. We walked over to the baseball field to catch the minor league game and grab a drink.

The next thing I know, I'm booking her a flight from Denver to Vegas for the following weekend. Now, I didn't know much about her, but she seemed like a cool chick and a person that I would genuinely like to get to know better.

The next weekend came, and when I went to pick her up at the airport, I have to admit I was kind of nervous to see her but still looking forward to a fun weekend. We were low-key the first night because the next day was Game Day, May 23rd. She seemed to have fun at the game, she got the chance to meet several of the players, and she seemed to enjoy being with Paul, Carmen, Doug, and Daniela. It got me thinking that maybe this could all go somewhere.

After the game, we left with Kelle and Dave and hit up some Italian restaurant for dinner and drinks. Afterward, Kelle, and Dave and I wanted to go have a drink at Red Rock Casino, but Miss Bunny's mood immediately switched. She turned into this… this … rigged stick in the mud to the point it was downright awkward.

Instead of going out to the casino, I went with her back to her place. I could tell by her body language and choice of words that the night was about to take a hard, sharp, shitty left turn. She was still not happy into the next day, so when I asked her what the issue was, she told me she had doubts about dating me. When further questioned, she told me that she was afraid of my "lifestyle" and started comparing me to her ex and how I like to drink and go out and party, yaddah yaddah yaddah.

She even went so far as to pull up a video from TMZ on her phone where TMZ interviewed her after her ex roughed her up and tore up their house. My first reaction to the video was *Who the hell is this blonde chick?* until I realized it was her I was looking at. When I asked her why she changed her hair she came back with how she's trying to hide her identity, put her past behind her, blah blah blah. The only thing I heard was *Warning: this chick has issues*, and it brought back so many memories from the past. The only difference with *this* chick is that she didn't need alcohol to flip her Jekyll/Hyde switch.

Nope. Once she started crying, I knew it was time to get the fuck out of there. I wasn't staying on that derailing train until it left the tracks. No, thanks. As she was packing her bags and still crying, her makeup was wearing off, and I saw exactly why she had to wear so much of it. Good Lord. I kept my cool, but honestly, I couldn't get her into the fucking car fast enough.

As we pulled into the airport drop-off area, I helped her out of the car, hugged her as I uttered some nice words that encompassed "It's better this way" or some shit, and I sent her on her way home. That's it. Nightmare prevented this time, thank you, God.

***

On June 3, 2015, I received a call from Mark (even though Mark was banned, he was still working his tail off to try and save this team), and he asked me for a favor. He was in Florida and the team was in serious trouble. We had until the end of the business day, *that day*, to pay two bills or the team wouldn't be able to play that weekend. It seemed that we owed the travel agent $9,261.00 for the team's flights on SW Airlines, and we also owed the Thomas & Mack Center a whopping $14,237.17.

Sohrob was done funding the team after already investing over $1 million into it. He had also grown tired of these clowns, so the only hope was to pay these bills and breathe another week's worth of life into the team. We needed to find a buyer or a partner who would inject cash, but it wasn't that simple. Mark told me that if I would handle these two invoices, he would make sure I would get the money wired back to me on Monday morning.

I knew it was a terrible mistake to do it, but I trusted Mark and I knew the only way to get my money back in full was to keep the team playing. Mark said Vince was very grateful to me for doing this and again assured me that I would be wired the money directly to my bank account come Monday morning. I only had about an hour to make it down to the Thomas and Mack Center before they closed so I stopped what I was doing and made my way there, which was about a 25-minute drive.

As I was driving, I paid the travel agent with my credit card and took care of that $9,261.00 detriment. When I arrived at the arena, I made my way to the offices and asked for Jim Sanders who was the Director of Merchandise & Senior Event Manager. As I pulled out my AMEX to pay the $14,237.17, he told me there would be a 4% credit card fee for using my credit card, which added an extra $569.49 to the tab, bringing the total bill to $14,806.66. My stomach was in a fucking knot because I didn't have an expendable $24,067.66 just laying around. I chose to continue to trust Mark even though Jim Sanders encouraged me not to pay with a credit card because he knew the stands were going to be empty. He told me I was wasting my money, and I told him to go ahead and run my credit card. I didn't know what else to do. I mean, we *had* to play that weekend.

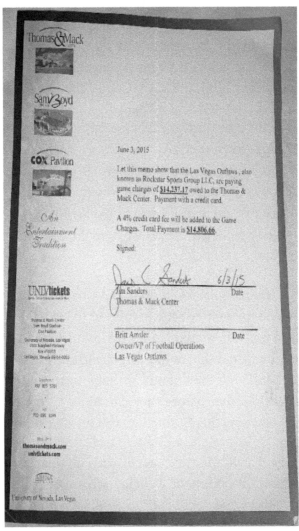

The next morning, I called my financial advisor to tell him what I did and that I needed to move $25,000 from my account with him into my Rockstar Investment Group account. I told him that I was going to be wired the money back on Monday and that we were close to making a deal and the plan would be for me to get my entire investment back and get the fuck out.

On June 4th, Sohrob sent out an email at 11:42 am to Bob, Mark, Vince, Chris & Cyrus (Sohrob's brother) and he copied the Commissioner. Sohrob had a deal on the table, a solution to hopefully stop the bleeding. He and Mark were working on a proposal to pay the League what we owed them so we could play the upcoming weekend. The new deal had Rockstar Investment Group (me, Bob, Vince, and Mark) owning 87.5%, Chris Salamone 5%, and Outlaws Investment Group (Farudi Brothers) with the terms that we had to pay $122,628.26 that day.

Mark replied that the deal structure presented did not work, but he was working the phones trying to find a path that will work.

On June 6th, Sohrob sent out an email at 1:51 am to Bob, Vince, Chris, Cyrus Farudi and included Bob's brother who was his attorney, and copied me, Mark, Commissioner Butera & Rahmeen Farudi stating that he and his brothers are no longer willing to fund the Outlaws. He stated that they had exceeded the obligation they made, funded $912,500.00 in cash, plus an additional $138,959.00 on the business AMEX, which is attached to his Social Security number, and that he is personally responsible to pay this bill. That now brought his total investment to $1,051,459.00.

Sohrob stated that over the last several months, his attempts to schedule board meetings to find a solution to the financial issues of the team have been ignored. In addition, he stated that his calls and texts to Vince and Bob have been for the most part unanswered, unreturned, and ignored. It was clear that without ever having a board meeting to make decisions and get board approval, there was no way we could successfully move this team forward. In his words:

"I sent out the full financial picture of the team to the board on April 14th, and since then have tried to schedule a board call many, many times to address the situation. Cyrus and I have made ourselves available and not one time have you all made yourselves available. As you are aware, on April 6th we received a notice from the league that we were in default. As of today, we have not cured that default and have fallen further behind in our payments and obligations to the league with a total amount past due of $332,567.49. The eviction process for our players and coaches will begin on the 11th of this month if we do not pay their rent. We will not be able to travel to next week's game if we don't pay for the tickets, which at this point, we do not have the money. We are in serious jeopardy of losing this team next week. I am sorry it has come to this point. I have worked tirelessly without pay for months to try and make this work. I can honestly say I have given this my all, and this decision to stop funding the team was not something I took lightly. I am never one to quit or give up, but you have left me with no other alternative. He closed with the game on Sunday will go on, but without a significant infusion of capital it will most likely be the last one we witness as owners of the Outlaws."

During that week, I got a phone call from Mark saying he spoke with our coach, Aaron Garcia. It was early in the morning when he called and said that per Aaron, Bob was supposed to be at practice that morning and give a speech to the team before practice, but he never made it.

Both Mark and I knew exactly why Bob didn't make it, but nevertheless, Mark asked me if I could go down and deliver the speech to the team after practice. I had a good relationship with the team even though I was a distant owner, but I knew the players were concerned about what was going on with the team. I had become close to three players and we had become good friends, two of which I remain close to still. Those folks would be known as our QB JJ Raterink, Tanner Varner, and Terrance Carter, the latter two who were both starters on defense.

JJ would share with me the inside scoop on team morale and even called me one day to tell me that eviction notices were being put on the front doors to the homes of the players. He even went as far as to tell me that many of the spouses of the players were getting really worried. They had no idea what was going to happen next, nowhere to immediately go if they got evicted from their homes, and they had every right to be worried about themselves and their kids. It was all so very fucking sad to me.

When I got to the field, practice was wrapping up, and it was a beautiful morning as the team took a knee in front of me. I was extremely honest with them and tried to give them some peace of mind by telling them that we were all in this together. I apologized on behalf of Bob that he couldn't be there, and I remember someone saying that he was probably still asleep from drinking the night before while everyone laughed.

I spoke about a potential new partner, some dude out of Cali that was wealthy and in the construction/real estate business. I told the team that he would be attending the game that week and that he had also just laid out a $50,000 deposit on a deal we hoped to close that week if all went well. Of course, I never saw that $50K, I was just merely told that this man made that down payment. The players genuinely seemed to appreciate me taking the time out to talk with them, and I got several high fives, handshakes, and "thank yous" as I walked away. Aaron came over to me, thanked me, and painfully reminded me how much we needed that deal to go down.

Even though we lost our game on June 7th, and even though that loss represented our fifth straight loss, and even though that loss of 63-44 to the Cleveland Gladiators hurt, the investor hopeful liked what he saw. By the grace of God, from what Bob told me after the game, this guy was in. Hellyeah!

We were all on our best behavior while he was around, but that façade was short-lived as the deal busted a mere two days later. Again, I was not present at that meeting, but I was told that Bob made the meeting a shit show and was arguing over percentage points to the point where this guy was like, "Fuck you guys, I'm out." Nice. Bob showed his ass again, and yet again, was nothing but a detriment to the team and everything he touched. This dumb motherfucker didn't have $1.00 invested in this team, yet he had the capability of fucking over every person who did. And that's when the emails of doom began.

On Tues June 9, 2015, at 2:20 pm, Jim Sanders sent out an email to all the owners and some folks from the arena league. It read, "Attached is the settlement packet for last Sunday's Outlaw game at the Thomas & Mack Center. The amount owed is $2,300.00 from the previous game. We have set a deadline of tomorrow for the payment process to be initiated. We do not want to set a hard deadline for next week as we did last game because that just got everyone in a frenzy and still with the exception of a credit card payment, no one showed any eagerness to step up and pay. I urge all ownership interests and league officials (if necessary) to convene and get all (not just the Thomas & Mack Center's) outstanding debts in order and plan accordingly for the rest of the season. Safe to say, we would also like this taken care of immediately to offset any future speculation of the franchise's health and long-term viability. Everyone knows that we are a public entity, part of the state of Nevada higher education group, we cannot take a loss to the unwillingness of event promoters to pay their contractually agreed to expenses. Thanks, Everyone."

At 6:40 pm we received an email from Michael Newcomb from UNLV asking Jim if there were any updates on payment.

At 6:48 pm, Bob replied, "Hi, Mike. Just got out of meetings in LA and saw this. It will be taken care of. Thanks, Bob."

Michael replied, "Thanks Bob… appreciate the response."

On Wed at 1:41 pm, Jim sent out an email to all the parties in the original email. "Greetings All. Will someone be coming by today to pay the TMC charges? An even better solution would be to start a wire transfer as the league did last week. The instructions are attached. Please let me know when the wire is initiated and what institution it is coming from. Everyone's mindset and attitude will be much better if this is taken care of now rather than later. Let's not get down to the final hour and risk the cancellation of games or the season. We know that you have the money so pony up! Thank you."

At 1:51 pm, Sohrob responded to Jim's email. "Jim, you guys we're days and days late on your payments to us for the first few games. Did I say anything about changing venues if you didn't pay by an arbitrary date? We are working on some things with the ownership group and would appreciate your patience and support as we get this done. This talk of canceling games or the season MUST stop. It is not helping anyone, and your support in the community instead of the swirling rumors that I have pretty good intelligence is being 'discussed' by T&M employees to people outside the organization, would do wonders for both of us moving forward. We will be in touch as we work through things today and tomorrow. Sohrob."

At 5:52 pm, Jim replied to Sohrob. "I know the first settlement took a little while to get money back to you but the second was much quicker. We have to utilize the University wire system and it sometimes takes longer than it should for that. I apologize. Since we have a quicker cost compilation system in place now, I'd like to think if this latest statement had money coming back your way it would be in your hands no later than tomorrow (Thursday) because I could have initiated the process on Tuesday for sure. We want to continue to support and partner with you and make this a successful season for all involved. This keeps everyone's dedication and morale at a peak. We will see what next week brings and good luck in Spokane this weekend."

On Saturday, June 13 at 2:01 am Jim sent out another email. Guys, congratulations on the big win in Spokane. Third place in the western conference with 7 games to play is very impressive for a first-year team.

I must admit I didn't know the game was tonight and I was working the circus. I've got to consult the game schedule more often. Really thought the game was tomorrow for some reason. Well, big win, and hopefully our fans were watching! Take care."

At 4:13 am that same night that Jim sent out that email. Bob replied. "Thx Jim! If we get in the tournament.... we will win it! Bob. Who the fuck is up at 4:13 am? Oh, that would be Bob!"

On Saturday at 9:18 am I replied, "Thanks, Jim. We needed that win and look to bring that momentum back to LV for a tough game next week. We appreciate your support!!"

On Monday, June 15 at 2:05 pm Jim sent out an email. "Gentlemen, I have to ask, any updates on payment status. Wednesday would be an ideal goal. Thanks."

At 3:11 pm, Jim Newcomb replied, "Can someone give us an update as to when payment will be made? Thank you."

On Tuesday, June 16, Jim sent out another email. "Hello, All. The deadline for the payment of the outstanding TMC bill from the last game is this Thursday, June 18th. We strongly encourage a wire transfer as opposed to credit card payment – the fee/cost of wire is hundreds less. Just shoot me back an email when the wire is on its way. This week's game will be canceled if no payment is received. Attached you will find all the info once again. Thank you."

At 2:12 pm Bob replied right back. "Thanks, Jim. We will take care of it."

At 2:20 Michael Newcomb replied to Bob, "Thanks for the response.... much appreciated. The lack of ticket sales out for this Saturday's game is concerning…is there any plan to increase the crowd? Thanks."

On Thursday, June 18th at 1:35 pm, Michael sent out an email to Jim. "The UNLV SI guys that handle stats have not been paid for a few games, so they need to get taken care of too or they won't work Sunday."

At 1:39 pm, Jim replied right back saying, "OK, good to know. I've copied them here. How much are they owed and how much a game do they receive? We will try to get them paid in advance for the next game."

At 1:51 pm Michael replied. "It's not a matter of trying to get them paid prior to the next game…they need to be paid in full for the outstanding games and prepaid for Sunday or there will be no stats…same as what we are looking for."

At 1:55 pm Christine, who is the AFL Executive VP, replied, "Our understanding is that they are paid $300 per game and are currently owed for the Outlaw home games on 5/23 and 6/7. Please confirm that the total amount for the stat crew is $900 ($300 per game on 5/23, 6/7 & 6/21). Thanks."

On a separate email chain, an email was sent out on June 15th at 5:05 pm from Wesley Friedman who is the AFL Corporate Council. A letter of termination of membership interest – Rockstar Sports Group, LLC.

Mr. Farudi:

The league recently received your e-mail (attached hereto) which explicitly states Rockstar Sports Group Inc's ("RSG") inability to fund the Las Vegas Outlaws Arena Football team ("Team") moving forward. As you are aware, violations of Section 15.2 (b) of the Arena Football One, LLC Limited Liability Company Agreement ("LLC Agreement") allow for automatic termination of a team if: "such member fails or refuses to organize and field a team to play in any scheduled League season."

It has come to our immediate attention that you have failed to pay the Thomas Mack Center in order to field a team to play this weekend's game (6/21/15). Furthermore, you have failed to pay Citi Lights Apartments for housing costs for team players and if payment is not made by tomorrow at noon Central Standard time, Citi Team Apartments will file for eviction of team players (see attached).

Please be advised that you have until tomorrow (6/16/15) at 11 am CT to pay all of your obligations in order to field a team to play this weekend. If payment is not made by that time, RSG's membership interest in Arena Football One, LLC (AF One") will be thereby terminated and the right to operate the team will revert back to the AF One as pursuant to Section 8.1 (d) of the membership agreement.

In addition, RSG has failed to pay its league assessments and fees in accordance with the deadlines established by the Board of Directors and subsequently, as of today's date currently owes $551,838.07 to the league. Irrespective of RSG's termination as a member, all financial obligations of RSG are immediately due and owing. It is your responsibility to make arrangements to promptly pay the outstanding amount immediately. Failure to pay the entire outstanding amount may lead to legal action against RSG and each of its members. Accordingly, the Board of Directors has granted RSG until tomorrow (6/16/15) at 11am CT to cover the existing liabilities and present a plan to ensure funding of the team moving forward. Regards, Wesley Friedman.

On June 16, 2015, an email addressed from Noble Park Manager went out to Mr. Wesley stating that the deadline has now passed and the rent is still delinquent. All 3 properties including Citi Lights, Sterling Summerland, and Noble Park will now begin the eviction process.

That led to an email from Wesley at 5:23 pm that said see attached termination notice. Sincerely Wesley Friedman.

At 5:51 pm the Commissioner sent out an email to all the owners. Gentlemen, as the current operator of the Las Vegas Outlaws team the league is now inquiring into whether there is interest, either as a group, by an individual, or any combination thereof, to fund and operate the

Outlaws team moving forward The league welcomes all offers and if interested please submit a proposal or term sheet to the league as soon as practicable. Best Regards Scott.

That is it. It's over. It's done. It's over, and it's done. The madness and shit show is now a bona fide reality. Yep. All of my hard-earned money was gone. Everything that I worked so hard for over so many years to attain was gone. Poof! Gone in a New York minute. I was devastated. Shattered. Flattened. Numb. I was … done.

Later that week, I emailed Scott Butera and asked him if he was cool with me coming out to the game on Sunday, 11 am June 21st to show moral support to the team. It was weird not sitting up in the stands and just hanging back at the end of the tunnel, at the back of the endzone. Bob and Vince made their entrance and we didn't even speak to each other. Quite frankly, we had nothing to say to each other. They sat in their normal seats and acted like nothing at all had happened, drinking, high-fiving, and celebrating a big play throughout the game.

I was mortified by their behavior. Even the players were like WTF are these two morons doing? A couple of players came over to me during the game and asked me why the two jackasses were even there and how they could be acting like nothing happened. It was so crude and disrespectful of those two, even for them. Here are these poor fucking families whose lives had been horrifically disrupted by their actions over the past few weeks, let alone all the drama that has built up over the season. I apologized for their behavior while it made me sick to my stomach to do so. And as the Outlaws lost the game to San Jose, 31-63, that "we" connection with those individuals dissipated as quickly as the team.

I went home after the game and couldn't believe what I had just witnessed. It was hard to digest that all my savings were gone, let alone we let all of the players, the staff, and all of their families down, as well. I was so bothered by it that I decided to send an email to Vince, Bob, Mark &

Chris, directly aimed at Bob and Vince's behavior from the day before at the game.

On Jun 22, 2015, I wrote:

*Gents,*

*I just wanted to share with you the perception the team has of our ownership group.*

*Yesterday I watched the game from the players' area and throughout the game, several players and a coach made comments regarding the current situation of the team. I thought you might like to know.*

> *\* This is a professional team, when are you guys going to get your shit together.*
>
> *\* I have a wife and two kids. We had an eviction notice on our door last week with 24 hrs to be out. My wife yelled at me, cried, and is worried about our living situation. What do we do, sleep outside?*
>
> *\* I thought you guys were better than this*
>
> *\* The league is charging us for our apartments now by taking it out of our weekly paychecks. I can barely pay my bills and support my family as it is.*
>
> *\* Who is in charge? Vince or Sohrob?*
>
> *\* You guys say things but don't follow through.*
>
> *\* Are we going to finish the season?*

*This is heartfelt and I am embarrassed. I apologized to each person on our behalf. The players/coaches trusted us to get it right. Instead, we mismanaged this team/organization and let them down. As everyone in this group knows, the league has taken the team as of Tuesday and everyone that put in their hard-earned money looks to have lost it.*

*Yesterday during the game, the players were watching as celebrations, high fives, etc were going on in the stands from members of our group. Their morale is down and I witnessed firsthand. We as a group look silly and should all be embarrassed.*

*Bob, I would appreciate it if you would not call or text me in the middle of the night as you did again last night. It's annoying, to say the least. If you would go to bed, like most people do at night, you would be able to operate as most business folks during the business hours of 9-5. You are grown-ass man. Act like it!*

*Thank you,*

*Britt*

I only got one reply which was from Bob as a reply to all -

*Quit being a girl, Britt. We all are fine, and our team is paid, professional athletes. They are paid to play.*

*Bob*

I was like, what a fucking douche! This heartless, piece of shit, jackoff, broke ass, gypsy fucking asshole will pay the price one day when he stands before God.

That was the end of my association with the Las Vegas Outlaws and with Vince. The team and season were a total flop, and in the end, it was all just a big fucking joke. My bank account had nearly $275,000.00 when I moved to Vegas, and now I had nothing left. Nothing. It was gone. All of it. All gone.

Where did it go? To funding a couple of clowns and producing a total shit show, that's where. The pressure from the resulting failure was heavy, and it was coming from many different angles: the disappointed players, the folks from Thomas & Mack, the AFL, the City of Las Vegas, our vendors, our families, our friends. My life had become a dark room with no visible light. Not even the hope for it.

The failure continued to eat away at me over time, and I became very bitter, very vengeful. By the Grace of God, I knew enough, however, not to pursue that vengeance for there was no fucking way I wanted to have to pay for those actions with *those* consequences. I had paid enough.

| Week | Day | Date | Kickoff | Opponent | Results Score | Results Record | Location | Attendance | Report |
|---|---|---|---|---|---|---|---|---|---|
| 1 | Monday | March 30 | 7:30 p.m. PDT | San Jose SaberCats | L 41–59 | 0–1 | Thomas & Mack Center | 6,569 | [4] |
| 2 | Saturday | April 4 | 7:30 p.m. PDT | Arizona Rattlers | W 70–53 | 1–1 | Thomas & Mack Center | 3,327 | [5] |
| 3 | Saturday | April 11 | 7:00 p.m. PDT | at Los Angeles KISS | W 61–48 | 2–1 | Honda Center | 8,565 | |
| 4 | | | | | Bye | | | | |
| 5 | Friday | April 24 | 5:00 p.m. PDT | at Jacksonville Sharks | L 28–60 | 2–2 | Jacksonville Veterans Memorial Arena | 9,682 | [6] |
| 6 | Monday | May 4 | 7:30 p.m. PDT | Los Angeles KISS | W 49–16 | 3–2 | Thomas & Mack Center | 2,452 | [7] |
| 7 | Saturday | May 9 | 7:30 p.m. PDT | at San Jose SaberCats | L 28–61 | 3–3 | SAP Center at San Jose | 8,600 | |
| 8 | Saturday | May 16 | 6:00 p.m. PDT | at Arizona Rattlers | L 41–60 | 3–4 | Talking Stick Resort Arena | 10,130 | [8] |
| 9 | Saturday | May 23 | 7:30 p.m. PDT | Spokane Shock | L 56–63 | 3–5 | Thomas & Mack Center | 2,273 | [9] |
| 10 | Saturday | May 30 | 3:00 p.m. PDT | at Philadelphia Soul | L 43–51 | 3–6 | Boardwalk Hall[10] | 6,514 | [11] |
| 11 | Sunday | June 7 | 2:00 p.m. PDT | Cleveland Gladiators | L 44–63 | 3–7 | Thomas & Mack Center | 3,255 | [12] |
| 12 | Friday | June 12 | 7:00 p.m. PDT | at Spokane Shock | W 62–56 | 4–7 | Spokane Veterans Memorial Arena | 7,497 | [13] |
| 13 | Sunday | June 21 | 2:00 p.m. PDT | San Jose SaberCats | L 31–63 | 4–8 | Thomas & Mack Center | 2,166 | [14] |
| 14 | Sunday | June 28 | 2:00 p.m. PDT | Portland Thunder | W 48–46 | 5–8 | Thomas & Mack Center | 3,497 | [15] |
| 15 | | | | | Bye | | | | |
| 16 | Saturday | July 11 | 6:00 p.m. PDT | at Arizona Rattlers | L 43–57 | 5–9 | Talking Stick Resort Arena | 11,891 | [16] |
| 17 | Saturday | July 18 | 7:00 p.m. PDT | at Los Angeles KISS | L 27–37 | 5–10 | Honda Center | 7,635 | [17] |
| 18 | Saturday | July 25 | 7:30 p.m. PDT | New Orleans VooDoo | Game canceled.[18] Result considered a tie. | | | | |
| 19 | Saturday | August 1 | 7:00 p.m. PDT | at Portland Thunder | L 33–64 | 5–11–1 | Moda Center | 14,055 | [19] |
| 20 | Saturday | August 8 | 7:30 p.m. PDT | Spokane Shock | L 34–51 | 5–12–1 | Thomas & Mack Center | 2,166 | [20] |

Over July 4th weekend, I went to the Bay Area with Dave and Kelle. We had a blast and we all needed the getaway. Unfortunately, the majority of our conversations centered around Bob, Vince, and the Outlaws, and one afternoon, I started exchanging text messages with dear old Bobby Boy. And another shit show ensued.

iMessage
Today 5:13 PM

Lol. Talked to JMAC about u today.

Dude I could care less. Your words have no value. You are a fool, loser, liar, and a pussy! I usually feel sorry for people at your level but I don't for you. Pigs always roll around in mud! Stay home where you belong on OPM = other people's money!

All good bro. Ur showing ur colors.

Later bro. See you at judgement day!

Ur a drunk mother ducker

Fucker

Why don't u send these comments to Vince?

Scared dude

All good bro.

U have no money. Jmac told me. That's why ur pissed

Why did u get involved with us. We t still going. U became an asshole.....

R

Only place you are going is to HELL bro. We are all laughing at you right now. Lol
Btw - food stamp line is open Tuesday in Miami because Monday is a holiday.
See you at Judgement Day!

Ur an asshole

With no money

That's why ur pissed. JMAC td me u didn't have it

Vince said if u invest in anything there a chance it won't work. Call Vince. Fuck you bro!!

---

Why don't u send these comments to Vince?

Scared dude

U call me out...lets play. U should have never invested anything cash or I our input team. U don't have it as JMAC told me. We r buying the team back. Now u showed ur colors. Luv u Brit.

Lol. Such a coward. And FYI, I just talked to JMAC.
Let me repeat myself -
Dude I could care less. Your words have no value. You are a fool, loser, liar, and a pussy! I usually feel sorry for people at your level but I don't for you. Pigs always roll around in mud! Stay home where you belong on OPM = other people's money

All good bro.

U have no money. Jmac told me. That's why ur pissed

Vince said if u invest in anything there a chance it won't work. Call Vince. Fuck you bro!!

I'm going to send this to mom. U have issues ....
Only place you are going is to HELL bro. We are all laughing at you right now. Lol
Btw - food stamp line is open Tuesday in Miami because Monday is a holiday.
See you at Judgement Day!

Ur

Please do. My mom wants to e you for breakfast. Lol if you do have her number let me know I'll give it to you.

As JMAC told me.... U shouldn't have invested in our team.... Keep blaming me.....

blaming me.....

And we r buying it back....

You r obviously drunk again ......

Until u do something ... Fuck u again for calling me out....

Lol. As your brother once said you are the only person to live out 15 mins of fame. Lol

Play baseball for somebody. Fuck u asshole. Stop contacting me

JMAC told me about u

Fuck u!

Today,

Fuck u again ....

And .....again......

Ur an asshole for doing this ...::

Let's play. Fuck you mother fucker!

Ur on testosterone

Let's play. I'll sue ur ass....

Ur obviously out of cash. Jmac told me

When I see you again, which I will, we will see how brave you are

U r a Weak dude...please d Stop contacting me

I will sue u

Fuck u again ....

And .....again......

Ur an asshole for doing this ...::

Let's play. Fuck you mother fucker!

Ur on testosterone

Let's play. I'll sue ur ass....

Ur obviously out of cash. Jmac told me

When I see you again, which I will, we will see how brave you are

U r a Weak dude...please d Stop contacting me

I will sue u

👍
Delivered

Please stop contacting me

And there you have it. That was, I believe, the last time I ever communicated with Bob. Did you happen to notice all the poor grammar, punctuation, and tone? He was really brave now that he was back in Miami and confronting me via text, don't you think? He wouldn't dare say that to my face or text me while he was in Vegas.

One night at the Cosmopolitan Hotel not long before the team collapsed, Bob and I were sitting at a bar having a cocktail. I was trying to get Bob to understand that we needed to change our business mode immediately by using our office, and not a bar, as a place to set goals. I stressed that we needed to set short-term and long-term goals and that we needed major organization. I stressed the need for us to be successful and how we needed to have weekly meetings to talk about planning, working the city for investors, and doing it all with a sober mindset.

That set the alcoholic in him off like a hot potato. He told me that we did not need to change our business model, that everything was working just fine, and that I had no idea of what I was talking about.

I will never forget what happened next. He struck a nerve with me and I shot straight up like a bullet, looked right deep into his eyes, and said "Fuck you, Bob!"

He immediately jumped up with his eyes as big as pool balls, took off running with his arms and hands waving above his head, yelling, "I'm going to tell Vince! I'm going to tell Vince!"

He stopped right before he turned the corner, looked back at me, and started yelling again as he continued to run away like a little bitch. I sat back down at the bar, ordered a drink, and as I started to walk away with that drink, I got a text from Kelle asking me if I was okay. Apparently, Vince had just called her to tell her that "Britt is about to kill Bob."

Hey, at least those fucking liars got *one* thing correct. I told Kelle what happened, she laughed, and I laughed my ass off all the way home.

***

Months had gone by, and another football season rolled around. It was week one and I told Dave I was coming to the Redrock to meet him and of course I knew Vince would be there along with Dip Shit Johnny, who had now become Vince's right-hand bitch.

As I walked in, I saw Vince at a table so I walked over to him, extended by hand, and said hello to him. I laid down my Terrible Towel and my phone on the table, and he shook my hand back even though I could tell he was a bit startled to see me Didn't matter. I was there for one reason, and one reason only.

As I knew Bob was back in Florida, I wanted to take the opportunity to tell my side of the story. It had been a few months since I had spoken to Vince, and I admit, it was awkward leaving the table to go over to Starbucks, but I was determined to be heard. I needed to tell Vince that Bob was the core nucleus of all our problems. Dave knew that was my plan, and he supported it.

My plan was short-lived, though. Very short-lived. Next thing you know, I saw Johnny walking my way, holding my phone and my Terrible Towel. As he walked up to me he said, "I'm sorry bro, but Vince doesn't want you here today. Please go!"

Chicken shit little fuck. It was funny to me that Vincie Poo always had to send people like Bob or Johnny to do his dirty work. He was never a real fucking man and never handled anything directly.

My first instinct was to walk over to the table and confront the diminutive Mr. Neil as my blood started to flow and my adrenaline started to pump.

I started to walk over that way, towards the table with Johnny by my side, but something happened.

As I reached the point where I needed to turn in order for me to make my way over to the table, I swear something took over my body and wouldn't let me turn right. It was like this invisible force just took over my entire body and guided it, kept me walking straight out the door to the valet.

As I walked out that door, I looked over to my left and there was Vince's car, sitting there and oh-so-nicely parked right up front. As pissed off as I was, it was all I could do to stop myself from going back into that casino and body-slamming that little fuck right there on that table.

Instead, I took the high road, laughed, and reminded myself that a miserable piece of shit like that is *not* worth going to jail over. Instead, I went home, sat on my couch, and just replayed in my mind everything that had happened.

Two days later, I decided I just wasn't ready to let it go yet. No. He wasn't going to get off that fucking easy.

That was the last time Vince and I exchanged any type of communication with each other. When he sent that text back, I could just see him typing and hear it in his voice like a junior high kid would say "Loser" while waving his hand.

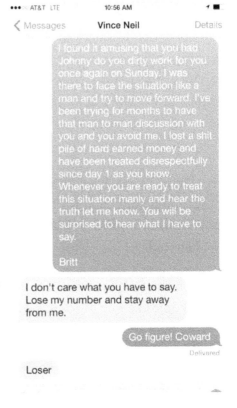

> •••○ AT&T LTE          10:56 AM          ◀ ■
> ‹ Messages          **Vince Neil**          Details
>
> I found it amusing that you had Johnny do you dirty work for you once again on Sunday. I was there to face the situation like a man and try to move forward. I've been trying for months to have that man to man discussion with you and you avoid me. I lost a shit pile of hard earned money and have been treated disrespectfully since day 1 as you know. Whenever you are ready to treat this situation manly and hear the truth let me know. You will be surprised to hear what I have to say.
>
> Britt
>
> I don't care what you have to say. Lose my number and stay away from me.
>
> Go figure! Coward
> Delivered
>
> Loser

I smirked and reminded myself that there was a time in my life where I actually wanted to be like this man. Shit. I wanted to *be* this man! And I wanted it so bad, that I had to learn an extremely valuable lesson. I had to realize, on my own, that my life is better than his, and I'm a happier, better person than he is. I Thank God for teaching me this valuable lesson, for this lesson has humbled me, made me a better man, and absolutely changed my life forever.

Every time I hear the word celebrity, I cringe now. I do. Every time I see someone on social media wanting to be known for "being famous," I'd love to be able to step in and tell them why they don't *really* want that. Take it from me, a private life that you can make your own is *way* better. Take it from me and stay in your own tree.

As I look back on this experience today, the bitterness is gone but the scars remain.

# MAKING CHANGES

## PART 7

# LEAVING LAS VEGAS

## CHAPTER 14

W hen it was all said and done, as the season was winding down, and when I had reached a point of utter mental exhaustion and financial ruin, I realized that my time in Las Vegas was going to be short-lived. What was once imagined as an incredible life experience was now a complete turn in the wrong direction with no U-turn option. What was done, was done, and I had to accept the fact that I allowed it to happen. The destruction was caused by my bad decisions, ill choices, and affiliating with too many of the *wrong people* in Las Vegas. Becoming entwined with the group behind the Outlaws shit show sealed my fate, and not in a positive way.

That December, the downfall started. I met up with Kelle and Dave for a drink at our favorite spot in Downtown Summerlin we had named the Wine Bar. It was a cool place, and, on many occasions, some cool folks met up with us there like Carrot Top, Vince, and Alice, Nick Cage's wife. This one particular night we were hanging out, Dave had to leave to go to band rehearsal so Kelle and I decided to stay and have a few more drinks and catch up. Kelle and Dave were like family, and I welcomed some one-on-one time with someone who had become like a sister to me.

With the crash of the Outlaws came the loss of all of my savings, a massive fallout with Vince, Bob, and Mark and the rest of the posse, and a crippling fear of an unknown, seemingly bleak future. I was completely on edge and felt like my entire life was falling apart. Stress and anxiety were at an all-time personal high, and the tension between those in that warped, dysfunctional inner group of people was growing at an alarming rate.

That night, the relationship between Kelle and me took an unforeseen sharp right turn, went off a cliff, and crashed and burned. Kelle and I were just chit-chatting along when, all of a sudden, our conversation turned sour. Part of that was my fault because I did have a negative attitude toward life. Out of respect for Kelle, that conversation will stay between us, but I will say she got extremely upset, said a few not-so-nice things to me, and out the door she went to walk home.

This was a final blow for me. I was totally taken off guard by her reaction, and by the time I paid the tab and went after her, she was nowhere to be found. I walked around the shops, in the parking lot, kept calling her, and then got in the car and looked around for her. No sign of her anywhere, nor was there any communication with her. I was in shock. Kelle was my closest friend in Vegas and I knew in my gut that our friendship was over. The thought made me sick to my stomach.

When I got home, the first thing I did was grab Lola, climb into bed, and cry. I laid there, reliving the moment, and telling myself that she was emotional and just overreacting. I kept searching for answers to justify how she reacted. Then I told myself to stop being an idiot and realize this was her way of maybe just cutting ties with me, to just accept it, and move on.

This is what my life in Vegas had become, a life of loss and betrayal on a somewhat grand scale. There weren't many people that I could trust as a friend, so this one really hurt. Kelle and I were tight-knit as friends, but I knew her loyalty would remain to Vince at all costs and above anyone else. Even though we spent a lot of time with each other, I look back on it now and I wonder if she was criticized and given a hard time by Vince for being my friend. It wouldn't surprise me. He seemed to be in competition with me when it came to everything else, so why wouldn't that also pertain to people?

As I laid there, torturing myself about what happened, I got a text message from Kelle. It was long, very harsh, and after I read it, I just left it at that. I was too damned tired and emotionally drained to respond and didn't trust myself to reply under those conditions.

The next morning, I woke up and before my feet hit the floor, my soul told me to "get out of Las Vegas and go the fuck home!"

I went down to my office, opened up my calendar, and circled March 13th, the day I would get my bonus check. I sat there in my chair, my thoughts spiraling, my emotions swirling, and drafted my resignation letter. My plan was to confirm that my bonus was deposited into my checking account and then simply send the email to my boss in New York, giving her my official two-week notice.

I had made my decision, and I wasn't looking back. There wasn't one good reason for me to stay in Las Vegas, but there were a thousand good reasons to leave it.

***

The next two and a half months encompassed some of the darkest days of my life. I only had a few close friends left, like Paul Shortino, Bob Golden, Vinnie Paul, Jeff Molitz, and a couple of others, some of whom I consider family to this day.

Not to take away from any of those fine people, but my ultimate, most trusted, and most loyal friend was my English bulldog, Lola. She was undeniably my best friend. Literally. We used to sit out on the second-floor bedroom patio for hours together. She would be in her chair and I would be in mine, drinking a glass of wine, and we would both gaze out at the Vegas Strip and the desert sky. We spent hours like that together, and those were the most genuine moments for me the entire time I lived in Las Vegas. But when Vegas life took a wicked turn, so did my thought process. I no longer looked at the Vegas skyline with optimism, wild wonder, and excitement. I now looked at it with disdain, contempt, and a shit ton of resentment.

I would look out at the beautiful horizon only to wonder what the fuck just happened and wonder why it had to happen to me, even though I already knew the answer to that question. As much as I didn't want to admit it, I was part of the problem. Me, and the bad decisions that I made, which included affiliating with the wrong people.

One night, it hit me like a bolt of lightning. This entire experience was God's plan, and he was using my own weakness against me to get me to see the light. I had idolized, almost worshipped, Vince Neil since I was a kid, which is the exact reason why God brought us together. God was going to teach me the ultimate lesson and leave a permanent etching on my soul whether I asked for it or not. I had to learn the hard way, and so it came to fruition as such.

See, when you idolize people other than God, and you want to be someone else versus being happy with your own self, you commit yourself to a life of disappointment, unhappiness, and false fulfillment that can be taken away at any moment. Most people on the planet are obsessed with celebrities, and I was no different in some ways.

Pay attention, folks, because this is where I want to convey to others how to learn from my mistakes. This is where I stress the need for everyone out there to recognize that each person's life has meaning and that you are the only one who can find that meaning in your own life. Don't rely on someone else, or something else, to justify your life for you, to make you whole as a person, to give you a life that you want to lead. You need to do all that for yourself, or it just won't work. Trust me on this.

I not only met my idol, but I also went into business with him and befriended him on some warped, dysfunctional level. Even though I may have accomplished what some are only able to dream about doing, in the end, I didn't feel I accomplished a damned thing other than ruining my life and feeling like an asshole. The ending of this dream left me with shit on my face, depleted savings, and a broken heart.

To top it off, the destruction was orchestrated, in great part, by that same person I idolized, the same person that was the reason for me being involved in the first place. I was heavily influenced by the persona of that person and not the actual person.

\]=,k]\I should have put all that trust and faith into myself and taken control, but I didn't. It's so easy to wish to be somewhere else, walking in someone else's shoes and following their successful, colorful footsteps. It's easy to understand why people fantasize about being famous, walking red carpets, and dating the most beautiful people in the world. It's obvious. Famous people are put on pedestals for nothing more than being famous, even though fame is not a measure of who that person is inside, of who that person is as a basic human being, and that's dangerous.

I'm guilty of sacrificing my own happiness because of putting a mortal on a pedestal, only to find that my life was actually better than his. To this day, I cringe when I hear the words "celebrity" and "famous." I mean, what does "famous" really mean, anyway? Does it mean that a person is on TV or in a magazine? Does it mean that a person lives in a mansion, drives expensive cars, and is married to, or destined to be married to, a famous spouse? Does that all mean, then, that these "famous" people are better than you and have better lives?

No, it doesn't. I'll tell you what it means. It means that a "famous" life is probably way more fucked up than yours and not all what it appears to be on the surface. The entire Las Vegas experience may have brought me to my knees, but I now see I needed to be on my knees to become closer to God and gain a greater understanding of myself and what I was capable of doing in my own life, by my own right. I now maintain a staunch belief that when you deny God and look for others to lead you down the road of your own life, you will always find yourself at the end of a dead-end road. Always.

I see now that I had to take that dead-end journey in order for me to move forward with my life. It was time to acknowledge defeat and turn my life around, and it was time to do that somewhere other than Las Vegas.

***

On March 26th, a few days before leaving Vegas, I met up with Vinnie Paul, Carrot Top, and Jeff Molitz at the Luxor. Carrot Top was doing a DJ gig after his show, so it was a perfect opportunity to meet up with the guys one last time in Vegas. Flavor Flav was also in the house that night and joined Carrot Top in the DJ booth to spin some tunes and it was pretty cool.

I didn't stay long and neither did Vinnie because the nightclub scene was definitely not Vinnie's scene nor mine, but we had a blast while we were there. I told Jeff and Scott that I was leaving on the 30th and would be by the show one more time to say goodbye to them. I shook hands with Vinnie and told him I would see him back in Dallas, gave him a dude's hug, and left.

The move was becoming real. I was done with Las Vegas, and I was moving away from all that I knew of it, willfully.

I kept my word and went to see Jeff and Scott at Carrot Top's show the night before I left. Both Jeff and Scott were great people and they were both always gracious to me, and still are to this day. I had a picture taken of all of us then hopped over to the Tropicana to see if I could say goodbye to Paul Shortino and Doug Aldrich. Paul had already left, but I caught Doug, took a picture with him, and said my goodbyes. I told Doug I would look forward to seeing him come through Dallas with the Dead Daisies.

Moving day arrived in the early morning of March 30th, and I left Las Vegas before sunrise, ready for the drive that would take me back home to Texas. I couldn't wait for that one last look in my rearview mirror as I headed over the mountain going towards Arizona. I was ready for it. I wanted it. I needed it.

When that moment of looking at Las Vegas one last time arrived, I stuck my hand out the window and flipped off fucking Sin City. Fuck you, Las Vegas. Fuck YOU. FUCK. YOU. I had nothing but hatred, repulsion, and disgust for that place. It was nothing more than an endless black hole of losers and users that I let whip me, beat me, abuse me, and ultimately destroy me. Sin City is an appropriate name for that fucking place. You either learn to live with it, work with it, or be consumed by it.

Unfortunately for me, I jumped into the shark pool way too soon in the game. I was uninformed, naïve, bedazzled by a rock star piece of shit, and I became prey, got bitten, and drowned. It's as simple as that.

I pulled into the Lone Star State on April 1st and it wasn't a fool's joke. It was real, and I was home. And honestly, I never felt better. I was happy to be where I was again, and it felt amazing. It was peaceful, too. No more sounds of ringing slot machines, no more neon casino lights blaring, no more dodging drunken idiots, no more neighbors that never spoke to me.

I was back to the sounds of birds chirping, watching pine trees waving, and the smell of fresh green grass, which was an appreciated change from the unmistakable odor that can only come from urine-soaked sidewalks. I was finally back home in Dallas with my true friends and my family, back to my security, back to my support system.

I even started a new career with Stoli Group, USA, which was cool because Stoli Vodka was my all-time favorite brand. Being back in that type of nurturing environment gave me overwhelming relief from the loneliness I had felt for so long. It's like it was all just lifted away from my soul and it never existed.

When I saw my mom, man, I felt safe again. It's so true that there is no place like home. One thing I learned about people and relationships in Vegas, if someone doesn't bring any "value" into your life, but they somehow still have the label of "friend" attached to them, cut them loose. Trim the tree. Weed the lawn. As you get older, you really do find out how your true friends are, and you learn to appreciate your roots. You truly learn to appreciate those people and relationships, even more, when those people date back to your beginnings. Those are the people that were there with you because of *you* and not what you could offer, who you knew, or where you worked.

Facebook can be the devil but most of us have it and use it to show off our lives. I admit I am 110% guilty of doing that. When I was in Vegas and running around with many of the people mentioned in this book, I had more friends than I knew what to do with. So many people wanted to be near me just so they could be part of the scene. I constantly got Facebook friend requests from people I didn't even know, but when the party crashed, so did their friend requests.

***

It's been five years since I left Vegas. Hard to believe how fast time flies. It took me quite a while, too, before I went back to visit. I had so many horrifying memories that they outweighed any of the good ones and I really didn't want to go back to that environment. I stayed in touch with Paul Shortino, Vinnie Paul, Bob Golden, Jeff Molitz, and Chance McDaniel, so on my first trip back out, I made it a point to see them all because those were the good times that were worth revisiting.

My buddy Robert Olivares made the trip with me and we had dinner with Paul and Carmen Shortino. They brought their good friend Christine Scott who I briefly knew. Paul had the night off from singing in Raiding the Rock Vault, which is one of the best shows you could ever see in Vegas. At dinner that night, Christine brought up the concept of writing a book about my experience with Vince and the Outlaws. She told me about her history of writing and that writing a biography was her ultimate goal. I was shy about agreeing to it, blushed, and kind of left it at that. Funny, though, because I can't tell you how many people have told me over the years to write a book. Christine told me to think about it and let her know, and the thought stayed with me.

The next night was all about Carrot Top, Jeff Molitz, and Vinnie Paul. Positive people, positive remembrances. Christine and I stayed in touch and a few months later, I agreed that she should be my ghostwriter. I was ready to write my book, tell my story, share my side of things.

We met at the Hard Rock Hotel for our first collaboration session in October of 2017. It felt weird sitting in that back Circle Bar again as we began laying out this book. That was the same spot I sat with Vince and Bob on many occasions, having drinks and discussing the Outlaws business. This was the spot that entertained one of the darkest eras of my life, but here I was again, turning it into something positive. It's like I came full circle at the Circle Bar, and this was my chance to undo some of the scar tissue that Vegas left on me.

As time has passed, most of the pain and hard feelings have lifted away from my soul and went into the atmosphere somewhere, although some scars remain. The process of writing this book has been a welcomed form of therapy for me. It has forced me to have several chats with God in hopes of gaining an understanding of not only what exactly happened to me, but how to let it go and move on with my life.

It has only been recently that I was able to forgive some of those people who intentionally caused me harm. It took almost 5 years to have that conversation with God, but once I did it was like a huge grey cloud lifted and I could actually see rays of hope, rays of light. That grey cloud drifting away was the finite ending of that chapter of my life. I was finally able to look ahead and start to dream about the new chapters that lay ahead. The pages of my future were blank, and it was time for me to write a successful script.

Throughout it all, I remained true to my rocker self, and part of my recovery from the Outlaws fiasco was getting back out there, getting back to enjoying the music, getting back to enjoying being around people with common interests again.

On Aug 21, 2017, that's exactly what I did. Doug Aldrich rolled into Dallas with his band, The Dead Daisies, for a show at the Gas Monkey. JMAC and I went to the show and we got the chance to hang out with Doug afterward. Doug is a really good dude, very genuine, and has become a great friend.

John Corabi joined us, and Doug filled him in on how I used to be partners with Vince in the whole Outlaws fiasco. Since John was the singer who replaced Vince when he left Motley Crue for that brief period of time, he was privy to stories about Vince. Doug didn't hang out too long because he was tired, but it was so great to see him and catch up.

Good people bring good energy, and it was a long time coming for me for that. It was funny, though, that it then became John and I hanging out like this was a planned piece of my Vince Recovery. Turns out, John and I had met back in 1994 in Tyler, TX, when Tommy Lee invited me on his tour bus for drinks and he told me he remembered that night.

I brought up Vince and he said he had no hard feelings against him, nor did he feel like Vince did towards him. He said he lived in Nashville and that Vince had moved there recently, but he doesn't cross paths with him. We decided to have a little bit of twisted fun, so we all stood up, side by side with our hands up with middle fingers extended, shit-eating grins on our faces, and I said that this definitely had to be texted to Vince. We laughed, shook hands, and I didn't see John nor Doug again until the following year.

Another form of rock therapy came shortly thereafter when I went to see KISS in Dallas on September 27, 2017. My buddy JMAC had a good friend that was connected with Doc McGhee who was KISS's manager, and who had also managed Motley Crue back in the day. So, needless to say, we had some great fucking seats and had meet-and-greet passes.

I was looking forward to reuniting with Gene Simmons. The last time I saw him was in Vegas when the Outlaws played the LA KISS., when Gene, Paul, and Doc were in attendance.

When I got the chance to approach both Gene and Doc, I reminded them of who I was and my connection to the Outlaws, justification came in two forms. Gene said that the AFL League was the worst investment he had ever made, and when I saw Doc, he jokingly asked me "which money pit league" I was referring to as we laughed. He told me that as soon as he found out Vince was involved in the Outlaws deal, he knew it was going to be a shit show. He also added that Vince never had $11.00 to his name his entire life, so that made me laugh pretty hard inside. What great therapy, indeed!

With my revelations and justifications came the personal losses, which we all suffer as humans, unfortunately. On June 19, 2018, my grandmother passed away of dementia. She had a tough road her last few years and even though she passed and was no longer physically with us, I was relieved that she was no longer suffering and living under such dire conditions. Dementia is a terrible disease that no one should have to encounter, let alone the suffering inflicted upon the family members who can only sit back and watch as their loved one deteriorates right before their eyes.

It was only four days later, on June 22nd, that I got the news that Vinnie Paul had passed away at his home in Las Vegas. I was blown away. Two of the most amazing people of my life had left this Earth within four days of each other. Then after I left the viewing of Vinne Paul, I was walking into Hotel Zaza in Dallas with Paul Shortino and JMAC to grab dinner and drinks when I got the call that my papa had passed away of a broken heart. I just sat there in denial holding back the tears over cocktails. I told my mom that after Vinne's funeral the next day, I would head home. I lost two other friends that week, which will go down as the worst two weeks in my life.

My papa was the greatest man who ever walked this Earth to me, and I miss him daily. Luckily for me, these three wonderful people will forever remain in my heart, my soul, and my most cherished memories. Loss teaches you to live life every day like it's your last, for you never know when that day will come. RIP Grandma & Papa. We love you!

# THE WHISKY
## WHERE IT STARTED, ENDED, AND STARTED AGAIN

## CHAPTER 15

On September 30, 2016, my buddy JMAC and I flew out to LA to see Rough Cutt play at the Avalon Club in Hollywood. Rough Cutt was kicking off the Monsters of Rock Cruise and this was the first show in decades where the original lineup was performing together. The show ended up being awesome, and it was beyond cool to see the original guys still rockin' it out.

Eddie Trunk was the guest host for the night and several rockers came out to support their fellow musicians, rockers like Doug Aldrich, John Corabi, and Sean McNabb. A whole bunch of them jumped on stage to join forces for the last song of the night, "Stars," as a tribute to Ronnie James Dio's project, *Hear 'n Aid*. I love that damn song, too! It immediately takes me back to the '80s, being a kid, glued to the tv watching MTV. This Dio song also had a cool video with all these rock stars making appearances in it.

Seriously, there was nothing better than growing up in the '80s, for so many reasons, like the birth of MTV and getting to actually *watch* rock idols doing their thing. It was definitely the coolest decade ever.

After the show, JMAC and I met up with Paul Shortino and his wife, Carmen, for a drink while we caught some of Jon Corabi's acoustic set. After the drink, JMAC and I headed over to the Whisky a Go-Go to check out Stephen Pearcy's show that had just started. It was always a dream of mine to go to the Whisky, and there was nothing that was going to stop me from getting into that club - nothing except for a fucking sold-out show with a long-ass line of hopefuls that wrapped around the block, all wanting to get in. Dammit. So close. No soup for you!

As we stood outside, listening to the muffled sounds of Ratt perforating the walls that were just a few feet away, I couldn't take it anymore. I instantly stepped through a time warp and reverted back to being in high school and feeling that vigorous determination of finding whatever means necessary to get into that fucking venue to see that fucking band.

I turned to JMAC and said, "I'm not missing this show. I *can't* miss this show."

He looks at me and says, "Fuck it. I'm gonna try something."

He walked up to the doorman, offered him $100 to let us in, only to face instant rejection. Strike two, but we weren't out yet.

After giving it a few minutes, I approached the security guard and asked him if I could speak to the manager, telling him that I was a vendor in the liquor business. When the manager came to meet me, I respectfully played the Stoli card and quickly gained her attention. I explained to her that although I knew California wasn't my market, I had to at least try and make a dream come true of being at the Whisky to see a show. At that point, I really didn't have anything to lose, so I may as well be honest about it, right?

She was so cool about it, too, and asked us to give her a few minutes. When she came back, she opened the door and told us to come inside and enjoy ourselves. I was so jacked! I immediately offered her the $100 that didn't go in the doorman's pocket as a tip, but she refused it and said to spend it on drinks.

We stood there, amongst the sold-out crowd, and caught the last few songs of the night, including the most important ones, "Back for More" and "Round and Round." Fuck yeah! That was some bucket list shit for me right there. The entire night was a bucket list item. I spent my entire childhood dreaming of the LA Rock Scene, and here I was, right in the midst of it, enjoying every aspect and facet of it. What an awesome way to pop my Whisky cherry!

It was almost the Thanksgiving holiday of 2018 when Paul Shortino called me to tell me he would be at the NAMM (National Association of Music Merchants) show in February. He was meeting up with Carlos Cavazo, Dave Alford, Chris Hagar, and he asked me if I wanted to come out and hang out with them for the weekend. Truth be told, "hanging out" also meant keeping out any creepers and not letting any undesirables get too close. Not a problem. I was looking forward to hanging out with the guys, and checking out their newly formed band, Rough Riot, which was a combination of former members of Rough Cutt and Quiet Riot, both of which Paul had been the singer at one time or another.

I made the necessary travel plans and off to LA, I went. #Hellyeah!

Since I lived in Texas, I didn't make it out to LA very often but whenever there was an opportunity to plan a trip out that way, I was all about it. The day before this trip, Paul contacted me to tell me he was too sick to make it out to LA but let me know that everyone else was still expecting me. I had never met Carlos before, but I had posters of Quiet Riot on my wall as a kid and could pick him out of a crowd if needed. I figured that if he was as cool a person as Paul, then it was going to be another great weekend ahead and I went ahead with the trip as planned.

Carlos, Dave, Chris, and I all spent an amazing day together, walking around the NAMM show and enjoying each other's company, and it carried on well into the evening. I don't know how many miles we walked that day from start to finish, but I would bet it was every bit of eight or nine miles. Easily. If you have never been to a NAMM Show, or don't know anything about it, you are in for a treat if you ever get to one. Just be prepared to walk. A lot.

The NAMM show is the world's largest trade show for any and all music or pro audio products and anything related to the event tech industry. Seriously, anything and everything that you can imagine is there on display, and the whole vibe of the event is just *cool*. There's always a cool crowd with a ton of cool musicians on-site, supporting their labels. For instance, Carlos was doing 'meet and greets' at the Gibson Guitar booth.

Needless to say, eclectic level people watching was guaranteed at these events, and on that day, I encountered so many crazy cool people it was mind-blowing. I ran into my good friend Doug Aldrich, an extremely talented and awesome human being, and saw others like Michael Anthony from Van Halen, Frank Hannon of Tesla, Randy Rand of Autograph, and, believe it or not, a friend of mine from high school, Monty Pitman, who was now the guitarist for Madonna.

The best, though, was running into Stevie Wonder on the way out. And yes, I literally ran right into the guy, not the other way around. No shit.

Once we all had enough of the show, we all went back to Carlos's room at the hotel to chill out and enjoy some wine and snacks. I sat there for a little while and listened to the real-life stories from back in the day, with everyone adding their own tidbits of personal history to the mix. It was awesome.

Was the evening wore on and everyone was growing tired, I wished everyone well and let them know that I would be back in a few weeks for their February show at the Whisky.

Seriously. What a cool fucking day that was for me. I made some new friends and saw a side of rock-n-roll that I could only dream about as a kid. I was now there, as an adult, able to socialize with a group of people that once represented my unapproachable childhood fantasies. Definitely a rare opportunity in life, and one that will live in my memory forever.

\*\*\*

When the date for the February show rolled around, I flew out the day of the show and caught up with Paul and the guys at the Whisky. When I got there, the guys were unloading gear, so I took the opportunity to go inside and walk around without being crushed by a crowd of people. I was able to take the time to appreciate where I was, really soak it all in.

When you walk inside, the first things you notice are the photos plastered all over the walls, creating this rock-n-roll time capsule vibe or museum of sorts. There's a lingering air of unspoken homage to all of the bands that have ever played there, to all the videos that have been filmed there, and to all of the fans in their fashion fad glory that have packed the floor, time and time again, cheering on the bands they loved. Man, if these walls could talk. It literally gave me chills to be there.

When I went upstairs to the infamous Green Room, fantasy versus reality smacked me in the face. I mean, wow. Here I was, walking where the footsteps of my idols have walked, and it was surreal. Not only in the Whisky, but I'm in the room that was fucking legendary. I've read a thousand stories about this room, some dating back to The Doors, Janis Joplin, and Led Zeppelin, to more current stories that involved bands like Motley Crue, Van Halen, and Ratt.

In fact, the Green Room faces the apartments across the street, and those are the apartments where Crue members once lived and had all those wild parties. Legend has it that same apartment is where David Lee Roth was sitting on the floor doing blow, when a mirror that fell off the door, hitting him over the head and he never quit snorting. Now *that's* a master, folks! Sound a little more familiar now?

When I sat down on the couch, I kept imagining the crazy stories and ya, okay, I also thought about what the hell I was sitting on. The walls may have had their own stories, but I bet those couches had a few sleazy stories of their own to tell as they looked as if they were the original ones from the '80s. I sat there, imagining what it would be like to be there in the '80s when Diamond Dave was there, partying hard with the groupies in tow.

As my thoughts returned to modern-day and the Dave that sat before me (Dave Alford) told stories of Vince and him being best buds back in the day and how the nickname "Rockin' Dave" was given to him by Vince. Apparently, Vince was in hot pursuit of this chick, and he was told to back off by Dave Alford because that chick was with Diamond Dave. Vince looked at him and drunkenly said, "Yeah, yeah, yeah, and you're Rockin' Dave, so fuck it." And the name stuck with Dave Alford ever since. To this day, when you see Dave play, you'll see his bass drum is tattooed with "Rocking Dave!"

Dave also somberly recalled the night they were all at Vince's house partying their balls off when they heard the horrid, unmistakable sound of a car crashing. That was the ill-famed night that Vince drove drunk, had a horrible accident, and killed his passenger, Razzle from Hanoi Rocks. Damn. Such a fucking tragedy. We paid homage to Razzle and snapped back to reality, refocusing on getting good energy buzzing for the show as it was time to lead the guys down to the stage. I still couldn't believe I was there, doing what I was doing.

We went down those famous stairs where legends and my favorite bands once walked to take the stage. It was time to rock out because that's what you did at the Whisky. The show was incredible. Paul's vocals never disappoint, Carlos manhandled his guitar, Dave pounded the shit out of his drums, and Chris and Sean ripped their guitars to shreds.

The show closed with the customary tribute to one of my all-time favorite songs, "Stars," from *Hear 'n Aid,* and then finished it off with "Bang Your Head." I was immediately pole-vaulted back in time, watching the MTV Videos for both songs.

I went home the next day, and left Los Angeles satisfied, gloriously happy, and extremely grateful for the over-the-top rock-n-roll experience I just received.

***

Rough Riot was scheduled to play the Whiskey again on January 2, 2020, so naturally, my buddy Robert and I grabbed some dates and took a weekend trip to catch the show. Dave and Chris weren't with the band anymore, but Sean was still on bass, and Greg d'Angelo, the former drummer for White Lion, took over on the drums. Paul called the afternoon of the show and asked me if I wanted to introduce the band on stage, and of course, I said, "Hellyeah!"

We showed up early to catch soundcheck and caught the guys performing "Piece of My Heart" by Janis Joplin, and they killed it. After soundcheck, we hung out in the Green Room as the guys wrote out the setlist for the show. "Piece of My Heart" didn't make the cut, so it was totally a bonus that we heard it at soundcheck, like an insider. In true rock and roll fashion, Robert, our dates, and I walked over to The Rainbow Bar & Grill for dinner with Paul while the rest of the crew went for burgers.

For those of you who don't know, The Rainbow Bar & Grill is another historical, very cool, infamously fabled rockin' place that has seen more than its share of mythological patrons and partygoers over the years. It is absolutely one of my favorite dive bars of all time and just up Sunset Boulevard 0.2 miles.

Paul shared some of his stories about this legendary venue, and right there, hanging on the wall by the front table, was a picture of Paul and Rough Cutt from back in the '80s. Fucking amazing. When it came time for me to be standing on the stage at the Whisky to introduce a rock band, it was another moment in time that was making my dreams become reality. I mean, there I stood, again, at the top of those famous stairs, once again standing in the same place where my favorite bands had stood over the years.

If you have ever seen a live KISS show and have been there for the very beginning of the show, then you've heard a deep-ass voice announce, "You wanted the best, you got the best! The hottest band in the world! KISS!" Well, that's what I was there to do that night. Obviously, using different words, but totally in that same style. I walked out onto the stage, leaned down as I grabbed the microphone, and yelled in that voice, "Hollywood, California, Are you ready … to take 2020 back to the 1980s? Please welcome ROUGH CUTT!" And that would have been super fucking cool and all if it weren't for one thing. Just one small, little thing. As I looked over at Carlos, I read his lips "we are Rough Riot!" so I immediately yelled back into the microphone, "ROUGH RIOT!"

I couldn't believe what I just did, and I felt like such a jackass. I swear I jinxed myself, too. Earlier that afternoon, Sean and I were chatting, and he said, "Don't be like the last guy, our manager, and introduce us as Rough Cutt." We laughed it off, and here it is, happening in real life. Fuck What did I just do?

As I walked off the stage, being greeted by a smiling Paul who high-fived me as I walked by, I felt like a dick. I really did, and I was hoping that I caught my error in enough time to minimize any negative backlash towards the band. I couldn't believe I fucked up my friend's introduction like that. Seriously. My one and probably only time to ever have the honor of introducing a band at the Whisky, and I go and fuck it up! I felt bad and I beat the shit out of myself for a while over it. Fortunately, everyone else was great about it and treated it like no big deal, which helped me to laugh at myself over a Stoli cocktail while the band started to play. It didn't take long for it all to become cool again, and Rough Riot put on an awesome show.

In the Green Room after the show, pictures were taken, and goodbyes were said. The band was heading to Las Vegas for the next gig, and I was off to my hotel to continue enjoying my weekend in LA. As I walked out of the Green Room, it occurred to me that this might be the last time I will be in this room, at this bar, here in this frozen fantasy moment in time. As I took a deep breath, I inhaled the essence of this historic room, forever locking it in my mind and my soul. As I turned the corner of those famous stairs that led to the back door below, I gave one final thought to all the feet that have walked them. As I looked up, my eyes stopped on a throwback picture of Ozzy that was hanging above the lower staircase. In the picture, Ozzy was ironing a kid who was wearing clothes and laying on the ironing board. Some funny shit. I grinned and said, "That must have been one hell of a party" as I walked down the stairs and out the door.

I left feeling a genuine connection to the Whisky, to the history of it like it didn't matter that I was a few decades late to arrive. Deciding that our Hollywood night couldn't end just yet, I suggested that we go to the Rainbow for a nightcap. Closing out the evening there sealed the deal for a night in true rock-n-roll fashion.

It was just the four of us sitting there when I noticed a familiar face walk by. I was like, "Holy shit, that's Ron Jeremy!" I had met Ron on several occasions and I knew that we had mutual friends, so I called, "Hey Ron!"

He looks over and I said, "Get your ass over here."

As he approached the bar where we sat, I asked him who he was fucking these days and he answered, "Everybody!" Classic Ron Jeremy. I bought him a drink (Bailey's on the rocks) and we started shooting the shit, talking about Paul Shortino's show to asking Ron why he's always wearing pajama pants every time I see him.

Out of nowhere, he asks me about the girl I'm with. I tell him that I'm dating her, and he then looks at me and asks in a very sincere voice, "Can I fuck her?"

It made me laugh, it did, but I still wasn't letting him fuck my girl. I told him that was my job, and the look on his face was utterly priceless, but he wasn't giving up just yet. He then ups the ante by offering Jenna Jameson in exchange for my girl. Robert and I almost spit up our drinks as I managed to choke out, "No, thank you."

Now, truth be told here. In my mind, I was thinking that if this happened back in the late '90s? Umm, ya, then we might have had a deal. But hey, no hard feelings. I had to give him credit for trying. We took a few pictures with Ron and although it took my date a few minutes to catch on, realize who he was, and what his proposition was all about, once she did she was totally a good sport about it. I did have to pry him off her once, but we all just laughed about it.

When it was approaching 2 am, and Ron had been trying to hook up with my girl for about 30 minutes, he didn't give up even as we were standing by the door taking one last picture. He offered the Jenna deal one more time but with a bonus, Jenna and two of her friends. As the security guys were laughing their asses off, I turned him down and walked away laughing.

Robert said, "Are you sure bro?" and we both were in tears laughing. I wonder how many times his persistence worked for him though. I mean, the guy never quit. It must work for him sometimes … it had to!

***

As I walked out of the Rainbow Room and my boots hit Sunset Boulevard, I paused for a moment to take in the Hollywood surroundings one last time. When you look down Sunset Boulevard from the Rainbow Room, the first thing you see is the glowing, bright red Roxy sign and then your eyes connect with the Whisky a Go-Go just a tad further down. As I glanced past the Whisky, I looked over the famous Sunset Strip, the Hollywood road that was known for being all about rock-n-roll.

As a young kid, I fantasized about walking down this road one day. As I climbed into the Uber that was waiting for me, it brought a notion of the past that was now mixed with modern-day me.

As we drove away, I laughed at myself at how I was once a young, very immature idealist, a no holds barred type of person with starry eyes, a wild imagination, endless dreams, and a lifetime of mistakes yet to make. There I sat, an adult by society's standards, supposedly as a person who has learned some lessons the hard way, and yet, I remained a hopeful person who accepts the fact that he still has lessons to learn.

I sat there as a person who will most likely live with some very deep regrets that will never fade and with scar tissue that will never completely heal. I sat there as a person with wounds and emotional injuries that will serve as constant reminders of the battles that were sorrowfully fought and miserably lost.

Yet, somehow, I also sat there as a person who managed to retain hope in his heart and as a man who was willing to forgive some and forget the others. I was ready and willing to continue to test fate in order to achieve the best life possible. Through it all, I somehow managed to still be there, in the present, with some shred of optimistic enthusiasm that I had when I was younger. The only difference now was that it all came with boundaries, with all this caution, and with all this need to have a plan – but it was all still there nonetheless, and still my driving force.

So many things about me had changed over the years, yet many remained the same, and it was now all about finding the right balance. I haven't quite found that balance yet, but I'm working on it.

When I look back on it all, it wasn't always me who willingly changed things. Many times, circumstances were changed due to self-serving people who remained consistently rotten to the core. I can admit that I naively got tangled up in the web of deceit and I'm grateful that I was able to break free from it.

My clarity came about by some people simply taking off their masks, while others that remained true to who they were forced me to remove the mask of idolization that I had foolishly placed upon them. I had to learn a hard lesson to "know better" when it came to idolizing a person and trusting them for their person, and not their persona. Trust me when I say I learned that lesson, I learned it the hard way. Fuck, did I learn that lesson!

Here I was, years later, physically touching the things that I could only dream about at one time in my life. Luckily for me, it was no longer done by dangerously mixing the level of fantasy with the reality of who I was as a person. Sure, on the higher end, I had my share of the girls, the money, the cars, the celebrities, and some fame … and I enjoyed it. Who wouldn't? All of those things had been presented to me as manifestations of my illusions brought into real life, but not all of them came with positive outcomes. Guess it goes back to the "be careful what you wish for" saying.

To be safe, I think that the saying needs to be expanded to include "you just might get it" because you never know what that wish is going to bring you. I honestly did my best to hold onto what was *me,* and as much as I could have been altered by it all to a detrimental level, I don't feel I was altered at all. I don't. Not to where it, like, permanently changed me as a person or anything on the extreme end, for which I am thankful to God for, too. Yes, it made me look at things differently, and it may have made me more cautious about how I approached things, but it didn't alter me as a *person.*

As I sat there in that Uber, I recognized that I had come full circle in my life. I had come to the current, real version of a past hypothetical place where I once believed it all began, where it all started, where it all came to life, where it all mattered.

The difference was that this place now had names to the unknown famous faces, and there were tangible, viable things that had my name connected to them. This place that once had the label "want to go there someday" now had "been there, done that" attached to it, and those people that I "need to meet" were now in the category of "met" and "knew." Some people even came with the unimaginable label of "friend" attached to them.

This current place now had my footprints in the sand instead of a picture of someone else leaving the trail. My paths of fantasy had turned into traveled roads. What did it all mean? Shit, I don't know. I'm not sure what my future holds, I really don't. What I do know is that my life has been one hell of a ride so far, throughout the ups and downs, the wins, and the losses, and I'm grateful for all of it.

I've got the next half of my life still left to live, and this time, I'm taking with me the lessons that will make me wiser for the time in learning them. I've made the conscious decision to leave behind the negativity and all the people associated with it.

I no longer have false hopes with regard to some things, but I do still have hope for some, and I will forever maintain that hope. I hope that one day my daughter will want to know me and that I can truly be a part of her life one day. I hope that one day I will hold that "dream job position," and I hope that one day I'll have a kick-ass woman by my side enduring life's challenges and rewards with me, like a true queen. And, on the flip side, I also hope that karma is real, and I hope that all those out there who should fear it are given a damned good reason to fear it.

As the last paragraphs of this literary journey were being written, I was blessed to turn 50 years old. To some, this is the halfway mark of life where you can either just start to live, or just start to fade away and slowly die. For me, I've never been one to just sit in the shadows and fade away, so I don't see any valid reason why I would start now at 50, right? Right.

I choose to continue to celebrate my life and express true gratitude for being blessed with these crazy 50 years on this Earth, and you can bet your sweet ass I celebrated this personal milestone in true Britt fashion. Before my birthday I flew out to Vegas and spent the entire day at Paul Shortino's studio where we recorded a version of the famous song, "Here I Go Again" by Whitesnake. I chose this song because it mirrors my own life right back to me, and for that reason also, I choose it to be the title of my book. I recorded some video footage of us singing the song in the studio, and once I got the final version back from Paul, I had someone make it into a video, incorporating some of the footage and photos that represent my life's journey. Pretty fucking cool, right?

Then, in the week before my birthday, I flew out to Las Vegas for a warm-up party for my actual birthday coming up in Cabo 10 days later. The first night Paul Shortino and I had dinner and after went to the Luxor Casino to see the Carrot Top Show and we laughed our asses off. After the show, Jeff Molitz and JMAC met us at the bar for a couple of drinks and lots of laughs.

The next day was a pool day at Encore Beach Club where my buddy Robert flew in and my buddy Seth Stokes joined us. We partied at the pool and managed to run up a $2,435.17 tab. I was like "WTF I'm turning 50, so who cares," and whipped my credit card out and paid the tab. No regrets.

That night Kelle and Dave came out and joined us for dinner at Michael Morton's Steakhouse located inside the Virgin Hotel. It was so awesome to see Kelle and Dave again and we had a wonderful evening laughing like we used to do back in the old days. It warmed my heart. I have truly missed them both and I sincerely feel we will always be in touch with each other. Always.

It gets even better. During my actual birthday week, I flew to Cabo for the official 50th Birthday Bash where I lost count of attendees after it hit 65. A good friend of mine, Jerry Natividad, took me and 15 of my friends and family out on a 120-foot yacht for an afternoon. What an amazing experience that was, let me tell you!

The yacht came with a full crew with a stocked bar and a freshly cooked meal. What was even cooler was the fact that Jerry jumped through hoops to make my day special. He had planned to take us out on his 110-foot yacht, but it turned out it was rented that day so instead of canceling the plans, he borrowed his buddy's bigger yacht so we could still go. It will be a gesture that I will never forget. What a great friend he is to do something like that for me. I hope one day I can pay that kind of gesture forward for someone. Dang!

On the yacht, Paul Shortino played his ukulele and sang for my friends, and on our last night in Cabo, Paul jumped on stage with the house band at Baja Brewing Co. Man, he rocked the fucking house in front of all my friends and all of the other patrons that were there that night. It turned into a full-blown jam, from Led Zeppelin's "Whole Lot of Love" to Journey's "Don't Stop Believing" and Guns & Roses "Knockin' on Heaven's Door," with the evening being closed out with "Hotel California" by the Eagles. Folks, it just doesn't get better than that. And when you add over 65 friends and family members to the list, it made for one hell of a party that I will never forget.

Luckily for me, the older I've gotten, the wiser I've gotten, and I now look at myself as that fine, unique rare bottle of 1971 vintage red wine. Not only does it get better with age, but this bottle also comes with an adapted ability to remove its own toxins from the bitter grapes left behind by some really bad, venomous people.

By the grace of God, I can forgive some of those people who hurt me along the way, and I can wholeheartedly move forward as a better person by doing so. Over the last several years, every time I heard a Motley Crue song I would cringe, but now, I find myself being able to just enjoy the music again. Like I did when I was back in high school, rocking out and just having a good time. It's been said that you should never meet your idols because chances are, it won't go as you imagined, and it becomes nothing more than a huge, disappointing, soul crunching letdown. Based on my own experiences, it turns out that theory can be true after all.

Meeting one of my idols humbled me in ways that you could never imagine, but the lessons I learned from it remain invaluable. For most of my life growing up, I wanted to be someone else. I wanted to lead someone else's life. I wanted someone else's achievements and I wanted to feel what I thought they were feeling. As it turns out, the key to my happiness has been inside me the whole time. When I left Las Vegas, I left a broken man. But that was then, and this is now. Today, I am okay with the man that I am, I really am, and I genuinely believe that the best is yet to come.

As I move into my 50's, may I live by my words of gratitude and not just utter them. If you only live once, then you better be damned sure to make it so that once is enough!

> *"In the end, only three things matter: how much you loved, how gently you lived, and how gracefully you let go of things not meant for you." Buddha*

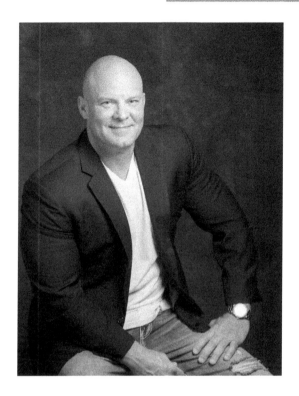

# BRITT AMSLER

Britt is always adventurous and has never scrapped his sense of childhood wonder as he grew. Britt sees the world as things can be and not as it is. And it's that sense of optimism that has fueled his passion for life, business and friendships. Britt loves motivating audiences and listeners from stages and podcast interviews to find their true passion and find fulfillment in life.

Author can be reached at BrittAmsler.com